THE STORY OF COLONIAL
TIMES

BY

Barker*
Grimm*
Hughes*

Row,Peterson & Comp.

Foreword to the Teacher

THE STORY OF COLONIAL TIMES is the concluding volume in a single cycle history program for the middle grades. The series includes two earlier volumes: THE STORY OF EARLIEST TIMES, which deals with civilization from earliest man to the end of Roman times, and THE STORY OF OLD EUROPE AND NEW AMERICA, which tells the story of the Middle Ages and of the period of discovery and exploration.

That the single cycle history program has an essential contribution to make to elementary social science is confirmed by the *Conclusions and Recommendations* of the Commission on Social Studies of the American Historical Association, 1934. The report asserts that, "The critical character of the present epoch in American and world history, with its social stresses and strains, makes especially imperative the organization of a program of social science instruction coherent and continuous from the kindergarten through the junior college. . . ." The Commission recommends an organization of materials in the elementary schools which "would acquaint the child as fully as possible with the evolution of American culture—local and national —and to some extent with the origins of American culture in the Western world."

In accordance with the Commission's further recommendation that the "materials and activities selected must be within the range of the capacity and the experience of the learner," THE STORY OF COLONIAL TIMES is self-administrative in the hands of the pupils. . . . Its basic vocabulary is limited to the first 6,000 words in the Thorndike list of words used by children; unfamiliar historical terms are carefully defined; and quoted materials are freely translated into terms the children can understand. . . . The content stresses the everyday things that touch children's interests and experiences: food, clothing, houses, trading, farming, money, schools, churches, amusements, travel, and communication. . . . Simple approach stories and "short story" summary activities make the organization of the book into *units* natural and comprehensible for the child. Pictures, maps, and time lines are not only identified closely with the text and especially designed to appeal to the interest and understanding of intermediate children, but are linked with child experiences by a strong then-and-now emphasis in the legends.

"The great purpose of the American public school," states the Commission on the Social Studies, "is to prepare the younger generation for life in a highly complex industrial society that is committed to the ideal of democracy and . . . is in rapid transition . . . to an economy essentially co-operative and integrated in character. . . . The achievement of this far-reaching purpose requires the introduction into the school curriculum of materials which will equip the younger generation, as fully as possible, to understand, to appreciate, and to evaluate the great changes under way." To that end, THE STORY OF COLONIAL TIMES systematically stresses the contrast between the simple agricultural past and the modern industrial present and traces the development of democratic ideals in text, pictures, maps, cartoons, time lines, and end activities.

THE PUBLISHERS

CONTENTS

Pronunciation Key

The first time any proper name or unfamiliar word is used, it is pronounced according to the following key:

ă as in at	ĭ as in it
ā as in face	ī as in mine
ä as in father	ŏ as in not
a̠ as in ask	ō as in open
â as in ball	ô as in long
ĕ as in end	o͞o as in too
ē as in be	ŭ as in up
ẽ as in her	ū as in use

û as in turn

Full-Page Maps and Time Lines

To the Boys and Girls

THE STORY OF COLONIAL TIMES is *your* book. It is planned so that you can easily learn for yourselves how to use it.

Turn to the table of contents and notice that it names six main ideas, or *units* of thought. Look at page 1; you will find a short story of Unit One to give you an idea of what the unit is about.

As you read the unit, study the pictures and cartoons. The legends beneath them will help you to see that many of our ways of thinking began in colonial days and to recognize how greatly times have changed since then. Look on the picture maps for the people and places you read about, and compare the maps to see how our country changed with the passing years. Turn to the time line at the end of the unit whenever you want to see when anything happened in relation to other events. Notice that a date worth remembering is marked with a white circle.

Find the answers to the questions and work out the activities at the ends of chapters and units. Make use of all the outside helps you can find: papers, magazines, library books, atlases, encyclopedias, museums, and motion pictures. In finding information through such helps and in putting them to use in class activities, you will learn two very important things: how to get facts that you need as a foundation for sound thinking, and how to work with other people.

THE STORY OF COLONIAL TIMES will help you to understand how American life has changed since the days when most of the people lived on farms and manufactured by hand nearly everything they used. It will help you to realize that we live in a changing world, and that people are constantly changing and improving their ways of living and of thinking to suit new conditions.

THE PUBLISHERS

In colonial times, raising great crops of tobacco required many laborers and quickly took the richness from the soil. How did this help to make problems for the South today?

UNIT ONE

The South Became a Great Farming Land

In colonial times the lives of people in America were shaped by geography even more than they are today. The English colonies which grew into the United States were, in fact, divided by geography into three groups: the cold and rocky North, the mild and deep-harbored middle colonies, and the warm and rich-soiled South.

Colonial times began with the coming of the first pioneers to the South in 1607. The southern colonies were Virginia, Maryland, the two Carolinas, and Georgia. The people in all these colonies made their living by farming. There was plenty of rich land watered by many rivers flowing toward the ocean. The climate was pleasant enough for outdoor living all the year around, neither too cold in winter nor too hot in summer. Because of these geographical advantages, farming was profitable. The South soon grew into a land of farms and plantations, raising corn and pumpkins and pigs for food at home and great crops of tobacco and rice to be shipped across the ocean to England.

There was not a single white man living in the
South before 1607 where today more than ten million people live. The first people who made their
homes in the colonies suffered almost unbelievable
hardships from sickness, starvation, and Indians.
It is difficult for us to understand how any of those
who lived through those terrible early years had
courage to stay, or why new immigrants continued to
come from England after hearing of the suffering
and dangers that awaited them in America. But the
truth is that most of the colonists were much better
off than they had been in Europe. Very few of them
wished to go back after living a few years in America.
You will find out why this was so in:

Chapter   I.   Making the First English Homes in
                 America

Chapter   II.   Self-Governing Tobacco Planters in
                 Virginia

Chapter   III.   Later Farming Colonies in the South

Outline of Chapter I

I. Making the First English Homes in America

  A. Why Starting a Colony Was Hard Work

    1. A trading company sent colonists after gold.

    2. Jamestown was not a healthful spot.

    3. The Indians were dangerous.

    4. The colonists could not support themselves.

    5. The company demanded quick profits.

  B. How John Smith Helped Start the Colony

    1. Captain Smith had experience and ability.

    2. Smith traded with the Indians.

    3. Smith governed the colony wisely.

  C. Jamestown in Its Worst Year

    1. The "starving time" nearly wiped out the colony.

    2. The company finally sent enough food.

3

CHAPTER I

Making the First English Homes in America

Why Starting a Colony Was Hard Work

A trading company sent colonists after gold. On an April day in 1607, three small ships sailed along the shores of Virginia. They were English vessels— the "Susan Constant", the "Godspeed", and the "Discovery". They carried the people who were to start the first lasting English colony in America.

A year before, a number of London merchants and business men had formed a trading company called the London Company. They planned to send settlers to Virginia, the region that Queen Elizabeth had once given to Sir Walter Raleigh (rô'lǐ). Because they saw that the cost of starting a colony in a new land far from England was too great for one man to bear, each member of the company was to pay a part of the cost. If the colony succeeded, each would share in the profits. If it failed, each would share in the loss, and none of them would be ruined as Raleigh had been by the failure of his colony twenty years earlier.

King James I had approved of the forming of the company and had given it a charter. A charter

4

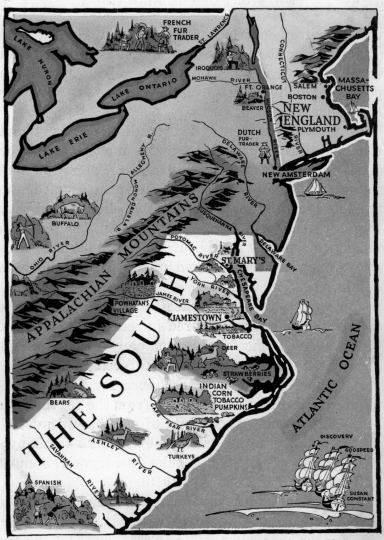

Looking at this map, can you tell why farmers in the South had more land and found it easier to take their crops to market than people in the middle and New England colonies?

5

was a written contract giving the company the land and granting it the right to govern a colony, for in those days trading companies were often given powers which today governments would keep for themselves.

Both the members of the trading company and the colonists expected to make money from the settlement in America. Since the Spaniards had found shiploads of gold and silver in Mexico, the members of the London Company believed that they might do the same in Virginia. As for precious stones, the colonists had heard tales of how diamonds and rubies could be picked up on the seashore as children gather shells.

Jamestown was not a healthful spot. For three weeks, the colonists explored in search of a suitable place to live. The trading company had given the leaders of the colony written directions about the sort of place they were to choose for their settlement. It must be some distance from the sea in order to be safe from chance visits of pirates. It must be on the bank of a deep river to enable the company's ships to unload goods and take on cargoes. It must be high and dry to be healthful.

After their long voyage across the ocean, the colonists were very glad to be on land once more. The season was springtime. Trees were green; the meadows were gay with flowers; and there were quantities of delicious wild strawberries. The clear waters of bays and inlets provided fish and oysters for the taking. No rubies or diamonds sparkled in the sands of the beaches, but the delighted Englishmen gave little thought to the lack of them. They thought Virginia the most beautiful country that they had ever seen—a land with "fair meadows, goodly trees, and fresh water running through the woods."

The natives were not so attractive. On the very first day the red men attacked an exploring party as it was returning to the boats and wounded two men. One of the colonists left an account of what happened: "At night," he wrote, "when we were going aboard, there came the savages, creeping upon all fours, from the hills, like bears, with their bows in their mouths. They charged us very desperately, hurt Captain Gabriel Archer in both his hands, and wounded a sailor in two places in the body very dangerously. After they had used up their arrows, and felt the sharpness of our shot, they retired into the woods with a great noise, and so left us." When the Englishmen found some of these same Indians at an oyster roast the next day, they drove them away and ate the oysters.

The leaders of the colony chose a spot for their settlement which would be easy to defend against Indians. It was a low peninsula jutting out from the north bank of the James River about thirty miles from the sea. At high tide the swampy neck of land connecting it with the mainland was covered with water so that the peninsula became an island. A low, damp location is, of course, not healthful. Many of the men fell ill and died, probably of a fever called malaria (mȧ-lā′rĭ-ȧ).

Jamestown was begun in May, 1607. Some of the colonists set about building cabins for shelter and a rude fort for safety, while others went on exploring the land along the banks of the river.

The Indians were dangerous. After their adventure on their first day ashore, the Englishmen found other Indians who received them as friends, smoked the peace pipe with them, feasted them on corn cakes, and entertained them with dancing. "After they had feasted us," wrote one of the men, "they showed us, in welcome, their manner of dancing. One of the savages stood in the midst singing, beating one hand against another, all the rest dancing about him, shouting, howling, and stamping the ground, with many antics and faces, making noise like so many wolves or devils."

The clothing of the Indians was made of skins. In summer time the men wore a girdle of skins around the waist. The description of the dancers tells how they adorned themselves in curious and awful ways: "They hang through their ears fowls' legs; they shave the right side of their heads with a shell; the hair on the left side they wear long and tied up in a knot with many feathers sticking in it. Some paint their bodies black, some red, with

Within sixty miles of Jamestown lived about five thousand Indians. What does this picture tell you about them?

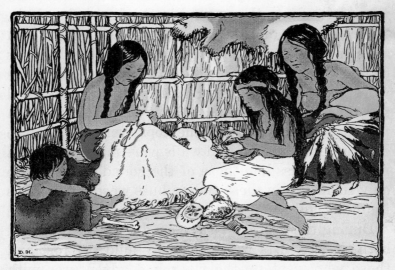

Sewing with needles of bone and strings of leather for thread, Indian women made suits of deerskin, or buckskin.

spots of different colors." The girdle sometimes had a pocket in which the wearer could carry a little dried corn when he was on a journey. On hunting trips the men wore moccasins and leggings for protection against briars and thorns. The women wore short skirts, and in winter both men and women wrapped themselves in robes of fur.

The Indians lived in villages in two sorts of houses: a small round house and a much larger long house. The round houses were occupied by one or two families and were used chiefly in the summer time. The long houses were winter homes and sometimes sheltered eight or ten families. Both kind of homes were built in the same way. To make a round house, poles were driven into the ground in the form of a circle. Then the tops of the poles were tied together and smaller poles and grass were laced around the sides to make the walls. To make a long house, the poles were placed in two long lines and the tops tied together to form arches. A row of poles was then placed at each end, and the tops were tied to the end arches. The roof and walls were made of woven poles and grass like those of the round houses. The only furniture in these Indian huts were a few skins for beds and some earthen pots for cooking.

During the first busy summer days at Jamestown, both the colonists who stayed to build the fort and those who went up the river had adventures with the Indians. The explorers, led by the captain of one of the ships and by John Smith, went up the James River to the point where Richmond now is, and found the Indians kind and friendly. They were entertained with dances and feasted on strawberries and cornbread, but they returned to Jamestown to find that it had been attacked by Indians.

The very first night at Jamestown, there had been an alarm, but the Indians went away without attacking. Four days later, one of the neighboring chiefs appeared with a hundred warriors armed with bows, arrows, and clubs. He said that he came in peace, and tried to get the white men to lay down their arms. When they would not do so, he pretended to welcome them and told them to take as much of his land as they wanted. A few days later he sent forty men to Jamestown with a present of a fat deer. The Indians wanted to stay in the fort all night, but the colonists would not let them. The men at Jamestown did not trust the chief or his men. They feared that he was trying to deceive them and take them by surprise. Their fears were justified, for a few days before John Smith and his party returned this chief attacked Jamestown and killed a boy and wounded seventeen men.

The colonists could not support themselves. Late in June, 1607, the last ship sailed back to England, leaving at Jamestown 104 men and boys. It was expected to return in December with more people and supplies. In the meantime, the first settlers were supposed to raise a crop of corn and vegetables sufficient to carry themselves and the later arrivals through the winter. But the plan did not work, partly because of the carelessness of the colonists.

By fall, famine threatened Jamestown. Sickness and wounds were carrying off the men at the rate of one or two a day. Forty-six had died by the beginning of September. Before the ship returned with supplies, the daily amount of grain for bread had been cut down to a small can of barley for every five men. During the winter, the fort burned down, and with it the clothing and living quarters of some of the men. Rats ate much of the seed corn stored in the corn houses. As one of the colonists declared, all would have starved had God not put it into the hearts of the Indians to bring them corn, fish, and game.

The company demanded quick profits. One of the causes of suffering and misfortune at Jamestown was the London Company's demand for immediate profits from the money that the colony cost it. The trading company expected the colonists to be able to raise most of their own food and to support themselves. The ships which took new people to Virginia rarely carried enough food to last the new colonists more than a few weeks after they landed. At the same time the directors of the company insisted that the ships must bring back something to be sold in England. The result was that the colonists spent much time hunting gold, making boards and ashes, and

The men who built Jamestown began at once to cut down the great forests of America. From then until now, for more than three hundred years, people have been cutting trees. Today we find that we must protect and replant our forests.

loading cargoes. They ought, instead, to have been clearing land, cultivating corn and vegetables, and building comfortable cabins.

The London Company continued to send people to Virginia as often as it could, but for the first three years the poor Englishmen died almost as fast as the ships could bring them across the Atlantic. Had it not been for the services of Captain John Smith in commanding the colonists and in obtaining food by his skillful trading with the Indians, it is probable that the colony at Jamestown would have failed completely.

How Captain John Smith Helped Start the Colony

Captain Smith had experience and ability. It was fortunate that John Smith was there to help the colony through its first few years. We have already met him in the party exploring the James River. He was only twenty-eight years old, but he was a young man of such ability that it was natural for him to take the lead when distress fell upon Jamestown.

Smith's adventures before he came to America had given him wide experience. When he was little more than a boy, he went to Holland to help the Dutch people in their war against Spain. Returning to England, he decided after a short visit to go and fight the Turks, who were making war on Austria (ôs′trĭ-ä). On the way, he was beaten and robbed in France, cast adrift on an uninhabited island in the Mediterranean Sea, rescued, and then attacked by pirates. But he finally reached the scene of the war and entered the Austrian army as captain of a company of 250 men. Captain Smith was captured in battle and carried off to Turkey, where he was sold into slavery. One day, while working in the field, he killed his Turkish master, jumped on a horse, and escaped into Russia. From there he made his way to Germany, and finally back to England. He arrived in England in time to become interested in the London Company and to go to America with the first shipload of colonists. This explains why we find Captain John Smith at Jamestown in the summer of 1607.

Smith traded with the Indians. In September of the first year, when new colonists arrived, Smith was made the trader for the colony. In a small boat that the ship's captain had left with the colonists, Smith visited the Indian villages along the banks of the James River and exchanged beads, trinkets, little pieces of iron, and an occasional hatchet for corn.

It was on one of his trading trips to the Indian country that Smith made a friend of the young daughter of Powhatan (pou′hä-tăn′), the most powerful chief in Virginia. The Indians killed Smith's two companions and captured and carried Smith himself before Powhatan, whose kingdom was far up the James River where the city of Richmond is now. The chief ordered the white man to be put to death. Smith's head was laid on a rock and the club raised to beat out his brains, when Pocahontas (pō′kä-hŏn′täs), the chief's eleven or twelve-year-old daughter, threw herself upon the white man and protected him with her body. This story has been doubted, but there are good reasons for believing that it is true. At any rate, Smith was released, and Pocahontas, as long as she lived, was a friend of the colonists. More than once she warned them when the Indians were about to attack, and, in that way, she probably saved the Virginia colony from being destroyed before it grew strong enough to defend itself.

Smith governed the colony wisely. In September of the second year, when Jamestown was a little more than a year old, Captain Smith took charge of

The Indians objected to the taking of their lands and fishing places. They would probably have destroyed the Virginia colony if John Smith had not won the liking of the great Chief Powhatan's young daughter, Pocahontas.

The corn for which John Smith traded in the villages of the
Virginia Indians was one of the real treasures of America.
Today it is the leading farm product of our country.

the government of the colony. He set everybody to
work, telling the men that those who would not work
should not eat. The church and the storehouse were
repaired, and new cabins were built for new colonists
who were known to be on the way. The boats were
cleaned and put in good condition for trading, and

fish traps were built. Some of the men were sent to the woods to make boards, and others burned timber and made ashes which were shipped to England to be used in making soap. Hard times continued, and the colonists were nearly always short of food,

Can you tell why less time and labor are needed today for the kinds of work at which the colonial laborers that are shown here are working?

but conditions would probably have been worse except for Captain Smith's energy and firm government.

Smith wrote to England advising the company to give up all hope of profit for a few years. It should send out people who knew how to work, such as "carpenters, farmers, gardeners, fishermen, blacksmiths, masons, and diggers up of trees' roots." It should keep the settlers supplied with food, clothing, and tools until they could build up a strong settlement. Then, he said, the colony would be in condition to support itself, and might begin to return a profit to the company. But the company could not understand the difficulties that the colonists had to overcome in Virginia. In spite of Captain Smith's plain speaking, it continued its unwise methods of trying to manage from London the affairs of the settlers three thousand miles away.

After having been a little more than two years in Virginia, Captain Smith was so badly burned by the explosion of a sack of gunpowder that he had to return to England for medical treatment. One of the colonists wrote of him after he left: "Justice was his first guide. He hated baseness, laziness, false pride, and meanness. He never took more for himself than he allowed to his soldiers; he would send them into no danger where he would not lead them himself. He would never see us want what he either had or could get for us. He loved action more than words, and hated falsehood worse than death. His adventures saved our lives, and his loss caused our deaths."

This was probably quite true. Smith undoubtedly saved the colony by his firmness and good judgment in governing the white men and his skill and daring in dealing with the Indians. But what did the writer mean by saying: "His loss caused our deaths"? It is easy to understand that statement after reading the story of the suffering of the colony during its third winter in Virginia.

Jamestown in Its Worst Year

The "starving time" nearly wiped out the colony. When Smith sailed for England he left nearly 500 colonists in Virginia. Three hundred of them had arrived only two months before. They did not bring enough food to carry them through the winter and the following spring. With so many mouths to feed, the supplies that the old colonists had managed to save soon disappeared. The Indians not only refused to sell their corn but stole the hogs that the settlers had begun to raise under Smith's direction. During that third winter, the colony suffered terribly.

Before the winter was over the unfortunate people of Jamestown were starving. Too weak or too lazy to bring in wood from the forest, they tore down fences and even cabins and burned them in the effort to keep from freezing. Of the 500 who began the winter, only 60 were living the next May when two little vessels arrived with more people and a small stock of provisions.

The new settlers had no heart to sacrifice their lives in these wild Virginia forests which had taken the lives of so many of their countrymen. In June they took the few who had managed to live through the "starving time" on their little vessels, and headed for home. It looked as if the English effort to settle the new world had failed. But fortunately this was not the end of the story.

The company finally sent enough food. At the mouth of the river the discouraged colonists met another ship carrying more settlers and the largest supply of provisions that the company had ever sent.

The new ship had arrived just in time to save Jamestown from being deserted. It brought more people to help do the work of the colony and enough food to last with careful management through the coming winter. But the colonists provided against famine. Two ships were ordered to sail at once to the English islands to the south and bring back wild hogs. One ship did not return, for its captain died, and the crew took the vessel back to England. The other went north to the Massachusetts coast and caught a load of fish. On the return voyage, the captain sailed up the Potomac (pō-tō′măk) River and obtained from the Indians a great quantity of corn. With this cargo of fish and corn, the colonists were safe from any danger of hunger.

Sickness carried off many of the people during the next few months, but Jamestown was never again in danger of being deserted. As time passed, the company sent out larger quantities of food with each shipload of colonists, so that the newcomers would not have to depend for the first year upon the small crops raised by the old settlers. And when the colonists became accustomed to the new country, they suffered less from fever and other diseases. The English were in America to stay.

Find the Answers

Be able to read directly from the text the parts of sentences, the sentences, or the paragraphs that answer the following questions:

1. Who settled Jamestown? When? Why?
2. What was a colonial charter?
3. Which one of the London Company's directions about planting a settlement was not followed by the colonists?
4. In what kind of houses did the colonists find the Indians living? How were the houses made?
5. When Captain John Smith took charge of Jamestown, whom did he put to work?
6. What was Captain Smith's advice to the London Company?
7. One colonist expressed his feelings about John Smith. What did the colonist say?
8. What saved Jamestown from failure after the "starving time"?

Picturing Colonial Times

1. Begin to save pictures, maps, and cartoons for a scrapbook showing how the people lived in colonial times and what we owe to them. Try to illustrate at least one idea for each chapter. Write brief notes beneath each picture in your scrapbook, explaining it (unless there is a printed explanation). Perhaps you can illustrate some chapters with your own drawings.

2. Ask your teacher to appoint a bulletin board committee to post the best of the illustrations so that the class may enjoy them. If a new committee is appointed for each unit, more members of the class will have the opportunity of serving the class. When you find or make a very good illustration, ask your bulletin board committee if they want to post it for a few days. Mark it in some way so that it will be returned for your scrapbook.

3. Draw a round or a long house like the ones in which the Indians on the Atlantic coast lived. Before you begin, look at the pictures on pages 9 and 17 in this book. See pictures in other books that you may find at home and at the school or public library. There are good pictures in *Compton's Pictured Encyclopedia* under the topic "Indians"; in George C. Eggleston's *Our First Century* (A. S. Barnes and Company), pages 31, 38, and 48; and in *The Pageant of America* (Yale University Press), Volume I, pages 11, 12 and 29.

4. If your class has a sand table, show the James River and the site of Jamestown. Use blue or green paper or cellophane for the river. Perhaps you can show, also, Powhatan's village up the river near the present site of the city of Richmond.

Outline of Chapter II

II. Self-Governing Tobacco Planters in Virginia
  A. How Virginia Became a Farming Colony
    1. Each man was given land by the trading company.
    2. The colonists began to raise tobacco.
    3. Laborers and slaves were shipped in.
    4. Women came to make settled homes.
    5. The Indians were forced to give up the land.
    6. Tobacco plantations spread up river valleys.
    7. Trade was carried on with furs and tobacco.
  B. How the colonists Gained a Share in Their Government
    1. The company allowed the colonists to help make laws.
    2. The colonists made their own tax laws.
    3. Virginia was made a self-governing royal colony.
    4. The frontier won a share in the government.

Each Virginia settler was given fifty acres of free land.

CHAPTER II

Self-Governing Tobacco Planters in Virginia

How Virginia Became a Farming Colony

Each man was given land by the trading company. Four years after the first people had come to Jamestown, the trading company sent Sir Thomas Dale to be governor of Virginia. Dale was in Virginia for five years, and much of the final success of the colony was due to his sense and firmness. He arrived on a beautiful day in May when all the men ought to have been busy planting their spring crops, but he found some of them amusing themselves at bowls, a game played with wooden balls on the grass. He promptly sent them to the fields, and gave them to understand, as Captain Smith had done, that men who did not work should have very little to eat. He enforced the rules of the company strictly, and punished people severely for idling and for small crimes. Those who broke the rules and suffered punishment thought him too harsh, but the industrious colonists who obeyed the rules said that severe measures were necessary.

One of the important things that Governor Dale did for Virginia was to see that each colonist was allowed to farm a little piece of land for himself. Before this time all of the colonists were expected to work together and put what they raised in the company storehouse. After a few years each was to receive an equal share of the profits. Dale found that this plan did not work well. It encouraged idleness because lazy colonists knew that they would get an equal share of everything, whether they worked or not. It discouraged hard work because it forced industrious colonists to share the profits of their labor with idle folk. So the governor allowed each colonist the use of three acres of land for himself. After paying the company part of his crop for the use of the land, a man could keep everything else that he raised. This plan caused everybody to work harder, and after a few years the company began giving each colonist fifty acres of land.

The colonists began to raise tobacco. During the first few years the colonists planted nothing but food crops in their little fields. It was necessary for them to raise corn and beans and pumpkins and other vegetables in order to keep from starving. After five years, however, when the danger of starvation was over, John Rolfe (rŏlf), who later married Pocahontas, planted a little crop of tobacco and sold it for a good price in London.

It was tobacco that really made the settlement of Virginia a success. The colonists continued, of course, to raise enough food for their own use, but they raised tobacco for a "money crop". They sold it in London and bought English goods, such as broadcloth, fine clothing, furniture, glass windows, china, silverware, and other things that they could not get in America. Many tobacco planters bought comforts and luxuries that they had never enjoyed before, and that they could never have owned if they had stayed in England. When men saw that they could make money in Virginia, even though there were no mines or precious stones in the country, they began to go there in greater numbers. Farms spread up the James River as far as the present city of Richmond, and before many years had passed, people were moving northward to take up land along the York and Potomac Rivers.

King James thought smoking a very bad habit, and did all that he could to prevent his subjects from using tobacco in any form. He declared that smoking was "loathsome to the eye, hateful to the nose, harmful to the brain, and dangerous to the lungs." But, in spite of all that the king could say, Englishmen went on smoking, and more and more people went to Virginia to raise tobacco.

By the time that the little Jamestown colony was fifteen years old, settlements had spread up and down the banks of the James River and around the eastern shore of Chesapeake (chĕs'ä-pēk) Bay. There were perhaps 4,000 English people in Virginia. The danger of famine was past. The deadly diseases which afflicted the first colonists affected people less. Spreading fields of broad-leafed tobacco were bringing industrious planters far greater comforts than they had ever enjoyed in England, and even giving rise to hopes of riches.

Laborers and slaves were shipped in. When the colonists got land of their own and began to grow tobacco for the London market, they wanted to hire farm workers, but there was nobody to hire. Every white man had as much work as he could do on his own land, and the Indians refused to be hired as regular servants.

The London Company solved the labor problem.

Here is a group of poor people whose "indentures" were sold by the ship's captain to some Virginia planters. They had to work for five years as laborers and servants to pay the cost of their journey to America.

There were plenty of men in England who wanted to go to Virginia but who had no money to pay the cost of the voyage across the ocean. The company made an arrangement with these men to send them to Virginia in exchange for an agreement to work for five years. Such an agreement, or contract, was called an *indenture*, and the men who signed it were called *indentured* servants. After getting them to Virginia the company sold their services to the colonists, who in this way got the laborers that they needed. When an indentured servant had finished his five years of service, he received a piece of land for himself.

In 1619 a Dutch vessel came to Virginia with twenty African Negroes on board. Some of the planters bought these Negroes as slaves. This was the beginning of slavery in the English colonies in America, though the Spaniards had been using slaves in their colonies for a hundred years.

Women came to make settled homes. There were no girls or women in the first three ships that came to Jamestown. The first English women came to Virginia in the second group of colonists in September, 1607. They were a Mrs. Forest and her maid. From that time onward a few women came over every year, but most of the immigrants were unmarried men without families.

Realizing that the men needed women and children to make them happy and contented in the new land, the company in 1619 sent a shipload of young women to the colony. The women did not have to pay for their passage, but when they married, as they soon did, each husband paid the company 120 pounds of tobacco for his bride. The company continued this happy experiment for several years, and, as a result, Virginia became a country of settled homes.

The Indians were forced to give up the land. Powhatan, the father of Pocahontas, was the most powerful chief in Virginia. Although he seemed to be friendly, the colonists never felt quite safe about him. Governor Dale finally decided to bring Pocahontas to Jamestown and keep her as a means of forcing the Indians to remain peaceful. When Dale sent for her, she was not at her father's village far up the James River but was staying with some Indians on the Potomac River. She came—whether willingly or by force, we are not entirely certain. We do know that, after saving Captain Smith's life, she had always liked the white people. She was probably glad enough to stay with them. She soon fell in love with one of the colonists, John Rolfe, and married him. Powhatan seemed pleased to have an Englishman in the family, and made a peace treaty which he kept as long as he lived.

A short time after her marriage, Pocahontas and her husband went on a visit to England. She was entertained as a princess, had her portrait painted by an artist, and was made much of. What she thought of it all, we do not know. No doubt the size of the buildings and the great number of people amazed her. She never returned to Virginia. When she died, she left a little son who was educated and grew to manhood in England.

There is an amusing story about one of the Indians who went to England with John Rolfe and Pocahontas. Before he left, Powhatan gave him a bundle of sticks and told him to cut a notch in a stick for each person that he saw in England. When he reached London, he saw that it would be impossible to obey the chief's orders and threw the sticks away in despair.

The Indians were beginning to see that the growing number of white people would force them to give up their lands. When the colony was fifteen years old, it suffered the most terrible Indian uprising that ever occurred in Virginia. The old chief, Powhatan, had died. His brother, who had attempted many years before to trap Captain John Smith and kill him, ruled in his place. This Indian had always hated the English. Working with the greatest secrecy, he had persuaded all the neighboring tribes to join him in an effort to rid their lands of the white invaders. One March day, he gave the signal for attack, and nearly everywhere the red men took the settlers by surprise. By nightfall, when the Indians left, 347 men, women, and children lay dead.

But the colonists were too many and too strongly attached to their homes and farms to be driven away. Under the leadership of their governor, the white men rose in defense and drove the Indians back to their wigwams. Later, when cannon and armor came from England, the colonists renewed the war and carried it on until the Indians begged for peace.

Tobacco plantations spread up the river valleys. The growth of the population of Virginia was very rapid. Within two years after the great Indian up-

With the coming of women Virginia's population began to grow. Men began to make lasting homes and to raise families.

rising the number of English settlers had again grown to 4,000, and within twenty years the white population had increased to 15,000. When the town of Jamestown was seventy years old, there were about 40,000 people in Virginia. By the time that the colony was a hundred years old, the population had grown to 100,000, including 23,000 Negro slaves.

Many of the later colonists were wealthy English nobles. They came to Virginia to live because a war in England between King Charles I and Parliament, as the national legislature of England was called, had ended in the death of the king, and had put the middle class in control of the government. These nobles who had supported the king were called *cavaliers*, a word meaning knights, nobles, or men who fought on horseback. So many of them came that it has been said that more noble families made their homes in Virginia than in any other English colony in America. This is probably true, although there were many people from the English upper classes in all the colonies.

There were many large plantations, some planters owning as much as twenty thousand acres of land. Most of them were along the river, for it was much easier and pleasanter to travel by water than by land, and the planters liked to load their tobacco at their own wharves when they shipped it to England. The first plantations, as we have seen, spread up the James River; later, plantations spread up the valley of the York River and, finally, up the Potomac River.

By 1700 English settlement had moved up the rivers past the falls, beyond which ocean-going ships could not sail. A few years later, the governor of Virginia led a company of explorers across the mountains to the beautiful valley of the Shenandoah (shĕn'ăn-dō'äh) River. Then people began looking forward to the growth of Virginia west of the mountains.

Trade was carried on with furs and tobacco. We should think it very inconvenient if we had to carry on trade as the colonists did. Today we go to the store and buy what we want with money, but the colonists very seldom had any money. Many of the men and women who grew up in America in colonial times probably never saw a coin.

If they were trading with the Indians, they used strings of beads made of shells, measuring the strings by the arm's length. Sometimes, also, they exchanged cloth, knives, hatchets, and cheap jewelry for beaver skins and other furs brought by the Indians to the settlements.

In trading among themselves, the colonists usually exchanged one sort of goods for another, or paid for what they wanted with tobacco or furs. Tobacco and beaver skins could always be sold in England in exchange for goods. That was the reason why merchants and traders in the colony were always willing to accept a hundred pounds of tobacco or ten pounds of beaver skins for goods that they had to sell. Nearly everything was priced in the chief product of Virginia, tobacco.

WHAT THE COLONISTS USED FOR MONEY

How the Colonists Gained a Share in Their Government

The company allowed the colonists to help make laws. For the first ten or twelve years Virginia was governed altogether by the London Company. The colonists took no part in their own government. The company in London made the laws for the colony and sent officers to Virginia to enforce them.

For a time the company governed through a council or, as we should say, a committee, of half a dozen men. This sort of government did not work very well, for the members of the council quarreled among themselves, and the colonists did not know whom to obey. The only member of the council who made a good leader was Captain John Smith. He succeeded because he was a man of great firmness and ability, and he really compelled the other members of the council to let him take the lead. As a result, the company soon changed the plan of government. It appointed a governor to be responsible for governing the colony and left the council only the duty of advising and assisting him in his work. One of the first governors sent out was Sir Thomas Dale, who, as we have already learned, improved conditions in the colony by giving each settler some land for himself.

In 1619 the company did a very important thing. It gave the settlers a share in making the laws for Virginia. The colonists had spread by this time to

The first elected legislature in our country met in the little
wooden church in Jamestown when the Virginia colony was
just a dozen years old. Here the governor is shown reading the first tax law passed by the House of Burgesses.

eleven different groups of plantations up and down
the James River. The company told the governor
to have each of these groups send two men to Jamestown to help make the laws. Each man was called
a *burgess* (bûr′jĕs). The burgesses represented the
people and acted for them as a part of the legisla-

ture. Their meeting was called the House of Burgesses. The other part of the legislature was made up of the governor and his council. It took the consent of both parts of the legislature to pass a law.

The meeting of the Virginia legislature in the little church at Jamestown, more than three hundred years ago, was one of the most important things that ever happened in the history of our country. It was the beginning of the practice of self-government by the American people.

The colonists made their own tax laws. The early Virginia legislatures passed some laws that seem strange to us now. The time for planting corn and the price of tobacco were fixed by law, and some laws were passed to try to keep the Indians weak and poor so that they could not make war on the colonists. It was against the law for a white man to live among the Indians for more than seven days at a time without the permission of the governor, or to sell the Indians guns, powder, shot, dogs, and hoes. These laws did not succeed, as we know, in keeping the Indians quiet, for just three years after the meeting of the first legislature, the Indians rose in defense of their hunting lands.

The most important thing that these first Virginia lawmakers did was to lay down the rule that nobody could collect a tax from the people without the consent of the legislature. The people claimed that neither the king nor Parliament could tax them

SOME COLONIAL TAXES

CHURCH TAX IN SOME COLONIES

ONE BARREL OF CORN AND TEN POUNDS OF TOBACCO

GENERAL PROPERTY TAX IN ALL COLONIES

OWNERS OF LAND AND OTHER PROPERTY WERE TAXED ABOUT ONE PENNY FOR EVERY FIVE DOLLARS WORTH OF PROPERTY OWNED

POLL TAX IN MANY COLONIES

EVERY GROWN MAN IN THE COMMUNITY PAID IN GRAIN OR CORN 6 SHILLINGS— $1.50 IN OUR MONEY

SOME OF OUR TAXES TODAY

INCOME TAX

PUBLIC SCHOOL   POST OFFICE

I help pay for many public services by giving the Government part of each year's earnings—

TAX ON INHERITED WEALTH

CAPITOL

THE HEIR GIVES THE GOVERNMENT A PART OF HIS INHERITANCE

SALES TAX

BILL OF SALE
2 doz. eggs

PRICE — $1.00
TAX DUE GOVERNMENT — .03
TOTAL — $1.03

In colonial days money was scarce, government services were few, and most taxpayers were farm owners. Today money is common, we enjoy many government services, and most people are wage earners. How have taxes been changed to suit modern conditions?

without the consent of the colonial legislature. We shall see later how important this American idea was in causing the United States to become an independent nation.

Everybody had to pay a tax to help support the church. If a man was unmarried, he paid the church according to the cost of his clothes. If he wore fine clothes, he paid a large tax; if he wore poor clothes, he paid a small one. If he was married, he paid according to the cost of the clothes that both he and his wife wore. People who cursed and used bad language had to pay a fine to the church for each offense, and everybody who was not sick or did not have a good excuse had to go to church on Sunday or pay a fine.

Virginia was made a self-governing royal colony. As you may remember, King James I had given the London Company permission to start the Virginia colony. After some years had passed, the king became convinced that the leading members of the company were his enemies. He feared that they might use the colony in some way to injure him. To prevent them from doing so, he broke up the company in 1624 and took charge of Virginia himself.

Fortunately, the king allowed the colonists to go on electing their burgesses, or representatives, to help make the laws, so that the change in government made little difference. About the only change that the settlers saw was that the king instead of the company now appointed the governor of Virginia.

The frontier won a share in the g o v e r n m e n t. One of the governors appointed by the king was Sir William Berkeley (bûrk′lĭ). He was governor of Virginia for twenty-six years, although not all in one term. The first time he was governor for ten years beginning thirty-five years after the founding of Jamestown, and the second time for sixteen years beginning when the colony was a little more than fifty years old.

During his first term Governor Berkeley was a popular officer and did many things for the benefit of the people of Virginia. He protected the colonists from the attacks of Indians. He encouraged them to raise cotton and flax and rice, as well as tobacco and corn, so that they would not be ruined if the tobacco crop failed. He made experiments with silkworms in the hope of making silk in Virginia, and he did all that he could to encourage the people to manufacture cloth and wear homespun clothing. In other words, he tried to make Virginia a self-supporting state.

During his second term, Governor Berkeley was not as good a governor as he had been during the first ten years. He did two things which finally caused a rebellion against him.

(1) First, he refused to protect the new settlements on the frontier from the Indians. The Indians stole cattle and killed innocent settlers, but Berkeley would neither lead a military force against them nor give anyone authority to protect the settlers.

(2) Second, the governor refused to allow a new legislature to be elected. Though the population of

Virginia was growing rapidly and new settlements were springing up, he kept the same legislature that had been elected when he began his second term. The result was that the people in the newer settlements had no share in making the laws. They believed that the laws that were not fair to them could be changed and that the governor would give them protection against the Indians, if they could have their own representatives in the legislature.

Nathaniel Bacon, a young member of the legislature who had a plantation on the western border, became the leader of a movement to make the governor treat the new settlements justly. In 1676, he led his neighbors in a defense against the Indians without waiting for the governor's permission. Then he marched to Jamestown and forced the governor to appoint him as an officer with authority to protect the border settlements. But Bacon had hardly led his men away against the Indians before Berkeley gathered together a company of his own followers with the intention of punishing the young planter. Bacon returned to Jamestown, put the governor to flight, and burned the town. A short time later, however, Bacon died. Then the old governor took a terrible vengeance upon the other rebels, putting many of them to death.

This struggle of the poorer farmers of the western part of Virginia succeeded in spite of the death of the leader and the killing of so many of his men.

The idea that all the people have a right to take part in making the laws that govern them was new in the 1600's. Even after Bacon's Rebellion, only property owners were allowed to vote for members of the House of Burgesses.

It led the king to remove Berkeley and give Virginia another governor, and caused the election of another legislature in which the new settlements had representatives. Bacon's Rebellion was an important event in the history of our country because it showed the determination of the common people in America to protect their rights and to insist upon a fair and equal share in their own government. It helped to build up for us and the people of our time the right of self-government.

GIVE AN EXPLANATION

1. How did Governor Dale help the colony?

2. Why was tobacco so important in Virginia?

3. Why did an indentured servant have a better chance than a slave?

4. Why were women necessary to the success of the colony?

5. In 1619 the London Company gave the Virginia settlers a voice in the government. Explain:

    a. How did the settlers take part?

    b. What other members of the government were there, and what did they do?

    c. How did the representatives take part in the government?

    d. How were laws passed?

    e. What was the most important law passed by the first Virginia lawmakers?

6. Why was Bacon's rebellion important?

LIBRARY READING ABOUT COLONIAL TIMES

1. Here is a list of books in which you will find interesting stories about early Virginia. Become

acquainted with several of these books. Perhaps you can find others of interest in your school or public library or at home.

Coffman, Ramon, *Our America* (Dodd, Mead and Company), Chapter XII.

Guerber, H. A., *Story of the Thirteen Colonies* (American Book Company), pp. 87-102.

Halleck, Rueben P., and Frantz, Juliette, *Founders of Our Nation* (The American Book Company), pp. 129-143.

Foote, A. E. and Skinner, A. W., *Explorers and Founders of America* (American Book Company), pp. 112-125.

Long, John A., *Early Settlements in America* (Row, Peterson and Company), pp. 125-172.

Woodburn, James A., and Moran, Thomas F., *Finders and Founders of the New World* (Longmans, Green and Company), pp. 93-115.

The Pageant of America (Yale University Press), Volume I, pp. 171-192.

2. Write a conversation to show how the Indians felt about the coming of the English. Have it take place between Powhatan and Pocahontas in Jamestown while Pocahontas is living there. Try to read more about the Indians before you write your conversation. The story of "Pocahontas, the Powhatan's Daughter" in *Explorers and Founders of America* by Foote and Skinner, pages 126-135, tells how the Indians along the Atlantic coast lived in colonial

times. The story of *The Golden Horseshoe* (The Macmillan Company), by Elizabeth Coatsworth, especially Chapter XII, will help you to understand how the Indians felt about losing their lands to the white man. Ask your teacher to choose, or allow the class to elect, some boy to play the part of Powhatan and some girl to play the part of Pocahontas in the best conversation written in your class.

3. Imagine that you are a planter in Virginia and tell the class why you are buying some slaves. Try to get the book, *The Colonial Twins of Virginia* (Houghton Mifflin Company) by Lucy Fitch Perkins, from your school or public library and read it before you plan your talk. It tells what the slaves did on the plantation of one of Nathaniel Bacon's neighbors. Good readers may also use A. B. Hart's *Colonial Children*, Source Book in American History, No. 1 (The Macmillan Company), pages 157-159.

4. Find out as much as you can about money in colonial times and the different things the colonists used for money. You can learn much from *The Pageant of America* (Yale University Press), Volume IV, pages 284-288, particularly from the pictures. Perhaps you can get that book in your school or public library. The last part of the story "How to Raise Tobacco," in Hart's *Colonial Children*, pages 63-64; Coffman's *Our America*, page 183; and Long's *Early Settlements in America*, pages 253, 259-261, 262-265, also tell about colonial money.

5. Report to the class on one of the following:
   a. farm life in early Virginia
   b. Bacon's Rebellion
   c. the House of Burgesses

Read as much as you can about your topic before you report on it. Facts are to be found in:

Gordy, Wilbur F., *American Leaders and Heroes* (Charles Scribner's Sons), pp. 55-63.

Singmaster, Elsie, *The Book of the Colonies* (George H. Doran Company), pp. 32-61.

Guerber, *Story of the Thirteen Colonies*, pp. 157-160.

Foote and Skinner, *Explorers and Founders of America*, pp. 253-261.

Encyclopedias.

Outline of Chapter III

III. Later Farming Colonies in the South
    A. The Settlement of Maryland
        1. Lord Baltimore owned and founded Maryland.
        2. The first settlers in Maryland prospered.
        3. The people gained the right to make laws.
        4. The people enjoyed religious freedom.
        5. Maryland became a great farming colony.
    B. The Carolinas
        1. A mixed population slowly settled the Carolinas.
        2. The people were finally allowed to make their own laws.
        3. People lived on farms and plantations.
        4. Pirates swarmed along the Carolina coasts.
    C. Georgia, the Last of the American Colonies.

Sap from the pine trees of Georgia was made into turpentine.

CHAPTER III

Later Farming Colonies in the South

The Settlement of Maryland

Lord Baltimore owned and founded Maryland.
Virginia, as we have seen, was founded by a company
of London merchants and business men. Maryland
owed its beginning to Lord Baltimore (bôl′tǐ-mōr),
whose family name was George Calvert (kăl′vĕrt).
He was a friend and officer of King James I. To
reward him for his services, the king had made him
Lord of Baltimore, an estate in Ireland. Lord Baltimore finally gave up his government position in
order to join the Catholic Church, for in those days
English laws did not allow Catholics to hold office.
But he did not lose the friendship of the king, or
of Prince Charles who soon became King Charles I.

Baltimore had started a colony in Newfoundland,
and after resigning his office, he went there himself
with his wife and their children. But it was not a
happy move. French fishermen attacked his men
and stole his property, and the bitter cold of the
winter was more than he could bear. He wrote to
Charles I, who had become king: "I have met with

difficulties and hardships here which I can no longer resist. They compell me to leave my residence here and move to some warmer climate where the winters are shorter and less severe. Here I have found by hard experience that winter lasts from the middle of October until the middle of May. Both land and sea are so frozen for the greater part of the time that one cannot dig a hole in the ice. Because of the cold and the salt meat that we had to eat, fifty of my people were sick at one time, and nine or ten died."

Baltimore ended this tragic letter by asking the king to grant him a piece of land in Virginia. Then without waiting for a reply, he set sail for Virginia. But the Virginians did not make him welcome. They wanted no Catholics among them.

Baltimore returned to England, and asked the king for a grant of land north of Virginia in the territory that we know as Maryland. King Charles was glad to reward his father's old friend, but Baltimore died before the necessary papers were prepared. The charter was given to his oldest son, who became the second Lord Baltimore, and the proprietor, or owner, of the new southern colony which the king named in honor of the queen, Maryland.

The second Lord Baltimore was a young man, only twenty-eight years old, but he was a very wise young man. By his careful planning he saved the colonists from the sufferings and hardships that the Virginia settlers had to endure. Though he never went to Maryland, he ruled the colony from England for nearly forty years.

The first settlers in Maryland prospered. The first colonists in Maryland were much more fortunate than those who first settled Virginia. There were two good reasons for this. In the first place, they had no trouble with the Indians. In the second place, they could get all the food they needed from the Indians and from their neighbors in Virginia and Massachusetts, who had passed through their hard times before the Marylanders arrived.

Early in March, in the year 1634, the first colonists sailed into the mouth of the Potomac River. They were in two ships, the "Ark" and the "Dove," and numbered more than three hundred men and women. Under the direction of Governor Leonard Calvert, Lord Baltimore's brother, they began their search for a safe and healthful place to start the colony.

All were delighted with the beauty of the country as they sailed up the river. A Catholic priest who accompanied the colonists thought that the Potomac was larger and more beautiful than any stream he had ever seen. The biggest river in England seemed to him "but a little finger to it. There are no marshes or swamps about it," he wrote, "but solid, firm ground. The woods are not choked by under-brush, and the trees are so far apart that a coach and four may travel through the woods without trouble."

On the bank of St. Mary's River, a stream flowing

into the Potomac, the governor found an Indian village which he thought would make a suitable place for the new settlement. What caused him to select this village for the first home of the Maryland colonists? An old book published three hundred years ago in London gives the answer to this question: First, the place seemed healthful, and the land was fertile and ready for planting corn. Second, the river was so deep that ships could come right up to the shore to unload and take on cargoes in a safe, deep harbor. Third, plenty of pure drinking water and firewood were near at hand. And, fourth, the place could be easily defended from hostile Indians.

Governor Calvert landed and had a talk with a peaceful chief and his principal warriors, who told him that they wanted to move away from that village as soon as their next crop was gathered. They were willing to sell him their huts and all the land around the village. For the present, they said, they would let the English have half of the houses and live in the other half themselves. In the fall they would move out and leave all the houses to the colonists. The governor gave the Indians some pieces of cloth, and some axes, hoes, and knives, and the bargain was made.

The colonists moved into the village which they named St. Mary and for the next eight or ten months lived side by side with the Indians in peace and

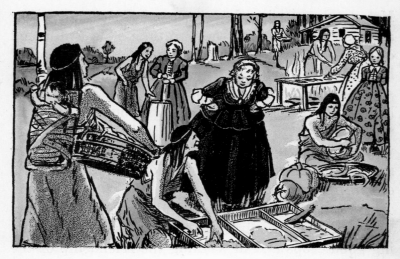

Some of the foods that we eat today are foods that the Indians taught the colonists to cook in early colonial days. These Indian women are shown teaching the women of Maryland to cook pumpkin and to make corn bread.

friendship. The size of the governor's ship very much surprised and puzzled the Indians. They thought that it was made all in one piece and asked the Englishmen where they could find a tree big enough to make such a canoe. The Indians had great quantities of corn saved up in their store houses, and they sold it cheaply for the beads and trinkets offered by the colonists. The Englishmen were able to ship a thousand bushels to Boston and trade it to the Massachusetts settlers for fish.

A year after the colony was started one of the colonists published a little book declaring that the

Marylanders enjoyed greater comfort and safety after six months than the Virginians did at the end of six years. "If you should go to Maryland now," he said, "you would find the people living in friendship with the natives. You would see comfortable houses, surrounded by cattle, hogs, poultry, and fruit trees brought from England and Virginia. And without boasting, one may say that this colony has made greater progress in six months than Virginia did in its first six years."

The population of Maryland increased rapidly. The success of the first group of 320 settlers in raising good crops and in winning the friendship of the Indians caused other colonists to come. Within a few years there were 10,000 white people in Maryland. Most of these came from England, but some came also from other colonies, such as Virginia and Massachusetts. Maryland was one of the most successful of the English settlements in America.

The people gained the right to make laws. Lord Baltimore owned all the land of Maryland, just as a man now owns a farm or a town lot. Because he was its owner, or proprietor, we say that Maryland was a proprietary colony. The charter, or contract, by which the king gave him the land, said that Baltimore must pay two arrowheads every year and give the king one-fifth of the gold and silver found in the colony. But no gold and silver was found, and Baltimore probably forgot to pay the arrowheads. Baltimore sold the land to his colonists, and they paid him a little sum of money every year, or a small amount of tobacco or furs, which he could sell in London. The charter seemed to Lord Baltimore to give him the right to make the laws of Maryland. It said that he could make rules "by and with the consent" of the colonists.

The colonists said, however, that the proprietor was mistaken. They thought that they should have the right to make the laws, and that the proprietor had the right to object to them and prevent them from going into effect if he did not like them. In the beginning, Lord Baltimore sent some laws to his brother and told him to read them to the settlers, but when Governor Calvert read them, the people refused to accept them. A little while later the men held a meeting and wrote some laws which they sent to Lord Baltimore. He let them go into effect, and in this way the Maryland settlers began to pass laws.

You can see that the government of Maryland was very much like the government of Virginia. In both colonies the people made the laws, but they did not have the right to elect their governors as the people do now. In Virginia the governor was appointed by the king, and in Maryland he was appointed by the proprietor.

In Maryland people enjoyed religious freedom. In our country, and in many other countries today, any citizen has the right to vote and hold office, no matter

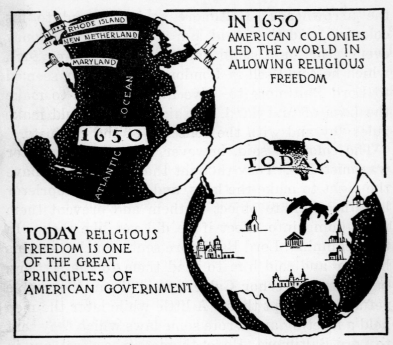

IN 1650 AMERICAN COLONIES LED THE WORLD IN ALLOWING RELIGIOUS FREEDOM

TODAY RELIGIOUS FREEDOM IS ONE OF THE GREAT PRINCIPLES OF AMERICAN GOVERNMENT

Religious freedom was a new idea in the 1600's. What country in Europe and what colonies in America led the world in allowing religious freedom?

what his religion is. All are free to belong to their own church, and the laws are the same for all. This was not so in England, or, indeed, in other European countries, when the first colonists began coming to America. The government of England tried to make everybody pay taxes to support the Church of England, and made it very disagreeable for those who belonged to other churches.

Lord Baltimore, like his father, belonged to the Catholic Church. The English laws were hard on Catholics, and he hoped that Maryland would become a home for members of his church, where they could be free to enjoy their own religion. But Baltimore allowed Protestants, as well as Catholics, to go to Maryland, and gave all the right to follow their own religion. Maryland was the first colony in America where the law gave people religious freedom. That is, it was the first colony where all Christians were free to practice their own religion and at the same time to enjoy the right to vote and hold office.

Maryland became a great farming colony. Nearly all of the Maryland settlers were farmers. The richer planters had large tobacco plantations and lived in handsome homes fronting upon Chesapeake Bay or upon the bank of one of the many rivers. The poorer colonists lived in cabins and cultivated little fields some distance from the water. A big planter's mansion was usually furnished with chests and chairs and beds and tables brought from England; but the backwoods cabin had only home-made furniture.

The ordinary clothing which everybody wore was made at home of woolen or linen cloth and of the skins of the wild animals which roamed the forests.

The poorer colonists did their own work. The planters owned slaves and had many indentured servants brought from England. When a servant became free after serving his master five or six years, the master had to fit him out with clothing, land, and tools, so that he could make a living for himself. It was the custom to give him a hat or a cap, a new suit of clothes, a shirt, a pair of shoes and stockings, one axe, two hoes, three barrels of corn, and fifty acres of land.

Every farmer tried to raise enough food for his own family, for his servants and slaves, and for his stock. Every farm and plantation raised its own corn, vegetables, fruit, hogs, cattle, and sheep; its own chickens, ducks, and geese. But the money crop was tobacco. It could be shipped to England and exchanged for fine goods that could not be raised in Maryland. Everybody tried to raise tobacco.

The Carolinas

A mixed population slowly settled the Carolinas. Some farmers from Virginia made the first settlement in North Carolina, but the proprietors sent the first colonists to South Carolina, where they settled near the present city of Charleston. King Charles II gave the two Carolinas to eight of his friends, just as his father had given Maryland to Lord Baltimore. They were the proprietors, or owners, of the territory.

The two Carolinas grew slowly. Charleston was begun in 1680. Settlers came to the Carolinas from England, Scotland, and Ireland; from the other colonies in America; and from the English islands in the Atlantic. The most important of the English islands were Barbados (bär-bā′dōz), a little island in the West Indies east of Puerto Rico (pwĕr′tō rē′kō), and the Bermuda (bĕr-mū′dä) Islands, not far from the Carolina coast. Still other colonists came from France. The people of the Carolinas came from many different places.

The people were finally allowed to make their own laws. The colonists had a good deal of trouble with the proprietors and with the governors that they sent out. The truth is that the proprietors knew nothing at all about the way the colonists had to live in America. Because of their ignorance, they tried to set up a government that was very clumsy and unsuited to the needs of the colonists. The settlers insisted that they must have the right to make laws as the settlers did in Virginia, Maryland, and Massachusetts, and they had many quarrels with the proprietors and their governors.

Finally, the proprietors grew tired of the trouble and expense and gave up their rights in the Carolinas to King George I. North Carolina and South Carolina then became royal colonies like Virginia. They had governors sent out by the king, but they had their own legislatures which passed laws for the colonies.

People lived on farms and plantations. Most of the settlers were farmers. In North Carolina they

In colonial days, wild turkeys flew past the North Carolina colonist's door, and Indian traders came with valuable furs. Today there are so few wild fowls and fur-bearing animals left in America that we protect them by law.

lived on little, scattered tobacco farms, and did most of their work themselves. In South Carolina, however, there were many large plantations, worked at first largely by indentured servants and later by Negro slaves.

The principal crop of the South Carolina plantations was rice, which grew in the low, moist coast lands and was shipped by the planters to England.

The South Carolina rice planter rode out on his horse to look at his flooded rice fields. Rice was one of the most valuable crops produced in the colony. There was a profitable market for it in England and in the West Indies.

Rice was the money crop of South Carolina. It could always be sold in Europe, as could the tobacco crop of Virginia and Maryland. Another important product of South Carolina, which was shipped to England, was indigo, a plant that was used in making blue dye.

Both North Carolina and South Carolina shipped large quantities of pine lumber, tar, turpentine, and furs to England and to the West India Islands. In exchange for such goods, the colonists brought cloth and household goods from England and sugar and molasses from the islands.

By the time that the two Carolinas were nearly a hundred years old, that is, about 1760, each colony had about a hundred thousand people. But there was a great difference in the kind of population that each had. South Carolina had about thirty thousand white inhabitants and seventy thousand Negroes, while North Carolina had some eighty thousand white people and sixteen thousand Negroes. You can see from these figures that South Carolina was a country of large plantations worked by slaves, while North Carolina was settled mostly by small farmers who worked their own lands.

Pirates swarmed along the Carolina coasts. The colonists suffered from Indian wars and from attacks of the Spaniards who lived in Florida. But the greatest damage was inflicted by the swarms of pirates who hid themselves in the bays and rivers along the Carolina coasts. We are told that at times there were as many as fifteen hundred pirates in Carolina waters.

The story of the pirates goes back to the time of Captain John Hawkins and Sir Francis Drake, who made war upon Spain and the Spanish colonies during the reign of Queen Elizabeth. As long as Spain and England were at war, the English rulers were glad to let their sea captains seize Spanish merchant vessels and treasure ships. The truth of the matter is, however, that many of these captains fought for profit, and they did not care whose ships they captured. They were sea robbers. When there was no war, they captured peaceful merchant vessels of all nations.

Some of the most dangerous pirates made a practice of watching the harbor of Charleston and capturing the vessels going in or coming out. They robbed passengers, as well as ships, and sometimes even took the best of their clothes. Occasionally they made flying trips northward and captured rich prizes along the coasts of Virginia, Maryland, and New York.

Two of the most heartless pirate leaders were Edward Teach, or Thach, and Stede Bonnet. Teach was also called Blackbeard, because he had a long, black beard, which he sometimes braided with red ribbons and curled around his ears. Bonnet had once been an officer in the king's army with the rank of major. He was a rich man, and seems to have become a pirate simply because he liked the wild, lawless life.

Once Blackbeard had some sick men in his crew and found himself without medicine. He captured a ship with some Charleston planters on board and sent one of them under guard to the governor, demanding medicine. He threatened to kill all the prisoners if the governor delayed, so, of course, the governor sent the medicine. A short time later Blackbeard was killed, and his vessel was captured by a warship sent out by the governor of Virginia. We are told that Blackbeard did not give up the fight until he had received twenty-five wounds.

Bonnet, too, was captured in a desperate battle which lasted five or six hours. The pirate begged piteously for his life, but he was tried for his crimes and hanged.

Georgia, the Last of the American Colonies

In February, 1733, thirty-five English families landed on the coast of the present state of Georgia near the mouth of the Savannah River. This was the beginning of Georgia, the youngest of the English colonies that later grew into the United States.

The leader of the Georgia settlers was General James Edward Oglethorpe (ō′g′l-thôrp) one of the most interesting and kindly characters in our early history. General Oglethorpe had been a member of Parliament, the law-making body of England. There he served on a committee which made a study of the heartless treatment given to poor men who had been thrown into prison merely because they could not pay their debts. One of his own friends, confined by a cruel jailer in a cell with other prisoners who had smallpox, had died of the disease. The general wished to free debtors from prison and to give them and their families a chance for a happy and useful life.

Oglethorpe laid his plan before the government and got permission from King George II to settle a colony in Georgia. The next step was to get money to carry his colonists to America. He used some of his own money, secured gifts from generous friends, and finally persuaded Parliament to give him ten thousand pounds, which would be about fifty thousand dollars in our money. Oglethorpe himself gave more than money. He gave his time and his services. He went to Georgia with the first colonists, and remained there nearly ten years, helping to get them started. He managed the business of the colonists, taught them how to farm their lands, kept them at peace with the Indians, and drove back the Spaniards who came from Florida to attack the little border settlement. Without his kind and fatherly care, the colony would probably have failed.

Georgia grew very slowly for the first few years. Fifty years after it was founded, when the colonies broke away from England and formed the United States, it had only about sixty thousand inhabitants. The people of Georgia made money from shipping furs and carrying on a valuable trade in the products of the great pine forests—lumber, tar, and turpentine. As in the rest of the colonies, nearly everyone lived on a farm.

IF YOU HAD LIVED THEN

1. Imagine you are one of the first settlers in Maryland, and write a description of your colony telling why you think it will prosper.

2. Pretend you are an indentured servant in Maryland. Give a talk before the class telling of your work and of your hopes for the future.

3. Write a conversation to be given before the class, in which a Maryland farmer and a South Carolina farmer each tells what crops he raises and why.

4. Imagine you are General Oglethorpe and that your classmates are the Parliament in England. Make a speech telling them your plans for a colony in America. Before you plan your talk, try to get one of the following books from the library and read more about early Georgia: Gordy, W. F., *Stories of Early American History*, pages 136-139; Nida, W. L., *Following Columbus* (The Macmillan Company), pages 232-236; Guerber's *Story of the Thirteen Colonies*, pages 164-166; Willis, Carrie Hunter, and Saunders, Lucy S., *Those Who Dared* (The University of North Carolina Press), pp. 83-90.

A Picture Map to Make

Make a picture map for your scrapbook, using drawings or magazine pictures. The maps on pages 169 and 288 will help you. Show the following:

1. the five farming colonies of the South
2. the chief settlement in each of these colonies
3. what the farmers in each colony raised
4. the James, York, and Potomac rivers

WHERE TO LEARN MORE ABOUT UNIT ONE

1. One writer says, "It was wiser for a man to stay in England in the 1660's than to migrate to America." Read more about the life in England in the 1660's and compare it with life in the colonies to see whether you do or do not agree with this statement. The interesting pictures in *Pageant of America* (Yale University Press), Volume III, pages 10-20 and 25-34, and in *A History of Everyday Things in England, 1500-1799* (Charles Scribner's Sons), by Marjorie and C. H. B. Quennell, will be helpful. Warren, H. P., *Stories from English History* (D. C. Heath and Company), pages 255-325, tells about England in the 1600's. Perhaps your library has *Merrylips*, by B. M. Dix (The Macmillan Company), which is the story of the adventures of an English girl during this period of history.

2. Arrange your illustrations for the unit in your colonial scrapbook. Try to have some pictures or drawings or graphs on the farming South, both in colonial times and today.

3. You will enjoy reading any of the following stories. Perhaps you have a school or public library which contains them.

Leetch, Dorothy Lyman, *Tommy Tucker on a Plantation* (Lothrop, Lee and Shepard Company), telling about Virginia in the 1700's.

Perkins, Lucy Fitch, *The Colonial Twins of Virginia*

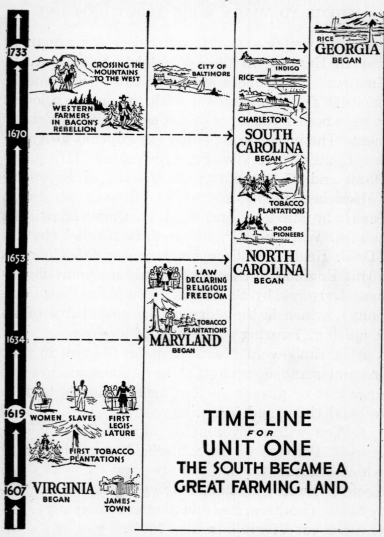

1733

CROSSING THE MOUNTAINS TO THE WEST

CITY OF BALTIMORE

RICE   INDIGO

RICE
GEORGIA
BEGAN

WESTERN FARMERS IN BACON'S REBELLION

CHARLESTON

SOUTH CAROLINA
BEGAN

1670

TOBACCO PLANTATIONS

POOR PIONEERS

1653

LAW DECLARING RELIGIOUS FREEDOM

NORTH CAROLINA
BEGAN

TOBACCO PLANTATIONS

MARYLAND
BEGAN

1634

WOMEN   SLAVES   FIRST LEGIS-LATURE

FIRST TOBACCO PLANTATIONS

1619

TIME LINE
FOR
UNIT ONE
THE SOUTH BECAME A GREAT FARMING LAND

VIRGINIA
BEGAN

JAMES-TOWN

1607

Follow this time line upward from the foot of the page.

68

(Houghton Mifflin Company), which tells about how pirates from the South Carolina coast tried to raid a Virginia plantation while its owner was away fighting Indians with Nathaniel Bacon.

Coatsworth, Elizabeth, *The Golden Horseshoe* (The Macmillan Company), which tells of a boy and girl on a Virginia plantation in the days when Governor Spotswood made his journey over the mountains to the West.

Daniel, Hawthorne, *Peggy of Old Annapolis* (Coward McCann, Inc.).

Heal, Edith, *The Topaz Seal* (Laidlaw Brothers), a mystery story about the Jamestown colony.

Sublette, C. M., *The Bright Face of Danger* (Little, Brown and Company). This is a story of the days of Bacon's Rebellion.

Holland, R. S., *Red Beard of Virginia* (J. B. Lippincott Company).

Varble, Rachel M., *A Girl from London* (Little, Brown and Company).

A SHORT STORY OF UNIT ONE

THE SOUTH BECAME A GREAT FARMING LAND

Colonial times began with the coming of the first English pioneers to the South, which from that day to this has been a great farming land.

A few people sent over by a trading company made the first permanent English homes in America at

Jamestown, Virginia, in 1607. During the first three years, a great many of the settlers died. Food was scarce; sickness fell upon the colony; and Indians with bows and arrows hid in the long grass. Had it not been for John Smith's services in managing the colonists and trading with the Indians for food, the Virginia colony might never have been the beginning of our nation.

Within a hundred years, Virginia became a strong colony of self-governing tobacco farmers. During the first half dozen years, the settlers began to grow tobacco and indentured laborers came to work for the planters. In the year 1619, three important things happened. The company helped in the making of homes by sending shiploads of young women to marry the men of the colony; it gave the colonists the right to take part in their own government; and the first Negro slaves were sold in Virginia. Five years later the king of England put an end to the trading company and began appointing the governors himself, but the colonists still made their own laws. For a time, one of the king's governors kept new settlers on the western border from electing members to the legislature. A rebellion led by a young western planter named Nathaniel Bacon gained them the right to take part in their government.

To see the South as a whole, we must turn to the story of Virginia's farming neighbors instead of taking up the thirteen colonies in the order of their founding. A quarter of a century after the founding of Jamestown, Lord Baltimore founded the tobacco colony of Maryland, which became the first colony in America to put the belief in religious freedom into practice. About twenty years later people began to settle and raise tobacco in North Carolina; and in another twenty years the rice-planting colony of South Carolina was begun at the present city of Charleston. Georgia, the youngest and farthest south of the thirteen colonies, was not settled until 1733, one hundred and twenty-six years after the beginning of Virginia.

All of the southern colonies were much alike. In all of them most of the people were farmers, living far apart on small farms or on large plantations, and there were few towns and few schools. In all of them the people helped to make the laws and thus to lay the foundation for our democratic government.

Ships built in New England carried much of the trade of the colonies. Look at the trade routes on the map, page 288.

UNIT TWO

Trade and Democracy Grew in New England

The interest of the people of New England from colonial times down to our own day has been attracted to trade. When we look at the map, we see that this is one result of the influence of geography upon their lives and industry. New England is a narrow strip of northern coast, crowded between broken mountain ranges on the west and the ocean on the east. Its stony land is not well suited to farming, but in colonial days the hills were clothed with ship-building timber, and the ocean invited trade.

During the winter of 1620, just a year after the Virginia colonists had gained the right to elect their own lawmakers, the first permanent New England homes were made at Plymouth, in Massachusetts. The Plymouth settlers had left England because of the laws requiring all Englishmen to support the same church. They were called Pilgrims because of their wanderings, first to Holland and then to the wild, new land of America. Before landing from their ship, these early immigrants signed an agreement to make just laws and obey them. This was the beginning of democracy, or self-government, in New England.

Massachusetts began to grow rapidly ten years later when a trading company settled nearly two thousand people in and near Boston in a single year. The trading company had been organized by Puritans. The Puritans were members of the Church of England who did not agree with all its teachings and said they wanted to purify it by making the church service simpler. Members of the trading company had the right to make the laws and to hold the offices in the government of the colony. Only a few members of the company went to Massachusetts, but they took in other members until about half the men in Massachusetts had a right to take part in making the laws for the colony. Men who were not Puritans were not allowed to vote or hold office.

In a very short time settlers were pushing their way into Connecticut, Rhode Island, and New Hampshire. Some of these bold pioneers came directly from England, but most of them moved out from Massachusetts because they wanted better land, religious freedom, and more democratic government. For that reason, Massachusetts is sometimes called the mother of the New England colonies.

The story of how trade and democracy grew in New England is told in:

Chapter IV. The Beginning of New England

Chapter V. A Trading Company in Massachusetts

Chapter VI. Democracy in Later New England

A friendly Indian, Squanto, taught the Pilgrims how to make corn grow in the rocky New England soil.

Outline of Chapter IV

IV. The Beginning of New England
    A. Why Hardy, Independent Settlers Came
        1. The colony was on a cold and rocky coast.
        2. The Pilgrims came for religious freedom.
    B. How Plymouth Became Self-governing
        1. Plymouth was outside the trading company's land.
        2. The government was based on the Mayflower Compact.
        3. Bradford was governor for many years.
        4. New settlers were represented in the government.
    C. How the Colony Succeeded
        1. Miles Standish led during early hardships.
        2. Peaceful Indians helped the Pilgrims.
        3. More settlers came.
        4. Farming helped in making a living.
        5. Trading and fishing brought prosperity.

CHAPTER IV

The Beginning of New England

Why Hardy and Independent Settlers Came

Colonists faced life on a cold and rocky coast. If you will look at a map or a globe, you will see that Boston is nearly five hundred miles farther south than London. It ought to be much warmer, but it is not. Why? Because the gulf stream, flowing like a great river through the ocean, carries the warm water of the Gulf of Mexico toward the shores of England and helps to keep the climate warm. At the same time a cold current from the icy waters of the Arctic Ocean flows southward along the shore of Massachusetts and keeps it cold.

Early explorers and colonists knew too little about American geography to be prepared for the cold winters the ocean current brought. A group of merchants and business men known as the Plymouth Company had tried to settle a colony in the North in the very same year that the London Company had started Jamestown. A year before, they had sent a ship to explore the northern coast, which we call New England, and select a place for settlement. After spending the late summer months on the coast of what is now Maine, the crew returned to report

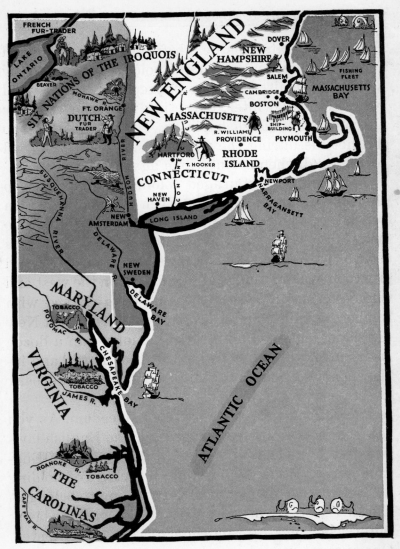

Note how the mountains come close to the shore in the North, and compare the narrow New England coast shown here with the wide, rich coast of the South shown on page 5.

that the climate was delightful and that they had found a perfect place for the colony. The company sent out colonists entirely unprepared for the cold New England winter, expecting no colder weather than during an English winter. The few settlers who did not die during the winter in America returned to England when spring came again.

This failure discouraged colonists from going to the New England country. Even if it had not been so cold, it was a land of hills and rocks not likely to be profitable for farming. A look at the map shows that New England is a narrow strip of coast crowded between broken ranges of mountains on the west and the ocean on the east. The hills were clothed with timber for ships and the ocean invited trade, but New England remained unsettled for more than a dozen years after this early failure. It took hardy and independent settlers to face life on that cold and rocky coast.

The Pilgrims came for religious freedom. As you learned in reading about Maryland, the English laws required everybody to belong to the Church of England and to follow its teachings and ways of holding services. Most Englishmen were willing to belong to the English church, and were satisfied with the laws; but two groups of Englishmen were discontented. One of these groups was the Catholics, who regarded the Pope as the head of their church and thought it a sin to belong to any other church. The other group were the Separatists or Independents, who wished to separate from the Church of England because they believed that each congregation had the right to make its own rules of worship and choose its own preacher. The first settlers in Massachusetts were Separatists, and were called Pilgrims because of their wanderings for the sake of religion.

One of these little independent church groups lived at the village of Scrooby (skrōo'bĭ) in northern England. For a time the members had their own church, but the officers of the English government compelled them to close it. Then they met secretly for awhile in a neighboring farm house; but again the officers hunted them down and broke up their meetings. William Bradford, who was a member of the Scrooby church, wrote a history in which he described their hardships after the meetings in the farm house were broken up. Three hundred years ago, some English words were not spelled exactly as we spell them today, and some of his sentences sound a little queer, but you will be interested in the way he told the story of his people: "Their former afflictions," he wrote, "were but as flea-bitings in comparison with the sufferings that now came upon them. For some were taken and clapt up in prison, and others had their howses guarded and watcht night and day, and hardly escaped the hands of the officers; and most of them had to flee and leave their howses and habitations, and their means of making a living."

Realizing that they must either give up their religion and go into the Church of England or leave the country, the members of the congregation decided to go to Holland. But it was a hard decision. They would have to learn a new language when they got there. Moreover, they would have to change their ways of living. They were farmers, but in the Dutch city of Amsterdam (ăm'stĕr-dăm), to which they were going, they would have to become bakers and shoemakers and clothmakers and learn to do the work of the city. Many of them hesitated, said Bradford, and thought the removal "a misery worse than death." Yet they went. The removal to Holland began in 1607, the very year that the London Company began the settlement of Virginia and the year that the New England colony failed.

Making a living in Holland was even harder than the Pilgrims had expected. Some who went there gave up the struggle and returned to England; while some who had remained in England, intending to go, decided to stay where they were. The men and women in Holland could bear the hardships for themselves, but they worried about their children. "Many of the children," wrote Bradford, "were good and obedient, and wanted to help their parents. But they were often so tired by their heavy labors, that although their minds were free and willing, yet their bodies were bowed down and their health was ruined."

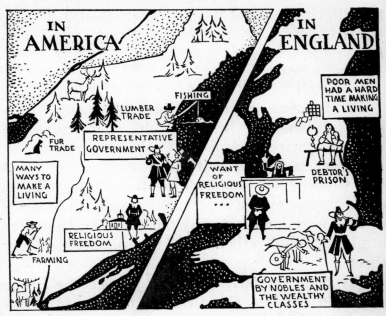

The conditions causing the Pilgrims to come to America are shown here. Try to find out why people come to America today and compare their reasons for coming with the ones pictured above for colonial times.

But the difficulty of making a living was not the worst worry. Some of the children, as they grew up, began to turn aside from the religion for which the Pilgrims had left their homes. Bradford said: "They were drawne away by evill examples into dangerous ways. Some became soldiers, some became sailors and made far voyages by sea, and others took up evil ways of living which grieved their parents and dishonored God." To escape from such dangers, the Pilgrims decided to move again, and to go this time to America where there was plenty of land to be had and a chance for religious freedom.

How Plymouth Became a Self-Governing Colony

The Pilgrims settled outside the trading company's lands. The first difficulty that had to be faced in moving to America was the matter of cost. It had taken all that the Pilgrims could earn in Holland to keep body and soul together. They had not saved enough money to pay their passage to America or to pay for land or to buy food to keep them alive until they could gather their first crop after getting there.

Friends in England helped them to get a promise of land in Virginia. Some English merchants agreed to furnish the ships and lend the necessary money, in return for the promise of the greater part of all that the Pilgrims made for seven years after they landed in America.

Two vessels were prepared to take the colonists across the ocean, the "Mayflower" and the "Speedwell." The plan was to carry thirty passengers in the "Speedwell" and ninety in the "Mayflower," but this plan had to be changed. After starting on the voyage, the captain of the "Speedwell" discovered that his little vessel needed repairs, so both vessels put back into the harbor. Again they started, and again the captain of the "Speedwell" declared that his ship was leaking too badly to go on. Both ships put back again into the port of Plymouth (plĭm'ŭth) in southern England. There the real trouble was discovered. The captain had wasted much precious time simply because he did not want to make the trip.

The Pilgrims knew that they could not reach America before the winter set in but, fearing that they might never go if they waited for the next spring, they made a third start. This time they had only the "Mayflower," heavily loaded with 102 passengers. They had had to leave some of the "Speedwell's" passengers because there was not enough room for them in the "Mayflower." This time there was no turning back.

Near the middle of November, the "Mayflower" sighted land. It turned out to be the coast of Massachusetts. The Pilgrims wanted to go on, as they had planned, to northern Virginia where they would be under the authority of a trading company, but the captain said that the weather was too stormy. Instead, he sailed into the quiet harbor of Cape Cod Bay.

The men began to search for a favorable place to start their colony. It was no easy task. The weather was cold, the winds were stormy, and the Indians might be dangerous. The Pilgrims had a little boat and sailed along the shore, stopping here and there to explore the land. They found some mounds of earth where the Indians had buried baskets of corn.

The Pilgrims landed on the cold and rocky coast of New England in the winter time. The first house in Plymouth was begun on Christmas Day, 1620.

They dug up the corn and saved it for planting the next spring, and later they paid the Indian owners for it.

Toward the middle of December they found a place which they thought would be suitable for the settlement. It was the last day of the week, however, and they spent Sunday in rest and worship. William Bradford tells us how the matter was decided on Monday: "On Munday they sounded the harbor, and founde it fitt for shipping, so that they could bring their vessel close to the shore. They marched into

The government of Plymouth was based on the famous *Mayflower Compact* in which the men on the "Mayflower" agreed that, since they were outside the lands of the London Company, they would make their own laws and obey them.

the land, and found several corn fields, and little running brooks, which would give them drinking water. The place seemed fitt for a settlement. At least, it was the best that they could find, and the cold weather and their necessities made them glad to accept it. So they returned to their shipp again with this news to the rest of the people, and the news made them very glad."

On Christmas Day they began to build the first house. This was the beginning of Plymouth, the first permanent settlement in New England. The Pilgrims had made their homes outside the lands of the London company by which they had expected to be governed.

The government of Plymouth was based on the Mayflower Compact. Before going on shore, the forty-one men in the "Mayflower" signed the famous paper called the *Mayflower Compact*. In it, the men agreed to make their own laws and to obey them. It was a plan for self-government, in which all were to share alike.

Bradford tells us in his history why it was necessary for them to sign this agreement. He says that some of the men joined the ship in England. They had not lived in Holland, as the Pilgrims had done, and were not as patient and helpful to one another as the Pilgrims had learned to be. While still on the ship, they began to say that they would do as they pleased when they landed, that there were no laws in that country and no officers to govern them. After signing the agreement, however, they kept their word and were good citizens.

Before landing, the men elected John Carver to be their governor for the first year. When he died, they elected Bradford governor, and kept re-electing him until he had governed the colony of Plymouth for thirty years.

William Bradford was governor for many years.
Bradford was born in an English village not far
from Scrooby, where the people lived who were to
become leading Pilgrims. He joined the group while
very young, and grew up a thoughtful, religious boy.

When he was about seventeen years old, he left
his grandfather's farm and started to Holland with
the first of the Pilgrims. But England did not want
its people to leave the country, and he was arrested
and put in prison before he could get to the ship
that was to take him to Holland. On getting out of
prison, he tried again to escape to Holland. This
time he succeeded. He went to the city of Amsterdam to live, and there he worked for a Frenchman
who owned a shop where silk was made. When he
had learned how to dye silk, the young Englishman
left the Frenchman's shop and started a store of
his own.

Bradford went to Plymouth on the "Mayflower,"
and the very next year the people made him their
governor. They loved and trusted him so much that
they made him keep the office almost all the rest of
his life. He lived in America thirty-six years, and he
was governor of Plymouth thirty years. The people
would have been glad to elect him again, but he
begged for a rest.

Bradford had a fine mind; he must have been a
good student. He could read Greek, Latin, and
Hebrew, and in his wanderings, he had learned to

speak the Dutch and French languages. He liked to read books in all those languages, but best of all he liked to study the Bible. He believed that God Himself was speaking to him when he read the Bible. It was Governor Bradford, you notice, who wrote the interesting history of the Pilgrims telling the story of how they left England, how they lived in Holland, and how they came to America to make the first permanent settlement in New England.

Bradford's book has an interesting history. When the governor gave it to his son, Major William Bradford, it had not been printed; it was hand written. Major Bradford passed it on to his son, John Bradford, who gave it to his son. So it passed on from father to son for more than a hundred years until, at last, nobody in America knew where it was. Then, strangely enough, a man wrote a book in England and quoted in it some paragraphs from an unprinted book which he said he had found in the library of the Bishop of London. Some Americans went to see the manuscript. They compared it with some letters that William Bradford had written, and saw that it was in the same writing. When they read it they knew that it was the long-lost history. How it got to England and into the library of the Bishop of London, nobody knew. Perhaps it was taken from Massachusetts by a British soldier during the American Revolution. Some years later the British government gave it to the government of the United States,

Democracy in New England began in the town meetings of Plymouth where all the citizens met to make the laws. Later New England towns all held town meetings.

and our government returned it to the state of Massachusetts. Without it, much of the history of the Plymouth colony would have been lost.

New settlers were represented in the government. As long as all the men lived in or near Plymouth, they came together and made laws for the government of the colony. When they spread to distant places, and it was inconvenient for all of them to meet in one place, each town began to elect representatives to speak for it at the assembly in Plymouth. These representatives, together with the governor, made the laws.

How the Colony Succeeded

Miles Standish led during early hardships. Captain Standish was somewhat like Captain John Smith of Virginia. He had not had such bold adventures and he did not talk much about himself, but he was a man of courage and experience just as Captain Smith was. Like Captain Smith, Standish had fought in the European wars, and he was always ready to protect the Pilgrims against the Indians. Even before they landed from the "Mayflower," the Pilgrims chose him for their captain. He led the party of sixteen men who went on shore and chose the place for the colony at Plymouth.

It was a bad time to begin a settlement. The colonists almost froze before they could build cabins to live in. Many months would have to go by before they could raise grain and vegetables, and they knew that many a night they would have to go hungry to bed if the hunters were unlucky or the fishermen caught no fish. For a part of the time they had nothing to eat but clams and eels. Hunger and cold brought sickness. During their worst misfortunes, there were only six or seven people, including Captain Standish, well enough to wait on the others.

By spring half of the colonists were dead, and those who were still alive were so weak from sickness and hunger that they could hardly creep around. One might suppose that they would have liked to go back to Holland, or even to England, but when the "Mayflower" sailed back to England in the spring not one Pilgrim returned.

Peaceful Indians helped the Pilgrims. Only a few years before the coming of the Pilgrims, there had been twenty-five or thirty thousand Indians in New England. All of these Indians had lived in much the same way as those in Virginia, by hunting, fishing and raising corn and other vegetables. After he had left Jamestown, Captain John Smith had returned to America to explore the New England coast. He wrote: "The country of Massachusetts is the Paradise of all that region. For here are many islands, all planted with corn; and there are groves of trees, mulberries, gardens, and good harbors. As you sail along the coast you see all along large corn-fields, and crowds of good looking people."

Three years before the Pilgrims arrived in America, some disease had carried off many thousands of the Indians and left only six or seven thousand of them in all New England. The Pilgrims found deserted corn-fields at many places along the shores of Massachusetts. The Indians who had worked the fields were dead.

One day, during the first spring, a friendly Indian

walked into camp and called out: "Welcome, Englishmen!" He had learned a little English from fishermen along the Massachusetts shore. The Pilgrims understood him to say that the tribe of Indians who had owned the land around Plymouth had all died of some sickness. The white people might keep the land and use it in peace. This Indian's name was Samoset (săm'ō-sĕt).

A few days later Samoset returned with another Indian, named Squanto (skwän'tō). This Indian had been to England, and could speak English very well. He told the Pilgrims that Massasoit (măs'ä-soit), the chief of the tribe of Indians about forty miles away, wished to live in friendship with them, and would sell them corn. You may be sure that this message pleased the colonists, because they did not want trouble with the Indians. The winter had left them too weak to defend themselves, and they were greatly in need of food.

Massasoit came and made a treaty of peace with the colonists. Bradford's history tells how the Indian chief agreed to five things:

"1. That neither he nor any of his people should injure our people.

"2. That if any of his people should ever take any of our things, he would send them back, and we should do the same if our people took anything from the Indians.

"3. That he would assist us if any other people

Compare the Thanksgiving dinners of today with the Pilgrims' first harvest feast pictured here. Where did the Pilgrims get turkeys? Where do we get turkeys today?

made war on us, and we should assist him if any one unjustly made war on him.

"4. That he would persuade all the tribes which were friendly with him to be friendly with us.

"5. That when his warriors came to see us, they should leave their bows and arrows behind them."

The Pilgrims tried to be kind to the Indians. Once, when Massasoit was sick, Governor Bradford sent the sick chief medicine and food. When the white men arrived, Massasoit was so weak that he could no longer see. His house was filled with Indians, howling with grief and making such a noise that the white men said it almost made them sick to hear it. They put a little of the medicine on the blade of a knife and put it on the sick chief's tongue. He got better almost at once and by the next morning was able to drink a little broth made out of corn-meal, strawberry leaves, and sassafras roots. The white men had a hard time keeping the Indian from over-eating and making himself sick again, but he was soon well.

Squanto remained with the colonists and taught them how to cultivate corn and how to hunt and trap game. He told them that the land was too poor to raise corn unless it was fertilized, and showed them how to catch fish and bury two or three in each of the holes into which they dropped the seed corn. The sick Pilgrims recovered with the coming of spring, and they went cheerfully to work digging up the ground and planting their crops of Indian corn. They sowed, too, the wheat and peas that they had brought from England.

In the fall the harvest was good, and the Pilgrims set aside a day for thanksgiving, and invited the Indians to join them. On the appointed day Massasoit came with nearly a hundred warriors. Both the Englishmen and the Indians had helped to prepare for the feast. Some had gone to the woods and some to the sea, and there was fish, deer meat, and wild turkey in plenty. This was the beginning of our custom of having a Thanksgiving Day in November.

Soon after the Pilgrims had made their treaty with Massasoit, another Indian chief sent them a bundle of arrows tied together with a snake skin. This was his way of saying that he was going to make war on the Pilgrims and drive them away. But when the Pilgrims sent the snake skin back filled with powder and bullets, he was so frightened that he would not accept the skin. He sent it back, and said that he would be friendly if they would not attack him.

When we remember how the Indians saved the first settlements in Virginia and Massachusetts from starvation, we should not be too ready to believe that all Indians were bad. The Indians often proved themselves good friends to the white people. Many times they were kinder to the English than the settlers were to them.

More settlers came. But the time of hardship and suffering at Plymouth was not yet ended. In November, just a year after the Pilgrims came to the American coast, a ship arrived with thirty-five young men to join the colony. Bradford was glad to have them, for he would need their strength when the time came to plant the next crop, but they had huge appetites, and before the winter was passed all had to go again on short rations.

The next winter and the next it was the same. With

all their labor, the Pilgrims could not raise enough food one season to last them until the next harvest. During the second year, two ships arrived with about sixty colonists, some of them being the wives and children of men who came in the "Mayflower." Families were happily reunited, but there were more mouths to feed.

For many years, people with the same religion as the Pilgrims continued to come to Plymouth, but the colony grew very slowly. Ten years after its beginning there were only 300 people, and in fifty years there were only 5,000. As the people increased in number, they spread to other villages, north and south of Plymouth and even as far west as the Connecticut River.

Farming helped in making a living. You remember that the Pilgrims borrowed the money which enabled them to come to America, and that they promised to work to pay it back. But Governor Bradford saw that some of the men, and some of the women, too, were unwilling to work very hard when they realized that the London merchants would get nearly everything they made beyond a bare living.

The governor therefore set aside a little piece of land for each family and told the mothers and fathers that they could work this land for themselves and keep all that they raised on it. What they raised on the rest of the land was to be divided with the merchants. Bradford wrote in his history of Plymouth that this arrangement worked successfully. Everybody now raised as much corn as possible. Even the women went to the field with their little children and planted corn.

A few years later Governor Bradford bought the rights of the London merchants, and the colonists gave up working the company fields. They worked much harder for themselves than they were willing to work for others.

Trading and fishing brought prosperity. While the Pilgrims lived in England, they were farmers. Those who went to Holland learned to trade and to work in stores and workshops. In America, they had

The "Mayflower" returned to England in 1621 loaded with beaver skins and lumber, but fishing was more important to Plymouth than fur trading. There were good markets for dried fish both in Europe and the West Indies.

to become farmers again; but the land was poor and produced hardly enough for their own use, leaving them nothing to sell.

However, the sea was on one hand and the forest was on the other. In the forest were beaver and other fur-bearing animals, while the sea held countless fish. So the Pilgrims added to farming the occupations of fishing and of fur trading. They could sell their fish in the West Indies and in the other English colonies in the South, Virginia and Maryland. They could sell the furs in England. You see how important an influence geography has upon the way people live.

How Did It Happen?

1. How did the name *Pilgrim* happen to be given to the settlers who landed at Plymouth?

2. How did the Pilgrims happen to go to Holland? Why did they leave Holland for America?

3. How did it happen that the Pilgrims drew up their own rules before landing in America?

4. How did the Plymouth settlers plan for self-government?

5. How did it happen that the Pilgrims had fewer hardships than the Virginia settlers?

6. How did it happen that for several winters the people of Plymouth did not have enough food? Could this happen to people today? Explain.

7. How did it happen that the Pilgrims began the custom of celebrating a Thanksgiving Day?

RE-CREATING PILGRIM DAYS

1. Read about Captain Miles Standish and write a sketch about his life and services in the colony for your scrapbook. You will find good material in Foote and Skinner, *Explorers and Founders of America*, pages 136-148.

2. You will enjoy reading Henry W. Longfellow's poem, *The Courtship of Miles Standish* (Houghton Mifflin Company). You might ask your teacher to read some of it in class.

3. Make a "movie" about the Pilgrims. On a long, narrow strip of paper draw from twelve to sixteen pictures to show why the Pilgrims left England, why they came to America, and what happened during their first difficult year in America. You might attach each end of this picture strip to a spool or a small round stick. As you unroll the strip from one spool and roll it onto the other spool you will have a moving picture. Try fitting the spools into a box in which you have cut an opening big enough for one picture to be seen at a time. Invent a way to turn the spools and show the pictures.

4. Dramatize the preparations for the first Thanksgiving feast.

5. List the ways in which the Indian helped the white man. Illustrate this list if you wish.

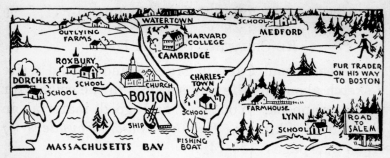
Every colonial town in Massachusetts had a public school.

Outline of Chapter V

V. A Trading Company in Massachusetts
  A. The Coming of Many Puritans
    1. Puritan merchants organized a trading company.
    2. The Massachusetts Bay Company became a self-governing colony.
    3. Many Puritans crossed the ocean.
  B. The Success of Massachusetts Bay Colony
    1. Thousands settled around Boston.
    2. The Puritans faced danger and hard work.
    3. The Indians were few and weak.
    4. Geography encouraged trade.
    5. The colony had strong leaders.
  C. Growing Democracy in Massachusetts
    1. The company charter became the constitution of the colony.
    2. More people gained a share in the government.
    3. Only Puritans could vote or hold office.

Salting and drying fish was an important business in Salem.

CHAPTER V

A Trading Company in Massachusetts

The Coming of Many Puritans

Puritan merchants organized a trading company.
In the summer of 1628 Captain John Endicott
(ĕn′dĭ-kŏt), with a little band of Puritan colonists,
landed on the shore of Massachusetts Bay and began

a settlement that grew into the village of Salem. Endicott was a member of the group of Puritan merchants who formed the Massachusetts Bay Company. Before sending a great number of colonists to America, the group secured a charter for a trading company from King Charles I. The charter gave the company a wide strip of land extending clear across North America from the Atlantic to the Pacific Ocean. The members of the company could sell this land or give it away. They could govern it as they pleased, making their own laws and electing their own governor. They could also take new members into the company whenever they wished.

The Massachusetts Bay Company became a self-governing colony. It is probable that the only purpose of the company at the beginning was to make money by fishing and by trading for furs with the Indians. But the leading members soon changed their minds and tried to make Massachusetts a home for colonists who had the same religious beliefs as the leaders.

Some of the leaders then agreed that they would go to the colony and set up the government there. Among those who decided to go, the most important was John Winthrop. He was elected governor of the colony for the first year and for many years afterward.

Many Puritans crossed the ocean. Today a steamship as long as two city blocks can cross the ocean from England to Boston in five days. The little sailing vessels which made the voyage in 1630 were on the ocean for two months or more, tossed about by storms, crowded and uncomfortable.

Governor Winthrop, who sailed in one of the larger vessels, kept a diary and we can read in his own words about some of the things that happened on the voyage.

"Thursday, April 8: We set sail. In the morning we saw eight vessels following us. The captain thought they might be enemy vessels and made plans for battle. Our cannons were loaded, and the chests containing our powder and balls were opened. We armed the men, and then we all met for prayer on the upper deck. It was fine to see how cheerful and brave all the company were.

"Not a woman or a child showed any fear, though we had only four ships and there were eight vessels following us.

"About one o'clock our captain said that he was not going to try to run away. If a battle had to be fought, he wanted to get it over with before night. So he turned around and sailed to meet them. Imagine our joy when we found that they were our friends.

"Our danger being over, we saw two fishing boats; and each of our vessels sent a skiff to them and bought a great quantity of fine fish.

"Saturday, April 10: Two young men were punished for quarreling and fighting, which was against the rules that we had made. They were compelled to walk the deck until night with their hands tied behind them. Another man was put in chains for using improper language. He was punished until he said that he was sorry and promised that he would behave himself.

"Saturday, May 8: About four o'clock we saw a whale just in front of us, his back about a yard above the water. He would not move, so we passed within a stone's throw of him as he lay spouting up water.

"Friday, May 21: We had to punish one of the servants. He had sold a toy to a child, the little boy promising to give in exchange for it three biscuits a day as long as the voyage lasted. The greedy fellow had already gotten about forty biscuits, and we found that he was selling them to other servants. We tied his hands to a bar over his head and hung a basket around his neck filled with stones, and so he stood for two hours.

"Monday, June 7: The sea was calm, and, our salt fish being used up, we decided to try to catch some fresh fish. In less than two hours we caught sixty-seven codfish, some of them a yard and a half long.

"Saturday, June 12: We came to port. Most of our people went on shore upon Cape Ann and gathered a great lot of fine strawberries. An Indian came aboard and stayed with us all night.

"Monday, June 14: The voyage ended."

More than two thousand people came to the shores of Massachusetts Bay in 1630. Seventeen ships brought men, women, children, indentured servants, cattle, horses, sheep, goats. The map, page 100, shows how towns sprang up about Boston.

The Success of Massachusetts Bay Colony

Thousands settled around Boston. Winthrop's ships were the first of a little fleet of vessels bringing settlers to Massachusetts. During the year 1630, more than two thousand colonists went to Massachusetts and began the settlements that grew into Boston, Cambridge, Charlestown, and other large modern cities. In his diary, Winthrop described the arrival of later ships, and he tells us something about the fortunes and misfortunes of each ship as it crossed the ocean.

"Thursday, July 1, 1630: The "Mayflower" and the "Whale" came into Charlestown harbor. Their passengers were all in good health, but most of their cattle were dead.

"Friday, July 2: The "Talbot" arrived. She had lost fourteen passengers.

"Saturday, July 3: The "Hopewell" and the "William and Francis" arrived.

"Tuesday, July 6: The "Success" arrived. She started with a herd of goats, and lost many of them, and many of her passengers were nearly starved.

"Saturday, July 20: The French ship called the "Gift" came into the harbor at Charlestown. She had been twelve weeks at sea, and lost one passenger and twelve goats.

"October 29, 1630: The "Handmaid" arrived at Plymouth, having been twelve weeks at sea. She lost all her masts, and of twenty-eight cows, she lost ten. She had about sixty passengers, who were all well."

For ten years Winthrop's diary continued to report the arrival of many ships, bringing colonists, cattle, horses, sheep and goats. Many animals died on the long voyage across the ocean, but most of the colonists arrived in good health.

By 1640 there were nearly twenty thousand people in the colony. It continued to grow very much more rapidly than the Pilgrim settlements, and in 1690 Plymouth became part of Massachusetts.

The Puritans faced danger and hard work. Many rich families came to Boston and the other towns near by; and most of the ships that brought colonists for the Massachusetts Bay Company had good cargoes of food and clothing on board. For these reasons the settlers did not have such a hard time as the Pilgrims had at Plymouth.

Nevertheless, the Puritans did not find it easy to live in the wilderness. Two hundred people died during the first two months at Salem, and others became discouraged and returned to England. Once the bread supply was almost at an end when a ship came in from Virginia with a load of corn. Once hogs got into the corn-fields just before the harvest and ate so much that the colonists had very little left for food. It was hard to avoid fire, for most of the houses were cabins built of wood with roofs made of brush and straw and with wooden chimneys plastered with mud and clay.

Nearly every week some colonist lost his cabin or his haystacks by fire. Winthrop tells how a servant went to a neighbor's to get some coals of fire. On the way home he carelessly dropped some hot coals, which set fire to the grass and burned his master's haystacks and house. In another case, when a man placed sixty pounds of powder in bags at the side of his wide fireplace to keep dry: "It took fire,

Was it easy to stop a fire such as this colonial servant started by dropping a live coal? Compare the dangers from fire in colonial times and now.

and some went up the chimney. But some of it exploded in the room and blew out the end of the house. A maid had her arms and neck so badly burned that she died. A little child in the arms of another servant was burned about the face but not killed. Two men were scorched, but not much. Several loaded guns went off but did no harm."

The colonists worked hard, finding the New England soil generally rocky and not very fertile. They learned from the Indians, as the Pilgrims had, to fertilize their fields with fish when planting corn. The little farms yielded food for the settlers, but rarely produced enough to sell outside the colony.

The Indians were few and weak. The Indians were friendly enough at first. It was not until they saw more and more white men coming in their ships and taking possession of the Indian hunting grounds that they began to fight.

Governor Winthrop's diary tells about the early relations between the Indians and the Puritans. Soon after the beginning of the settlement at Boston, a neighboring chief went, with his warriors and squaws, to present the governor with a hogshead of corn. He told Winthrop that he wanted some English clothes, and the governor fitted him out in a new suit and entertained him at dinner. This was the beginning of a friendship that lasted until the chief's death from smallpox several years later.

Perhaps it was smallpox that caused the death of so many thousands of Indians before the coming of the English to New England. At any rate, a great many died of it afterward. The white people were kind to the Indians and nursed them. They tried to save the children by taking them into their own homes, but not many escaped the terrible disease.

Six years after the founding of Boston, the governor made a treaty with some tribes in Massachusetts, in which the Puritans and the Indians agreed to be friendly with one another and to carry on war against the Indians living in what is now the state of Connecticut. The next year a terrible war with the Indians of Connecticut began and went on until nearly all of the tribe were killed. The removal of this tribe made it possible for the settlers who were moving into Connecticut to live there in peace.

The last serious trouble with the Indians, King Philip's War, came when the colony was nearly fifty years old. Philip was the son of Massasoit. When he became chief of his tribe after his father's death, he saw that the farms of the white people were destroying the Indians' hunting grounds. There were only three things that the Indians could do: (1) they could move; (2) they could change their ways of living and settle down and farm like the English; or (3) they could drive out the English and continue to live in their old homes as they had always lived before.

Philip decided to fight. Very secretly he made a treaty with the other tribes in New England and in 1675 they struck. The war, which lasted about a year, was terrible, but Philip had waited too long. The English were too strong; they killed him and destroyed his people. King Philip's War was the last effort of the Indians to drive the white people from New England.

Geography encouraged trade. Geography, as we have seen, not only delayed the settlement of New England, but shaped the habits of the colonists after they arrived and influenced their ways of making a living. The waters of New England swarmed with fish, and the forests produced lumber and masts and tar and pitch for shipbuilding. So fish and lumber combined with the poor soil to make the Massachusetts colonists shipbuilders, fisherman, and traders.

The ships that came into the Massachusetts ports brought cattle, horses, goats and sheep; corn, potatoes and fruits; sugar and molasses and salt; guns and tools and household furniture. Most of the ships which sailed away carried dried fish, furs, and lumber. Some of the trade was with England, but the most profitable market for the New England products was the islands of the West Indies.

The colony had strong leaders. Many fine and noble leaders had a part in the making of the Massachusetts Bay Colony. We have already met Endicott at the beginning of this chapter. He led the first group of colonists to Salem and prepared the way for the settlements around Boston. When the company began to carry out its plans, Endicott became an important man in Massachusetts. He served the colony for many years, sometimes as governor and sometimes as military commander in the Indian wars.

John Winthrop, as we have seen, was governor many times. In England, he had been a rich landowner and lawyer, and had had powerful friends close to the king. It was Winthrop and his friends who persuaded the king to sign a charter saying that the freemen of the trading company could manage their own government in America. He and the members of the company then took the charter with them to America so that they could choose their own governor and make their own laws. Winthrop lived nineteen years after he came to America, and served as governor of the settlements around Boston for a dozen years. The happiness and success of the early settlers in Massachusetts were largely due to his wise and kindly government.

Although he was rich, Governor Winthrop shared the hardships of the people, because he did not want them to be made unhappy and discontented by seeing the governor living in greater comfort than they could afford. He was kind and generous and always gave freely to the poor. The story is told that he used to send his servants on errands to his neighbors about mealtime to see if they had enough food on their tables. If they seemed to need anything, he sent it to them as a gift. According to another story, one very cold winter when wood was scarce in Boston, someone reported that a needy neighbor was taking Winthrop's wood. "Does he so?" said the governor sternly. "Go call that man to me; I'll cure him of stealing." When the man came, the governor said kindly, "Friend, it is a severe winter, and you are but poorly provided with wood; wherefore I would have you supply yourself at my woodpile till this cold season be over." Later Winthrop asked his friends jokingly how they liked the way he had "cured this man of stealing" his wood.

One of the most interesting New England leaders

Massachusetts started a public school system in 1647. The law required every town of fifty families to have a school for all the children.

was John Eliot. He was pastor of the church at Roxbury, near Boston, and preached there for fifty years. He is best known, however, for his work in education both among the Indians and the colonists. He took an Indian into his home and learned from him the Indian language. He then translated the Bible so that he could read and preach to the Indians in their own language. Eliot also wrote an Indian primer and a catechism in the Indian language. Here is a sentence from the Lord's Prayer in Eliot's Bible:

Noo-shun Kes-uk-qut, qut-tian-at-am-unch,
Koo-we-su-onk, Kut-ket-as-soo-tam-oonk
pey-au-moo-utch,
Kut-te-nan-tam-oo-onk ne nai, ne-ya-ne
Ke-suk-qut Kah-oh-ke-it

He taught a number of bright young Indians to read and sent them among their people to teach and preach. During King Philip's War, however, many of Eliot's Christian Indians were cruelly treated by settlers who thought that all Indians were bad. Eliot tried to protect the red men and made an effort to carry on his good work after the war was over; but the Indians no longer trusted the white men. Most of them gave up the Christian religion.

Two other great preachers and leaders in education were Increase Mather (mă'thẽr) and his son Cotton Mather. Both were born in the colony and were educated at Harvard College, the first college to be founded in America. Both preached at Boston, wrote many books, and had a powerful influence upon the people of Massachusetts.

Growing Democracy in Massachusetts

The company charter became the constitution of the colony. The government of Massachusetts Bay was not as democratic as the first Plymouth government. We have already seen how the Plymouth colonists set up their own government under the Mayflower Compact, in which they agreed to make their own laws and elect their own officers. Their government was entirely democratic, that is, every free man had a right to help make the laws and to hold office.

The king's charter gave to the members of the Massachusetts Bay Company the right to make the laws and govern the colony. In the beginning very few colonists were members of the company, so they could not take part in the government. Governor Winthrop and eight or ten assistants had all the power. The charter gave the company the right to take in new members, however, and Winthrop and the assistants very soon did so.

More people gained a share in the government. A quarrel over taxes led to more democratic government. The governor and his assistants passed a law saying that the people should pay a tax. The money was to be used to build a fort, and the people knew that the fort was necessary. They were willing to pay for it, but they denied the right of the governor and the assistants to tax them. They said that nobody had a right to take an Englishmen's money without his consent.

This important question was finally settled by giving the property owners in each town the right to elect representatives to sit with the governor and assistants and help make the laws. At first they all

The governor and assistants met in one room, and the people's representatives met in another.

sat in the same room and talked subjects over before voting. Later, the governor and assistants met in one room and the representatives in another. Most of the states now have legislatures divided into two parts like this early legislature of Massachusetts, which was called "The General Court."

Only Puritans could vote or hold office. The government of Massachusetts was never as free and democratic as was the government of Maryland. You remember that Lord Baltimore gave the people the right to help make the laws without regard to religion. No matter what church they belonged to,

free men in Maryland had the right to vote. The Puritans would let nobody vote who did not belong to the Puritan church.

We have seen that the people who came to Plymouth and the Massachusetts settlements were determined to worship God according to their own beliefs. They suffered great hardships for the privilege of enjoying such freedom, but they were not willing to let others have the same freedom in their settlements. Let those who disagreed with them go elsewhere. If they insisted on staying in Plymouth or Massachusetts, they must keep very quiet. They were not allowed to preach their beliefs or to vote or hold office in the government.

FIND THE RELATIONSHIP

1. between the purpose of the Puritan settlement and the purpose of the Plymouth colony
2. between the Puritans and the Indians

3. between the geography of Massachusetts and the ways in which the Puritans made a living

4. between the government of Massachusetts and the government of Plymouth

5. between the General Court of Massachusetts and our present state legislatures

6. between church membership and voting in Massachusetts

Choose Your Own Activities

Select the activities that interest you. Do as many as you like.

1. The first public schools and the first college in our country were founded in Massachusetts. Read all you can on education in early Massachusetts. If your library has *The Pageant of America* (Yale University Press), chapter IX tells about schools.

2. Try to read the first education law, passed in 1647 by the General Court of Massachusetts, in *The Pageant of America* (Yale University Press), Volume X, page 257. Perhaps you can copy this famous law and post it on the bulletin board.

3. Imagine that you are a Puritan settler in early Boston, and write a letter to a friend in England giving him reasons why you think he should join you. Warn him that he will not find life always easy, and tell him how you live. Try to read Foote and Skinner's *Explorers and Founders of America*, pages 150-159, before you write your letter. Or at

the library get M. E. Freeman's *The Green Door* (Dodd, Mead and Company), which gives a vivid description of the hardships of early New England.

4. Perhaps you can find one of these books in your library and enjoy reading it: In Caroline Sherwin Bailey's book, *Children of the Handcrafts* (The Viking Press), the stories called "The Silversmith's Adventure" and "The Christmas Ship," tell about trade and shipping in the two famous colonial trading towns, Boston and Salem. In *An Island Story*, by H. E. Marshall (Frederick A. Stokes Company), pages 358-362, you will find an interesting story of the Pilgrims. In *The Story of the Marys*, by Grace Humphrey (Penn Publishing Company), pages 27-40, you will find a story of a Plymouth girl.

5. Begin a booklet about "Famous People." Include in it pictures of the people you study, a short sketch of the work of each, and pictures relating to some interesting event in the life of each. Illustrate the events by drawing stick figures or crayon sketches if you wish.

6. Compare the help given the Puritans by Governor Winthrop with the aid given Jamestown by John Smith.

7. Imagine that you are an Indian child in Massachusetts and that your classmates are your Indian companions. Tell them what you saw when the Puritans arrived and what you thought about the white people.

An Indian trail ran through the forests to Connecticut
from Massachusetts.

Outline of Chapter VI

VI. Democracy in Later New England Colonies
    A. The Democratic Beginning of Connecticut
        1. Traders and farmers started Connecticut.
        2. Good land brought many people from Massachusetts.
        3. Puritans from England settled New Haven.
        4. Thomas Hooker helped to form a democratic government.
    B. Free Speech and Religion in Rhode Island
        1. Massachusetts denied free speech and religion.
        2. Roger Williams founded Rhode Island.
        3. Anne Hutchinson and others moved to Rhode Island.
        4. Rhode Island became a real democracy.
        5. Rhode Island helped to give us religious freedom.
    C. New Hampshire's Government

CHAPTER VI

Democracy in Later New England Colonies

The Democratic Beginning of Connecticut

Traders and farmers started Connecticut. The valley of the Connecticut River quickly attracted settlers from Massachusetts for the geography of the country made it easy for traders and farmers to make a living. Its forests and streams gave rise to a rich fur trade with the Indians, and its land was far more fertile than the rocky soil of Massachusetts.

The first white men to settle in Connecticut were traders, Dutch traders from New York and English traders from Plymouth. Both groups came in 1633. The Dutch arrived first. They built a little fort on the Connecticut River, where the city of Hartford now is, and tried to keep the English out of the valley by saying that the country belonged to Holland. But the Plymouth traders sailed by the Dutch fort and started a settlement ten miles further up the river.

Farmers were not far behind the traders. The real beginning of Connecticut dates from the coming of about a dozen home-seeking families to the valley of the Connecticut River from the settlements about

121

Boston in 1635. They came at the end of the summer, traveling overland, driving their cattle and carrying a few household goods. Their furniture, tools, and provisions for the winter were to come by sea from Boston; but the ship was delayed, and the river froze in November. The people found themselves facing a terrible winter without shelter and with little food. Some were discouraged. They found an abandoned boat at the mouth of the river, chopped it free of the ice, and made their way back to Boston. The others decided to stay. They threw up hasty shelters, bought a little corn from the Indians, dug acorns and roots out from under the snow, and managed to live through the winter.

Good land brought many people from Massachusetts. On the last day of May of the following spring, Governor Winthrop in Boston wrote in his diary: "Mr. Hooker, pastor of the church of Newtown, and most of his congregation, went to Connecticut. His wife was carried in a horse litter; and they drove one hundred and sixty cattle, and fed of their milk by the way."

Who was this Mr. Hooker? Where was Newtown? And why did the people want to go to Connecticut?

Thomas Hooker was one of the finest of all the New England leaders. He had a splendid education, for he was a graduate of Cambridge University in England. He had been a preacher and a teacher in England until, like the Pilgrims, he was forced to flee to Holland because he did not follow the rules of the Church of England. Like the Pilgrims again, he left Holland to come to America. There the leaders of the Massachusetts Bay colony welcomed him, and made him minister of the Newtown church.

The village of Newtown was just across the river from Boston. In the very year that Hooker went to Connecticut, it became the home of Harvard University, the oldest university in the United States. A few years later the name of the village was changed to Cambridge.

Hooker was a wonderful preacher and a man of very fine judgment. The members of his church admired and loved him, and asked his advice about the management of their business. One thing that they asked his advice about was this: Their town had so little land around it that it could not grow. There was hardly enough land for their little farms and their growing herds of cattle. What should they do? Hooker said it was a mistake to have towns so close together, and he advised his people to move to the Connecticut valley where there was plenty of fertile land.

At first Governor Winthrop and the Massachusetts leaders tried to prevent the Newtown settlers from leaving. The villages of Boston and Watertown gave them more land, but that postponed their removal for only a little while. Soon several shiploads of colonists came from England, wanting to settle

Hooker insisted that Connecticut's plan of government, the Fundamental Orders, should allow all free citizens to vote.

near Boston. Here was the chance that Mr. Hooker and his people had been hoping for. They sold their cabins and little farms to the newcomers and took up the march for Connecticut. Winthrop tells us how many cattle they had, but says nothing about the number of people. About one hundred people took the trail—men, women and children.

The distance from Boston to Hartford is about a hundred miles. A fast automobile can make the trip

today in an hour and a half. It took these early travelers nearly two weeks, going only seven or eight
miles a day, camping at night, and milking the cows
night and morning. Finally they reached their journey's end and settled at Hartford, where the Dutch
had their fort and trading post.

By the following summer there were nearly a
thousand white people in Connecticut. That was

The people of New London had their grain ground into flour
at a mill built by John Winthrop, the younger, who became
governor of Connecticut. Political affairs were often discussed at the colonial mill.

the year of the war with the Connecticut Indians, which, as we have already seen, made the country safe for white settlement. The members of Mr. Hooker's congregation were not the only inhabitants of Massachusetts who wanted to go to Connecticut. A great many families went also from the villages of Dorchester and Watertown, near Boston. John Winthrop, Junior, the son of Governor Winthrop, started a settlement called Saybrook at the mouth of the Connecticut River.

Puritans from England settled New Haven. Two years after Hooker's settlement was started at Hartford, a Puritan preacher, John Davenport, and his wealthy merchant friend, Theophilus Eaton, came to Connecticut and started the village of New Haven. Davenport had been a preacher in the Church of England, but he became a very strict Puritan, and came to America in order to be free to practice his religion. Eaton came to America from London and acted as governor of New Haven for nineteen years.

Thomas Hooker helped to form a democratic government. Thomas Hooker believed that every man of good character should have the right to vote and help carry on the government. He did not agree with John Winthrop, who believed that only a few men should have the right to vote. The Connecticut towns of Hartford, Windsor, and Weathersfield formed a government in which the laws were made by representatives of the towns, and all citizens had the right to vote in the election of these representatives. Thus it was a democratic government, a government by the people.

The government of New Haven was not like that of the Connecticut River towns. Its leaders believed that none but members of their church should have the right to vote.

After governing themselves for twenty-five years, the Connecticut River colonies obtained a charter from the king of England. It united New Haven with them, and allowed the people to elect both their governor and their legislature. Connecticut had one of the most liberal governments ever established in the English colonies.

Freedom of Speech and of Religion in Rhode Island

Massachusetts denied free speech and religion. The church members and officers of Massachusetts were unwilling to give everyone in the colony freedom to worship God as he pleased or to hold any belief different from that taught by their church. They feared that people who did not believe as they did might some day be in the majority and begin persecuting the Puritans.

Roger Williams, an assistant minister of the church in Plymouth, held different religious opinions from the founders of the colony, however, and tried to persuade others to believe as he did. You can understand why the people of Plymouth did not accept his teachings. He said that the land on which the colonists had built their homes still belonged to the Indians unless the red men had been paid for it. Even the charter from the king, he said, could not take the land away from its native owners, the Indians, and give it to the white men. This sort of talk disturbed those who owned land because they wanted everyone to believe that the deeds to their property were legal and could not be questioned. Williams said, also, that each man should be allowed to choose how he would worship God and that nobody had a right to punish a man for his religious beliefs. When Williams asked to be transferred to Salem, the leaders of Plymouth were glad to have him go, because they thought that he was disturbing the peace of the colony.

In Salem, Williams continued to have trouble. When the Massachusetts government tried to force him to change his beliefs, he asked the church of Salem to separate from the other churches in Massachusetts and follow his teachings. This the church refused to do, and the legislature of Massachusetts then voted to banish Roger Williams from the colony.

Roger Williams founded Rhode Island. In the cold winter weather, accompanied by five friends, the great believer in religious freedom started on his journey from Massachusetts. Slowly the six men made their way through the forest, stopping at

We owe a great debt to the founder of Rhode Island for
championing religious freedom. Look at the diagrams on
page 56. Do you think Roger Williams had courage?

friendly Indian villages for rest and for food. At
last they found a place on Narragansett Bay, beyond
the control of the Massachusetts Colony. Here they
decided to stay. They bought land from the Indians,
and named the place Providence because they believed that God had guided them through the forest
to the place where they could build new homes and
worship as they chose. During the next few years,
others who disagreed with the beliefs of Puritan
Massachusetts came to Providence to live. Some of

them later moved to Rhode Island from which the entire colony finally took its name.

Anne Hutchinson and others moved to Rhode Island. There were still many people left in the colony of Massachusetts who did not accept the teachings of the Puritan church. One of their leaders was Anne Hutchinson.

This seemed very strange in those days because women were not supposed to make speeches or do anything which would attract attention. Instead, they were expected to take care of their homes and of their children. It took so much of a woman's time to prepare food and to make the clothing for her family that very few of them attempted to do anything else. But Mrs. Hutchinson was different. After the Sunday sermons, she gathered together some of the women and such men as cared to come. Then, in talking over the sermon which they had all heard, she criticized it. About a hundred people usually went to the meetings that she conducted.

Finally, Mrs. Hutchinson was called before the General Court because the members of the legislature thought that her teachings were dangerous. The legislature voted that she was guilty of "criticizing the ministers" and was "a woman not fit for our society," so she was banished from the colony.

With her husband and some friends Anne Hutchinson left Massachusetts and made a home in Rhode Island.

Rhode Island became a real democracy. As Roger Williams and his friends were soon joined by others who were attracted by the idea of religious freedom for everyone, it became necessary to form some sort of government. Two years after the founding of the settlement the men of the colony met and drew up an agreement something like the Mayflower Compact. They agreed that all should have the right to take part in making the laws; and they agreed also that everybody might follow his own religious beliefs. This was very different from the Massachusetts Colony, where the government was made up of church members who tried to make everybody in the colony attend the same church.

The settlers in Rhode Island bought their land from the Indians, but for some years they had no charter from the English government to give them a legal right to the property. Then the towns of Providence, Portsmouth, and Newport sent Roger Williams to England to get a land grant from the king. He returned with a charter which gave the settlers a legal right to the land and gave them the right to govern themselves. Twenty years later the people of Rhode Island secured from King Charles II a new charter which united all the towns of the colony under one government. It allowed them to go on electing their own officers, making their own laws, and choosing their own way of worshiping God.

Rhode Island helped to give us religious freedom. There were different churches in the colony of Rhode Island. There was no state tax for the support of any church and there was no law that forced anyone to attend church. A man could vote or hold office in the government without having his religious beliefs questioned.

Only when governments do not interfere in a man's choice of his religion, is there religious freedom. Rhode Island was founded on the idea that religion was to be separate from the state, and for this fact the United States of today owes Roger Williams a debt of gratitude.

New Hampshire's Government

North of Massachusetts, the country which was to become New Hampshire, Vermont, and Maine was settled partly by colonists moving from Massachusetts and partly by people who came directly from England. For many years these people lived in disputed territory. Massachusetts claimed it as part of the land given to the Massachusetts Bay Company by its charter. Some men in England claimed ownership of the same land under an earlier grant. Finally the dispute was settled. The region which is now Maine was governed as a part of Massachusetts for nearly two hundred years. New Hampshire was made a separate colony, claiming Vermont as part of its western lands.

New Hampshire then became one of the thirteen colonies with a government of its own. It had a governor appointed by the king, but the people elected the legislature which made the laws.

GIVE AN EXAMPLE

1. Give examples of two different kinds of conditions that made people move out of Massachusetts.

2. Give an example of democracy in Connecticut.

3. Give an example on the part of the Massachusetts colonial government of what in these days would be considered narrow-mindedness.

4. Give an example of religious freedom in Rhode Island.

5. Give an example of colonies that were settled by people from Massachusetts.

6. Give an example of our debt to Roger Williams.

MAPPING NEW ENGLAND

Make a picture map of New England for your scrapbook. On it show the following:

1. the colonies in the New England group

2. how the harbors, forests, soil, and climate determined the life of the colonists

3. the settlement of Plymouth

4. four early New England towns that are now modern cities

5. Harvard University

NEW ENGLAND YESTERDAY AND TODAY

1. In early New England we find the beginnings of democratic government, religious freedom, and public education. Be sure to have in your scrapbook some pictures, cartoons, or drawings showing that these are important today.

2. Picture the differences in the occupations of New England then and now. Use your geographies for information about present-day New England.

3. Compare the nations represented in the population of New England then and now.

4. Make a list of the conditions on Mr. Hooker's journey from Boston to Hartford that were different from those we would meet in journeying through Massachusetts and Connecticut today. Read about early Connecticut in Gordy's *Stories of Early American History* (Scribner's Sons), pages 12-14, or in some other library book, before you make your list.

5. List the ideas of government, religion, and education that were started in New England and that we still have in America today.

6. Reread the account of the trip from England to Massachusetts taken from Winthrop's diary, and give five ways in which a similar trip today would differ from it.

7. Read more about Unit Two in any one of the following books:

Albert, Edna, *Little Pilgrims to Penn's Woods* (Longmans, Green & Company).

Browne, G. Waldo, *Real Legends of New England* (Albert Whitney & Company).

Bailey, Caroline Sherwin, *Children of the Handcrafts* (The Viking Press).

Willis, Carrie Hunter, and Saunders, Lucy S., *Those Who Dared.*

Colonial Stories Retold from St. Nicholas (The Century Company).

Foote, A. E., and Skinner, A. W., *Explorers and Founders of America.*

Long, John A., *Early Settlements in America.*

Nida, W. E., *Explorers and Pioneers* (The Macmillan Company).

Pumphrey, M. B., *Pilgrim Stories* (Rand, McNally & Company).

Southworth, Gertrude, *Builders of Our Country* (Appleton and Company).

Usher, R. G., *The Story of the Pilgrims for Children* (The Macmillan Company).

8. The pictures in *The Pageant of America* (Yale University Press), Volume I, Chapter X; Volume V, pp. 9-18, and Volume X, pp. 256-259, tell many interesting things about how trade and democracy grew in colonial New England. Other good pictures and stories may be found in Bailey's *Children of the Handcrafts*, in Smith, Mrs. S. C. G., *Made in America* (Alfred A. Knopf), and in Faris, John T., *Where Our History Was Made* (Silver Burdett Company) pp. 80-84.

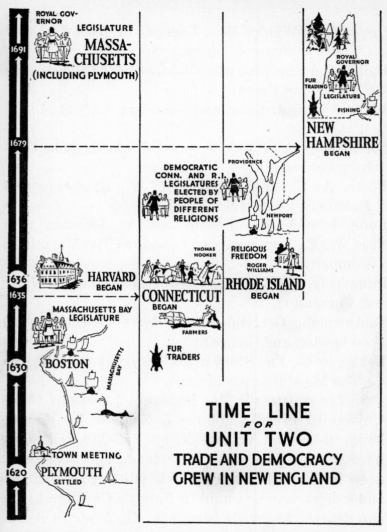

ROYAL GOV-
ERNOR
LEGISLATURE
MASSA-
CHUSETTS
(INCLUDING PLYMOUTH)

1691

ROYAL
GOVERNOR
FUR
TRADING
LEGISLATURE
FISHING
NEW
HAMPSHIRE
BEGAN

1679

DEMOCRATIC
CONN. AND R.I.
LEGISLATURES
ELECTED BY
PEOPLE OF
DIFFERENT
RELIGIONS

PROVIDENCE

NEWPORT

HARVARD
BEGAN

THOMAS
HOOKER

RELIGIOUS
FREEDOM
ROGER
WILLIAMS
RHODE ISLAND
BEGAN

1636
1635

CONNECTICUT
BEGAN

MASSACHUSETTS BAY
LEGISLATURE

FARMERS

FUR
TRADERS

1630

BOSTON

MASSACHUSETTS
BAY

1620

TOWN MEETING
PLYMOUTH
SETTLED

TIME LINE
FOR
UNIT TWO
TRADE AND DEMOCRACY
GREW IN NEW ENGLAND

Follow the time line upward, starting at the foot of the page.

136

A SHORT STORY OF UNIT TWO

TRADE AND DEMOCRACY GREW IN NEW ENGLAND

In colonial times there was much less farming and far more trading in the narrow strip of cold and rocky coast called New England than among the people of the South. Most of the New England colonists did some farming in order to have corn and pumpkins and a few cattle and sheep for home use, but they found it easier to earn a living by building ships and trading in furs or fish.

Trading New England, which today supports nearly eight and a half million people, had its bening in a little English settlement at Plymouth, Massachusetts, in 1620. These first New England pioneers came to America because England did not allow religious freedom. Democracy in New England began with their agreement to make and obey their own laws. When the colony grew so that all the men could not come together in one place to make laws, each town elected representatives to meet and make the laws for them, very much as we do now.

The real growth of Massachusetts began ten years later when a trading company sent more than two thousand people to settle north of Plymouth in the towns that grew into Boston, Cambridge, Charlestown, and other modern cities. The trading company had a charter, or contract from the king of

England, giving its members the right to govern the colonists. Bringing this charter with them, some of the members came to Boston and set up a self-governing colony in which only people who belonged to the Puritan church were allowed to vote or hold office. After some sixty years, the English government united this Massachusetts Bay Colony and Plymouth as the single colony of Massachusetts. From then on Massachusetts had a governor appointed by the king, but the people went on electing a legislature to make their laws.

The pioneers in New England were influenced more than those in any of the other colonies by a desire for religious and political freedom. Some of the hardy pioneers who pushed their way into Connecticut, Rhode Island, and New Hampshire came directly from England, but many came from Massachusetts. These later New England colonies had religious freedom and the most democratic governments in America.

UNIT THREE

People of Many Nations Came to the Middle Colonies

In our day, New York, Pennsylvania, New Jersey, and Delaware support a mixed population of more than twenty-seven million people. These are the states that have grown from the middle colonies of colonial times. Their geography has made them the richest commercial region in the whole of North America, for their broad, deep rivers flow through fine farm lands into excellent ocean harbors. From the beginning people came from many lands.

The first white settlers in New York were Dutch traders and farmers sent by a Dutch trading company from Holland, which was then the greatest trading nation in Europe. The purpose of the Dutch merchants, who had learned about the wonderful furs of the Hudson River valley from Henry Hudson as early as 1609, was to make money from trade. Accordingly, their trading company governed the Dutch colonists very strictly in the interests of trade. The colonists were allowed to follow their own religion, as they had done in Holland. The land was paid for so that they had little trouble with the Indians. But they were not permitted to engage in the profitable fur trade, nor to take part in their

German settlers flocked to Pennsylvania where they made a living weaving and farming. This family of stocking weavers lived in Germantown, now a part of the city of Philadelphia.

own government. As a result of such treatment, the settlers, who were used to more democratic government in Holland, were discontented, and the Dutch colony of New Netherland grew slowly.

In 1664 when the English, who claimed that New Netherland really belonged to them, seized the country, the Dutch settlers welcomed their coming. The New York of today owes much to its history as an English colony. From those early times come its belief in democratic government, its protection of religious freedom, and its great interest in trade.

The country taken from the Dutch included the three other middle colonies, Pennsylvania, New Jersey, and Delaware, where some Dutch and Swedish people were already living. All three of these colonies were rapidly settled when they came under the control of William Penn. His promise of religious freedom, cheap lands, and the right to take part in making the laws brought thousands of immigrants from England, Scotland, Ireland, Wales, and Germany.

The story of how the middle colonies became the home of people from many nations is told in:

Outline of Chapter VII

VII. When New York Was a Dutch Trading Post
    A. Why the Dutch Came to America
        1. Holland had become a great trading nation.
        2. Dutch merchants wanted a short route to India.
        3. The Dutch discovered the American fur trade.
    B. The Beginning of New Netherland
        1. A trading company founded the colony.
        2. Land was given to great landlords.
        3. There was religious freedom.
        4. The people had no share in their government.
    C. Dutch Friendship with the Indians
        1. The Indians were friendly.
        2. The Indians helped the colonists.
    D. Life in New Amsterdam
        1. New Amsterdam became a busy town.
        2. The colonists built Dutch homes.
        3. Schools were encouraged.

BOWLING GREEN IN NEW AMSTERDAM

CHAPTER VII

When New York Was a Dutch Trading Post

Why the Dutch Came to America

Holland had become a great trading nation. Holland, the home of the Dutch people, is on the shores of the North Sea in a low, flat country which has long been known as the Netherlands. The word *Netherlands* means low countries. The North Sea has always been both an enemy and a friend to the people of Holland.

The sea was an enemy because its waters always threatened the low fields on which the Dutch farmers grazed their cattle and planted their crops. In order to keep the water out, great walls called dykes had to be built. Sometimes the waves would beat against these high walls, break holes in them, and come flooding over the land. The Dutch had to be always on the watch so that the water would not overflow their fields, drowning their cattle and ruining their crops.

The sea was a friend to the merchants of Holland, for it gave the country a deeply indented coast with fine harbors such as the one where the city of

Amsterdam (ăm'stẽr-dăm) was built. From this harbor sailed many ships flying the Dutch flag. Most of these ships were in the "carrying trade," getting cargoes wherever they could and sailing wherever there was a market for their goods. Some came home from the long voyage to the East loaded with spices, silks, perfumes, and jewels. Some ships sailed to the American colonies and brought back cargoes of tobacco, grain, and furs. The Dutch were among the most successful seamen in the world.

Dutch merchants wanted a short route to India. In the days when great wealth could be won by trading in the rich products of the Far East, Dutch ship companies joined the search for a shorter route to India than the one around Africa. Many people believed that there was an opening through North America, a "Northwest Passage," which would let ships through to the Pacific Ocean.

The Dutch East India Trading Company wanted to be the first to find this passage and its officers engaged an Englishman, Henry Hudson, to search for it.

The Dutch discovered the American fur trade. Hudson, crossing the Atlantic in a ship called "The Half Moon," sailed one September day into what is now New York harbor. This was two years after the English had founded Jamestown in Virginia. He was met by friendly Indians, who boarded his ship and curiously examined the great boat that

Henry Hudson did the Dutch traders a great service when he made friends of the Iroquois. These powerful Indians controlled the Hudson Valley fur trade.

had come from across the sea. They saw coils of rope, black cannon, and shining brass tablets whose lettering they could not read. One said, "Honor thy father and thy mother." Another, which Hudson wisely obeyed, said, "Do not fight without cause."

The Indians traded tobacco for knives and trinkets. Tobacco was to prove almost as valuable to the trading companies of the old world as a "Northwest Passage" to the East might have proved. The Indians did not remain friendly. They killed one member of a small exploring party and wounded two others.

Hudson decided to sail on up the great river we now call by his name. He carefully guided the "Half Moon" past the Indian village on Manhattan (mănhăt'ăn) Island, past the high bluffs called the Palisades, and on toward the north. When the "Half Moon" reached the place where West Point now stands, Hudson went ashore. We have his own description of what took place. He wrote:

"I sailed to the shore in one of their canoes with an old man, who was the chief of a tribe consisting of forty men and seventeen women; these I saw there in a house well constructed of oak bark, and circular in shape. It contained a great quantity of maize, and beans of last year's growth, and there lay near the house for the purpose of drying enough to load three ships besides what was growing in the fields. On our coming into the house, two mats were spread out to sit upon, and immediately some food was served in well-made red wooden bowls. Two men were also dispatched at once with bows and arrows in quest of game, who soon brought in a pair of pigeons which they had just shot. They likewise killed at once a fat dog, and skinned it in great haste, with shells which they got out of the water."

Hudson and his men refused the chief's invitation to spend the night on land, although the Indians broke their arrows and threw them into the fire so that their guests might feel safe. The white men thought it better to go back to their ship. Continuing their explorations, they sailed on until they reached a place near where the city of Albany now stands. Here the water grew so shallow that they did not dare to take the ship farther.

Hudson had failed to find a "Northwest Passage" to India and the riches of the East; but he had discovered a new source of riches along the Hudson River. He reported to the Dutch that the woods were filled with fur-bearing animals such as beaver and mink and that these furs could be purchased from the Indians at the cost of a few trinkets. The merchants of Holland were pleased with Hudson's account of his voyage because they saw a way to make money from the fur trade.

The Beginning of New Netherland

A trading company founded the colony. Accordingly, in the summer following Hudson's explorations, the merchants sent a ship from Amsterdam to trade some cheap goods to the Indians for furs. By 1613 several such voyages had been made, and a little trading post had been established on "the island Manhattes," that is, Manhattan Island, now part of New York City.

Eight years later the Dutch West India Company was formed. One object of the company was to settle a colony on the Hudson River and carry on trade. So it happened that New Netherland was founded under the control of a trading company which had authority to govern, to bring in colonists, to appoint governors, and to do anything which would increase trade.

In 1623 the first shipload of colonists, thirty families, was sent by the company to New Netherland. A few of these newcomers joined the Dutch already on Manhattan Island. Most of them sailed up the Hudson River to the place where other Dutch traders had already established a fort and trading post called Fort Orange, where the city of Albany now stands. The ships of the Dutch West India Company brought all kinds of supplies to the colonists, such as horses, cattle, sheep, pigs, farm tools, furniture, and cloth.

When the ships returned to the mother country they carried great cargoes of furs. The company made much money from the trade in furs because the Indians did not know how valuable the beaver and mink skins were in Europe. They sold them to the traders for rum, firearms, beads, knives, blankets, and other goods of less value. To the Dutch colony furs were so valuable that they were often used as money. The salaries of officers in New Netherland were sometimes paid in beaver skins.

As the fur trade with the Indians developed, the Dutch established a number of trading posts, each one protected by a fort. The two principal forts were where the cities of New York and Albany are today.

Land was given to great landlords. Starting a new colony was always expensive. Ships had to be provided to carry the people across the ocean. The colonists had to be supplied with tools and seed for farming and with food until they could clear land, build homes, and become self-supporting. The Dutch West India Company offered large estates in New Netherland to wealthy men who would pay the expense of starting a small colony. These men were called patroons (pȧ-trōōnz'), and one of them has left us the following account of one of his estates in the new world.

"It was a fine place, situated along the river, under a mountain. At an hour and a half's journey there is a valley where hay can be raised for two hundred head of cattle, and where there is sixty acres of corn land, and where I have sown wheat which grew higher than the tallest man in the country. Here were also two fine falls from the mountains, where two good mills could be erected for grinding corn and sawing plank. It was a beautiful and pleasant place for hunting deer, wild turkeys, and pigeons."

Had the Dutch West India Company followed the advice of one of their ship captains, their colony might have had a different history. He said, in regard to the settlers: "For their increase and prosperous advancement, it is necessary that those sent out be first of all well provided with means both of support and defence. They should be given land, and all that they work for and gain should be theirs to dispose of and to sell it according to their pleasure."

No such arrangements were made, however, by the trading company. The patroon had great authority over all of the people on his estate. He could hold court, appoint officers, including sheriffs and hangmen, and could compel his tenants to pay him for having their grain ground at his mill. To each tenant, the patroon rented a piece of land which was to be paid for partly in the crops which the tenant raised and partly by labor. Every year the tenant gave the patroon a share of the fruit, vegetables, and grain which he raised. He also had to work a number of days on the roads and to cut wood not only to keep himself warm and to cook his food, but for the patroon as well.

In return for the land given him by the company, the patroon agreed to bring over fifty tenants or colonists and agreed also not to sell furs along the coast of New Netherland, although he could buy or sell anything else. The Dutch West India Company wished to keep the profits of the fur trade for the merchants of the company. Another harsh restriction placed on the patroon was that he could not make cloth of wool, linen, or cotton on his estate. This was because the people in Holland made cloth and wanted to sell it to the colonists in New Netherland.

Under such a system the patroon had many disagreements with the company, and the tenant was constantly in trouble with the patroon. The Dutch colonist knew that his neighbor, the English colonist, had a share in the government while he had none, and that the English colonist did not rent land from an overlord but owned it himself. The English colonist, too, could trade in furs, if he pleased, and his wife could make cloth and sell it to her neighbors or use it for clothing her family.

Besides the patroons with their tenants, there were in New Netherland other colonists who owned small holdings of land and were independent.

There was religious freedom. New Netherland welcomed colonists of different religious beliefs. People who were persecuted in their own country found shelter there; for Holland was the country of greatest religious freedom in Europe at that time.

Although most of the Dutch were Protestants in religion, they had long been ruled by Spain, which

was a Catholic country. Because Spain had not only
ruined their business by heavy taxes, but had tried
to force them to go to the Catholic church, the Dutch
had declared their independence. When, after years
of hard struggle, Holland became a free country,
the Dutch were willing to let others worship as they
pleased. Perhaps this was because the Dutch had
suffered for their religious beliefs at the hands of
the Spanish king; perhaps it was because of the
wise leadership of one of their great rulers, William
the Silent. Holland, at any rate, became a place of
refuge for many who, like the Pilgrims, left their
own country because of their religion. The Dutch
took their liberal ideas to New Netherland.

In a New England town, one of the first buildings
to be erected would be a church; but this was not
true of the towns in New Netherland. Before the
church was built, church services were held in the
loft over the mill or in the minister's house.

The first church building in New Amsterdam was
of stone, and it did not differ greatly from the other
churches of colonial days. It was so cold in the
winter that the women carried hot stones to keep
their feet warm and even men carried muffs. Men
and women did not sit together, as they do today. The
men took seats at the sides of the church, while the
women sat in the center. Contributions were taken
up by the deacons who passed a bag attached to the
end of a pole. From the bottom of the bag hung a

The Dutch colony of New Netherland was run in the interest of profits for the fur-trading company. The people were allowed no share in their government and were forbidden to share in the fur trade.

small bell that tinkled approvingly when a coin was added to the collection. At the beginning of a sermon the hour glass was turned and the minister did not stop preaching until the last grain of sand had run out.

The people had no share in their government. Since the Dutch West India Company had its headquarters in Holland, it was necessary to send over a governor or director-general to govern the colony.

Peter Minuit (mĭn′ū-ĭt), the first governor, bought the island of Manhattan from the Indians for twenty-four dollars' worth of trinkets. He established Fort Amsterdam on the tip of the island, built a ship of eight hundred tons which carried thirty guns, and gave the great landowners many trading privileges. Because these privileges interfered with the trade of the company, and because Minuit spent money in shipbuilding, he was removed, and another governor took his place.

After several governors had held office without satisfying the company, Peter Stuyvesant (stī′vĕ-sănt) was sent to New Netherland. The people in New Amsterdam expected great things of their new governor. Men, women, and children dressed themselves in their best clothes and went down to the dock to watch his ship come in and to greet him. When the new governor stumped ashore, the children, no doubt, looked at him curiously, for he had a wooden leg ornamented with silver nails. From this came his nickname, "Old Silver Nails". Governor Stuyvesant was richly dressed in velvet and silk and wore a wide hat decorated with a long plume. The men and boys stood with uncovered heads while the new governor made a long speech in which he told them that he would be a good ruler for he would rule them as a father guides his children. Perhaps he did feel like a father to his people; but his subjects were grown men, not children, and they wished to have a share in the government under which they lived.

Many of the men, feeling that Stuyvesant was not a good governor, met one day in convention, and drew up a list of complaints against him. This they called their "Remonstrance and Petition." In it they said that Governor Stuyvesant did not provide enough protection for them against the Indians, that he gave large grants of land to his friends, and made laws without the people's approval.

Governor Stuyvesant was very angry when he read their complaints and he ordered the men to leave the convention and to return to their homes. He said, "We receive our authority from God and The Company and not from a few ignorant subjects and we alone can call the inhabitants together."

Even though Stuyvesant refused to give his subjects a share in the government, he tried to be a good governor. He built schools so that the children could learn to read and write; he laid out the streets in New Amsterdam; he kept on good terms with the Indians much of the time; and he decreased the smuggling of furs into New England.

Dutch Friendship With the Indians

The Indians were friendly. Although some of the Dutch thought that the Indians were "a wicked, bad people," this was by no means the opinion of all the colonists in New Netherland. One wrote:

"The natives of New Netherland are found to be very well disposed so long as no injury is done them. But if any wrong be committed against them they remember it long, and should anyone against whom they have a grudge be peaceably walking in the woods or hunting, even after a long lapse of time they will slay him, though they are sure it will cost them their lives on the spot."

The very fact that the people of the town of New Amsterdam lived for some years outside the fort in no fear of the natives, shows the peaceable disposition of the red men. In a "Narrative of a Journey Into the Mohawk and Oneida (ō-nī′dä) Country," we are told that, though travelers were a little uneasy about what might happen to them, the natives allowed the strangers to enter their villages and to leave unharmed. In the native settlements an old traveler saw the famous "long houses" of the great Iroquois (ĭr′ō-kwoi) tribes. In one village there were, he said, "about 36 houses, in rows like streets, so that we could pass nicely. The houses are made and covered with bark of trees, and mostly are flat at the top. Some are 100, 90, or 80 paces long and 22 and 23 feet high." Then he gave the Indians credit for inventing fancy breads by adding, "We bought some bread, that we wanted to take on our march. Some of the loaves were baked with nuts and cherries and dry blueberries and grains of the sunflower."

Since the Dutch bought and paid for their land, they had little trouble with the Indians except when the colonists themselves gave cause for it. Friendly treatment of the Indians was encouraged because it greatly helped the fur trade, which was the chief business of New Netherland. But greed for profit caused many of the Dutch to trade firearms for furs. Thus armed, the Indians had the means of taking revenge when, as sometimes happened, they felt that they had been wronged.

Many of the struggles that arose between the natives and the colonists were the fault of the white men. In Governor Kieft's (kēft) time, a savage killed a Dutch settler in revenge for a previous attack by the Dutch. When the governor, in his turn, took revenge on the Indians, he brought on a cruel massacre of white settlers. Again, when Peter Stuyvesant was governor, war broke out because one of the Dutch colonists shot an Indian woman while she was stealing peaches in his garden. Stuyvesant was away from New Amsterdam at the time. Before he returned, there was much fighting and loss of life, as well as the destruction of a number of outlying farms to which the Indians set fire.

The Indians helped the colonists. The Indians, in the Dutch, as in other colonies, were useful to the new colonists. From the Indians the colonists learned how to plant corn, beans, and pumpkins, how to fertilize the soil with fish, how to make canoes for travel by river and lake, how to trap game in the forests, and how to use Indian money in trading.

The Indians made their money from the clam shells that were found in abundance on Long Island. White and purple beads were ground out from the shells and a hole was drilled so that the beads could be strung into strings and belts. "These wampums," a traveler of the time tells us, "are properly made of the purple parts of the shells which the Indians value more than the white parts. A trader who goes to trade with the Indians and is well stocked with them, may become a considerable gainer; but if he take gold coin, or bullion, he will undoubtedly be a loser, for the Indians who live farther up the country put little or no value upon these metals which we reckon so precious."

The Dutch had the advantage of being near a place where wampum was made and could readily be obtained. Not only that, they learned to make it, and, because of better tools, could make it more easily than did the Indians themselves. Thus the colonists of New Netherland had cheap money and plenty of it for carrying on the fur trade with the Indians. This meant great profits for the trading company, which used the Iroquois as middlemen in bringing furs down from the Indian country to the north.

Life in New Amsterdam

New Amsterdam became a busy town. In the town of New Amsterdam, homes and public buildings were built close to the fort. Here were the storehouse and government house of the Dutch West India Company, the church, a gallows for hanging law breakers, and the pillory. The pillory was a frame of wood with holes through which a prisoner's head and hands were put.

The lives of the townspeople were strictly regulated to prevent fires. At eight in the evening, when a bell called the curfew was rung, fires were covered, candles blown out, and old and young went to bed. It was the duty of the fire warden to inspect all chimneys. If he found them dirty, the owners were fined, and money collected from fines was spent for ladders and buckets. All through the long night the watchman tramped the silent streets, shaking his rattle to assure the head of each house that all was well in the town.

Morning found all the members of every colonial household busy. The boys had water to draw and wood to carry. The men had cows to milk and horses to feed before they started on their day's work. The women had corn meal porridge to make for breakfast and milk to care for in the dairy, for they made the butter and cheese for their families. The growing daughters found plenty to do in helping their mothers.

The first Roosevelt came to America from Holland about 1644. He was Klaes Martensen van Roosevelt, a Dutch merchant in New Amsterdam.

The colonists built comfortable Dutch homes. The first houses of the Dutch traders were shelters like those the Indians made, and were covered with bark. When the settlers began to clear their land, they built log cabins, often fastening the logs to-

From "*Der Amsterdammer*," Amsterdam, Holland, in Shaw's "A Cartoon History of Roosevelt's Career." Adapted by permission, Review of Reviews Corporation.

Theodore Roosevelt, 1910: "All this seems very familiar."
The Dutch Nation: "It is the home of your ancestors."

gether with wooden pins and pegs, for iron nails had to be made by hand and as a result were scarce and expensive.

Later, better houses were built. They were Dutch houses like those in Holland, with the gable end, which was usually of imported brick, toward the street. Their roofs were high and were usually topped by a weathervane in the form of a gay cock. The small windows were of glass, if the owner could afford it; if not, they were sliding shutters of wood. The door was cut in two, so that the lower part could be securely fastened while the upper half might be left open. In this upper part of the door, two small round windows served as peep holes through which the father or the anxious mother could see whether the knocker outside was lifted by a friend or an enemy. A heavy iron latch served instead of a door knob and in the early days metal hinges were so hard to get that leather ones were used instead.

The kitchen, the main room of the house, was heated by a great fireplace, where there were long hooks and cranes on which kettles could be suspended or meat roasted. In this room the women knitted warm socks for the cold winter days while the men smoked their pipes and talked of their growing crops. Here all food was prepared and eaten, and here, at night, in a great bed in the alcove the father and mother slept. Near them the children slept, snugly tucked into their low trundle bed, so called because it could be rolled, or trundled, under the large bed in the daytime. By the fireplace was the hooded cradle where the baby was sung to sleep by this Dutch lullaby:

Trip a trop a tronjes,
De varken in de boonjes,
De koejes in de klaver,
De paaden in de haver,
De eenjes in de water plas,
De kalver in de lang gras,
So good myn klein poppetje was.

*   *   *

(Tip a tap a toe catch
The piggies in the bean patch
The cows are in the clover
The horses by the oats bin
The ducks are in the little pond
The calves are in the long grass
So good my sweet doll baby was.)

Many Dutch homes had a front room which was opened for important guests or on great occasions, such as a wedding. Here the mother kept her treasures: a large four-poster bed piled high with feather mattresses, the Delft plates that came from her home in the Netherlands, and a huge chest filled with linen.

In the cool darkness of the cellar, apples, potatoes, beets, and turnips were packed in bins. Tubs of salt brine contained pork or corned beef. Butter and lard were packed in tubs.

In the attic strings of sausage, smoked hams, and home-cured sides of bacon hung from the ceiling.

Schools were encouraged. The first schoolmaster came to New Amsterdam ten years after the first shipload of thirty families had arrived. Being poorly paid, he added to his small income by taking in washing. A schoolmaster had many duties besides teaching reading, writing, some arithmetic, and the catechism, for he was usually the town clerk, the sexton in the church, and the grave digger. On Sunday he led the singing in the church and turned the hour glass when the minister began his sermon. In addition to all this, he was expected to read the Bible to those who were unable to read, and to visit the sick.

Toward the end of its control of New Netherland, the Dutch West India Company sent over a young man to teach Latin. His school became so famous that Dutch fathers no longer sent their sons to the Boston Latin School to be educated.

READ WHAT THE MAP TELLS

Turn to map on page 77 and answer the following questions:

1. Where did the Dutch settle in America?

2. What did the position of the Dutch settlement do to the English settlements?

3. How did the Hudson River aid the Dutch in the fur trade?

4. Why was New Amsterdam founded where it was?

5. Find on the map the place where the Indians found abundant material for wampum.

6. How did the Iroquois Indians keep the English and French apart?

7. Why would the land in New Netherland be good for farming?

Something You Can Make

1. Draw pictures; make models of clay, soap, wood, or paper; use the sand table; or make scenes in boxes showing some of the following:

a. a Dutch fireplace
b. a blockhouse
c. an Indian peace pipe
d. a stockade
e. an Indian bow and arrow
f. a string of wampum
g. Hudson's "Half Moon"
h. a doorway of a Dutch house
i. a Dutch hooded cradle
j. a four-poster bed and a trundle bed
k. supplies found in a Dutch cellar or attic
l. a Dutch kitchen
m. an Indian canoe
n. a long house of the Iroquois

More furs were shipped from New York harbor than from any other colonial port. What are its chief exports today?

Outline of Chapter VIII

CHAPTER VIII

The English in Early New York

Why New Netherland Became New York

Why did the English want New Netherland? The Dutch colony had several advantages that, with wiser leadership, might have led to rapid growth and power. There was the great Hudson River, whose branches led to the trade of the Indian country, and there was the splendid harbor to encourage trade with foreign ports. There was the great abundance of fur-bearing animals either within the colony or at no great distance. There were the Indians who were inclined to be friendly when the colonists first arrived. There were the fine Indian trails through the Mohawk and Hudson valleys over which the furs could be easily brought to Fort Orange or New Amsterdam. There was the fact that the Indian money could be easily and cheaply secured. There was plenty of rich land for farming.

Nevertheless, all these advantages were outweighed by the fact that the trading company in charge of New Netherland was so greedy for profits that it neglected the welfare of the settlers so that few colonists came.

England looked with longing eyes at New Netherland, wedged in between its New England colonies on the north and its other colonies farther south. English merchants were envious of the rich profits the Dutch trading company made from the fur trade up the Hudson valley. They claimed that the land was England's by right of discoveries made by the Cabots who had sailed along the coast long before Hudson had been sent out by the Dutch merchants.

The English seized the Dutch colony. In 1664, the English king sent a fleet of warships to take the Dutch colony. Commander Nicolls (nĭk'ŭlz) was to be the first English governor. When he reached New Amsterdam, the English commander ordered Stuyvesant to haul down the Dutch flag. The Dutch governor grew red in the face and stumped about on his wooden leg, angrily declaring that he would never surrender; but his people, to whom he had refused to listen, now refused to help him. They expected that under the English they would have democratic government as the English colonists did. So, without fighting, the Dutch colony went under English rule, and was renamed New York for the king's brother, the Duke of York, to whom it was given.

The transfer of New York from the Dutch to the English had the effect of bringing the English colonists in New England into closer contact with the English colonists to the south. No longer was

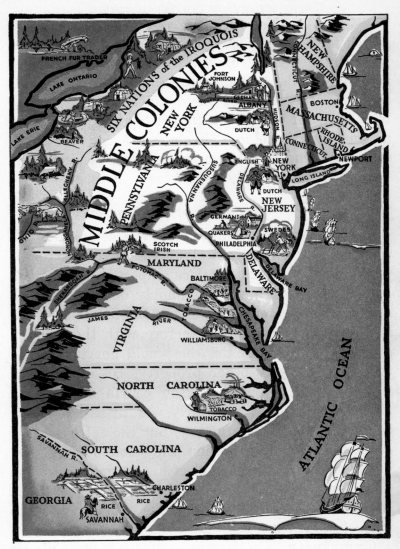

Can you locate in the middle colonies settlers from four different nations? Notice how New York makes a wedge separating New England from the colonies to the south.

169

Dutch territory wedged in between two sections of English territory. This change made it much easier for the English colonies to unite when union became of the greatest importance to them. The New York of today owes much to its early history as an English colony. From those colonial times come its democratic government, its practice of religious freedom, and its greatness in trade.

How New York Became Self-Governing

Early New York had no elected assembly. When the colony of New Netherland was given up to the English, the Dutch settlers expected to elect a legislature, as this was commonly done in English colonies. The commander of the English fleet promised that he would not interfere with the religion of the colonists and that he would not take away their land or any other property. He also agreed to have trial by jury in the courts and to tax all the people justly and fairly. As far as this promise went, it was satisfactory, but the settlers were greatly disappointed when they found that they would not be allowed to elect an assembly to make their laws. The governor and his advisory council, who were appointed by the Duke of York, were to rule New York.

Commander Nicolls was a good governor. He won the respect of both the settlers and the Indians. Without creating trouble, he helped them to get used to the change in government. He did much toward settling the boundaries of the colony, and seems never to have abused the great power that was his.

New York was next ruled by Governor Lovelace, who tried to establish the first regular mail delivery in America. His plan was to make one trip each way between New York and Boston every month. Writing to the younger John Winthrop at Hartford, Connecticut, the governor said, "By our monthly letters all public news may be carried from one colony to another, and our settlements may be more closely united, as the king has desired." Under Governor Lovelace, New York was still without a legislature.

Finally the people gained the right to make laws. Ten years after the English had taken the colony, Sir Edmund Andros (ăn′drŏs) was sent over to be the third English governor of New York. Although he was honest and hardworking, the new governor had little sympathy with or understanding of the people. Therefore, it was not long before the colonists were demanding a representative assembly. They had talked of such a body before Andros arrived in New York. Now they demanded it as their right. They sent a petition to the Duke of York, who decided to let them have what they wanted.

Accordingly, under a new governor, Thomas Dongan (dŏn′găn), an assembly was elected and held its first meeting in October, 1683. Before it had done very much, however, the Duke of York became King James II and withdrew the permit that he had given for the New Yorkers to have a legislature.

Fearing that the French would get the Indians to help them make war against his colonies in North America, the king had decided to unite New York, New Jersey, and the New England colonies, and to place one governor over all of them. He sent Sir Edmund Andros back to America with authority to unite all these colonies and to rule them without the help of an elected law-making assembly. Governor Andros tried to carry out the wishes of his king, and in doing so, as you can imagine, found himself very unpopular in all the colonies. But the king was as unpopular in England as Governor Andros was in America. After he had governed three years, Parliament forced him to give up his throne to his daughter, Mary, and her husband.

When the American colonists heard that the English people had invited William and Mary to rule England, the people of Massachusetts arrested Andros and sent him back to England. In New York, a German merchant, Jacob Leisler (lĭs'lĕr), seized the fort and took over the duties of governor. At first he was supported by most of the people, but he lost much of his popularity because he enforced unpopular laws and behaved in a very high-handed way. After about two years, he was hanged for refusing to give up his power when the new rulers of England sent over another governor to the colony.

After the revolution in the government of England, when New York had been under English government for twenty-five years, its colonists gained the assembly which they had desired for so many years. The towns and counties of New York were, at last, given the right to elect representatives to make the laws and assist the governor in ruling the colony.

New York a Wealthy, Powerful Colony

A mixed population grew and prospered. After the English allowed New York to have a legislative assembly, more men and women wanted to settle in the rich colony. Incoming ships brought new colonists both from Europe and from other colonies in America. In twenty years the colony nearly doubled its population.

With the increase of population came better living conditions. The fur trade became far more valuable than it had been under the Dutch, and farming prospered. Those who had grown wealthy built larger and better homes, in which silver plate took the place of the pewter which the Dutch had used. Even poor men no longer lived in huts. Good roads took the place of forest trails, and, with good roads,

Dutch and English farmers watered their cows at the town pump at the corner of Wall Street and Broadway in 1681. What are Wall Street and Broadway like today?

came the horse-drawn cart to replace the pack horse. Inns were built, where the traveler could spend the night in comfort instead of trusting to the kindness of good-natured settlers.

The mixture of people and customs showed in their amusements. Boys and girls still enjoyed sleigh rides and skating in winter and fishing in summer, as they had under the Dutch rule. Husking bees were still held in the fall, and in June the "Pinckster picnic" still gave the opportunity for gathering the beautiful wild pink azaleas that grew in the woods.

Many of the British colonists, however, liked horse racing better than any other amusement.

The friendly Iroquois gave New York a rich fur trade. The English inherited the friendly relation of the Dutch with the Indians who were spread over much of New York. These Indians were the powerful Iroquois with their villages of long houses, their cultivated fields, and their strong government of six nations under a council of chiefs. The Iroquois had never forgiven the French for fighting against them when Canada was being founded, but had given their friendship to the early Dutch settlers.

On taking over the Dutch colony, the English did what they could to keep the peace with the Indians, for they knew that the six nations were very valuable neighbors. They saw very clearly that the friendship of the Iroquois was necessary to the prosperity of the colony because these Indians controlled the fur trade and protected the western border against the French. Again and again the French tried to win the good will of the Indians in New York. Sometimes they almost succeeded; but the English always managed to appeal to the bond of friendship that had existed for so many years between them and the Iroquois. In this way the English had the help of the most powerful Indians in America in keeping the French out of the northern colonies and in carrying on the rich fur trade.

One of the most important citizens of colonial New York was Sir William Johnson, who was made superintendent of Indian affairs by the governor. He was an Irishman who came to America as a young man to look after his uncle's lands in the Mohawk River Valley on the New York frontier. He was not satisfied to be merely an agent on his uncle's land, but wanted land for himself. By the time he became Sir William Johnson, he was one of the great landowners and fur traders of the colony.

Before he had been in America two years, he had bought several thousand acres north of the Mohawk River. Here he built for himself a great stone house with walls four feet thick, and called his new home Fort Johnson. Beside the river which ran through his land, he built two mills, a sawmill and a gristmill. In the sawmill could be heard the busy hum of the saw as it made the logs of the western forest into lumber. In the gristmill corn was ground into corn meal and grain into flour for bread or into feed for horses and cattle. Some of the flour was made into bread for Sir William's own family, for his servants and slaves, and for his guests.

Many people went to Fort Johnson to visit and talk with Sir William—noblemen from England, officers of the colony of New York, Indians from the forest. All were welcomed. The Indians came in groups to sell furs to Sir William who bought many beaver and otter skins and other furs and sold them

Sir William Johnson grew rich shipping furs and lumber and flour down the Hudson Valley from his great estate in northern New York. Find Fort Johnson on the map, page 169, and trace the route to New York harbor.

in England. Often Indian chiefs came to counsel with their white brother whom they loved and respected.

The Indians had good reason to love Sir William, for he was honest with them when he bought their furs. He would not lie or cheat. He kept his promises to them. They feasted at his home. Sometimes as many as several dozen Iroquois came to Fort Johnson. Then tents were pitched on the lawn, and meals were served out-of-doors on long wooden tables built under the trees, so that the lawn of the great house looked like a picnic ground. Sir William exchanged valuable gifts with the Indian chiefs. He gave many a poor Indian hunter traps, a gun, powder, and warm blankets from the country store that he maintained. He trusted the poor Indian to pay him in beaver skins or in wampum when the hunting season was over and summer had come, and he was seldom disappointed. "The Indians are honest," he used to say.

The Iroquois made him a member of their nation and invited him to sit with them in their councils. When he attended an Iroquois council, he dressed like an Indian, putting war paint on his face, wearing a great feathered headdress, and wrapping himself in a blanket. He made long speeches in the Indian language and listened while the Indian chiefs made their long speeches. After his white wife died, he took an Indian wife, Molly Brant. She was an Indian princess, the granddaughter of a chief of the Iroquois and sister of the famous chief, Joseph Brant. "Lady Molly," as she was called, always made his Indian friends welcome, and could persuade them to do as Sir William wished when he could not control them.

Once some Indians sold to white men great

stretches of land near the place where the city of Schenectady now stands, thinking that they were only loaning the land to the white men for pasture land. When the white settlers claimed the land, the Indians complained to Sir William Johnson. On examining the papers, he found that the land had been sold. The Indian chiefs had signed the papers with their names or marks, and their totem signs. There were the totem-signs in the form of rude pictures of a wolf, a bear, or a tortoise. Sir William said that the papers proved that the Indians had sold the land which they thought was still theirs. Because he said that the white men owned the land, the Indians went peacefully back to their homes.

For more than thirty years Sir William Johnson held the Iroquois friendly to the English, and so kept them as a protection against the French on the north. Probably no other man of his time could have been successful in doing so.

What Do You Think?

(Give reasons for your answers.)

1. Was it important for the English to keep the friendship of the Iroquois?

2. Did England have any right to claim New York?

3. Were the Dutch settlers wise in surrendering to the English without a struggle?

4. Did the settlers in New York have a right to demand a representative assembly even though the governors were ruling the colony wisely and well?

5. Was it wise for the English to send Governor Andros back to America to try to unite New York and the New England colonies?

6. Does the story of Sir William Johnson suggest anything as to the best way to treat the Indians?

PICTURE NEW YORK

1. On the map on page 77, locate the Hudson River, New Amsterdam, and Fort Orange. Notice how New Netherland was like a wedge between New England and the English colonies to the south.

2. Give a word picture of New York harbor today. Look at the pictures in your geography. Some member of the class might like to write to the Chamber of Commerce, New York City, New York, and ask for pictures of New York City and of New York harbor.

3. Try to find a picture showing that New York still has a mixed population, and post it on the bulletin board.

4. Imagine a trading scene in New York today. Picture the difference between it and a fur-trading scene at Fort Johnson.

5. Make a collection of pictures of things that Sir William would never have dreamed of, which are found in New York at present.

Outline of Chapter IX

IX. Pennsylvania and Two Colonial Neighbors
- A. Why Pennsylvania Had Religious Freedom
  1. Few countries allowed religious freedom.
  2. Quakers were cruelly treated in Europe.
  3. William Penn became a leading Quaker.
  4. Penn turned to America for religious freedom.
- B. Why People Came From Many Lands to Pennsylvania
  1. Penn made a business of getting colonists.
  2. Penn made friends of the Indians.
  3. It was easy to earn a living.
- C. How Democracy Began in Pennsylvania
  1. Penn was landowner and governor.
  2. The people elected the legislature.
  3. The legislature and governors disagreed.
- D. The Mixture of Colonists in New Jersey
  1. Dutch, Swedish, and English came.
  2. Penn helped to give New Jersey self-government.
- E. Delaware and Pennsylvania Under the Same Governor
  1. Dutch and Swedes first settled Delaware.
  2. Delaware and Pennsylvania had the same governor.

CHAPTER IX

Pennsylvania and Two Colonial Neighbors

Why Pennsylvania Had Religious Freedom

Few countries allowed religious freedom. In colonial times, as we know, most people in Europe did not have freedom in religion. Although the people of England were divided into many religious groups, the Church of England was supported by the government, and the government tried to compel everybody to belong to that church. We have seen how the Pilgrims fled first to Holland and then to America so that they might have their own church. We have seen, too, how the Puritans settled New England for the same reason, and how Lord Baltimore made a home for Catholics and others in Maryland. In most of the countries of Europe conditions were similar to those in England; there were Quakers, Baptists, Presbyterians, Catholics, and many other religious groups. In nearly every country, there was great discontent and distress because the laws required all the people to practice the same religion as the ruler. This caused the rapid settlement of Pennsylvania, where the colonists were allowed to practice whatever religion they thought best.

Quakers were cruelly treated in Europe. Of all the abused and distressed groups who suffered for their religion, the Society of Friends fared the worst. They were disliked not only by members of the Church of England, but by Puritans and Catholics as well. They were given the popular name *Quakers* because, when one of their earliest leaders was arrested, he told the English judge to "tremble (quake) and fear God."

The Quakers' lack of a fixed creed, that is, of a statement of beliefs that all must accept, caused other religious groups to dislike them. The Quakers thought that each person should study the Bible and form his own beliefs. They had no church buildings and no regular church organization where members of the same congregation met for worship on certain days of the week. There were no regular preachers. Any man or woman might preach at any time and almost at any place. Having no church buildings, they often preached in barns, on the open roadside, and on village street corners.

The Quakers not only turned away from the religious customs of the time, but disapproved of some of the usual political and social practices. For example, they were opposed to war and would not serve in the army or navy. They would not take an oath and could not, therefore, perform some of

Penn wore a hat in the king's court, as he did in the company of common people, because Quakers did not believe in class differences. Can you see why the Quaker colony of Pennsylvania became a democracy?

the duties that were required of all good citizens, such as sitting on juries. They thought it a sin to show more respect to one person than another. Therefore, they addressed everybody as "thee" and "thou" and "friend." They refused to take off their hats when they appeared in court, or even when they appeared in the presence of the king. And many a noble resented the refusal of humble Quakers to lift their hats or to address him by his title.

William Penn became a leading Quaker. William Penn, who became the founder of Pennsylvania, was a man of great wealth and high social position. His father held high rank in the English navy. Although the king's brother, the Duke of York, was Lord High Admiral, Admiral Penn sailed on the flag ship and was the real commander when there was any fighting to be done. The king and his brother felt a warm friendship for Admiral Penn. They welcomed him at court and bestowed upon him many gifts and favors. The admiral's wife and daughter were the gayest of society women, and it was in this atmosphere of gayety, wealth, and influence that William Penn spent his boyhood.

The education of young William Penn was broadened by travel and business experience. Private teachers gave him his early training, and at the age of fifteen he went to Oxford University. After he had been at Oxford about two years, he was expelled from the university because he became interested in the Quaker religion and refused to attend the Church of England chapel. But his education did not stop when he left Oxford. His father sent him to France, where he traveled and went to school. On his return to England, he studied law for about a year. Then his father sent him to Ireland to manage the family estate. The wealth and power of his father and the social activity of his mother did not keep William Penn from being an earnest and hard-working student. He became one of the clearest thinkers and writers of his day. He spoke several foreign languages, including French and Italian, and could read and write Latin well. He was a serious student of the Bible and of other religious literature, and had a considerable knowledge of law.

It was while he was a student at Oxford that William Penn first heard a Quaker sermon. He was much impressed by the earnest, simple words of the preacher and by the absence of the forms and ceremonies to which he was accustomed in the Church of England. It seemed to him that this simple religion was better.

Penn's father tried to make his son give up the hated religion, and for a while it looked as if Admiral Penn had succeeded in getting his handsome young son to give up Quaker ways. In France the young man lived a gay life and seemed to have forgotten the Quakers. He returned to England and served a short time in the navy. When his father sent him to Ireland, William became a soldier, as no Quaker could do. But the same preacher who had aroused Penn's interest at Oxford happened to visit Ireland. Penn heard him preach and was again won to the Quaker religion. From that time onward he never changed. He was arrested and imprisoned for preaching on the streets. His father drove him from home, when he was released from prison, but he remained firm until, at last, the admiral forgave him.

William Penn became a rich and powerful man,

for he inherited his father's wealth and friendship with the king. A story is told of the friendly humor of the king toward Penn. Once, it is said, Penn wore his hat in the king's presence. King Charles removed his own hat. "Why does thee uncover, Friend Charles?" asked Penn.

"Because it is the custom," the king replied, "for only one man to remain covered, where the king is. We must not break the custom. You will not remove your hat, so I must take off mine." But everybody was not so pleasant as the king.

Penn was an important Quaker leader. He preached, wrote books on religious subjects, and tried to help Quakers who got into trouble with the government. He himself was arrested again and spent many weeks in prison.

Penn turned to America for religious freedom. Penn became interested in America when two Quakers who owned part of New Jersey, where Quakers were already settling, appealed to him to settle a dispute. He did so, and then got some friends to join him in buying most of New Jersey and sending many Quaker colonists there. His interest in the Quaker settlement of New Jersey led Penn to ask the king for land in America.

It happened that the king owed Penn's father a large sum of money, equal in our day to nearly half a million dollars. In payment of this debt Penn asked for a grant of land in America. King

Charles gladly gave him land and named it Pennsylvania, in honor of William Penn's father. The name means *Penn's forest*, or *Penn's woodland*, and since the word Penn means *high*, we may say that Pennsylvania means *high woodland*.

Why People Came From Many Lands to Pennsylvania

Penn made a business of getting colonists. Immediately after getting his territory from the king, Penn wrote a little book describing the country, telling the liberal terms upon which he would sell or rent land, and promising that all the colonists should have a share in making the laws that governed them.

This booklet and other writings by Penn spread through England, Scotland, Ireland, and Germany. There were already some Swedes and Dutch in Pennsylvania, and very soon there were English, Scotch, Welsh, German, and Scotch-Irish colonists on the way to the country. The Scotch-Irish were Protestants, usually Presbyterians, who went first from Scotland to Ireland and later came to America. In the beginning there were more different sorts of people in Pennsylvania than in any other colony.

Penn made plans for three different classes of people: (1) those who were able to buy land; (2) those who could pay their passage across the ocean but who had no money to buy land; and (3) servants who could not even pay their way to America.

German "redemptioners" flocked to Pennsylvania, becoming farmers when their terms of labor were ended. Often a sod hut dug in a hillside served as the first home of the farmer's family.

Those who were able to buy could get five thousand acres for a hundred pounds. Those who could not buy could rent land for a penny an acre. Those who could neither buy nor rent could borrow from Penn enough money to pay their way and work for a master in Pennsylvania for five or six or seven years. These laborers were called "redemptioners" in Pennsylvania, because they "redeemed" themselves from bondage by their labor. In the other colonies, as we have seen, they were usually called indentured servants. When the cost of their voyage was repaid by their labor, Penn would give each man fifty acres of land.

Penn himself arrived in his colony in October, 1682. There he visited various parts of the territory and the principal Indian settlements. He began to build a mansion on the Delaware River above Philadelphia, intending to bring his wife and children to Pennsylvania and live there the rest of his life. But business recalled him to England in 1684 and sixteen years passed before he saw Pennsylvania again. Then he returned for two happy years in the colony, and went back to England to stay. Thus, he was able to spend but four years in his beautiful "woodlands," as he called Pennsylvania.

During his first visit to Pennsylvania, Penn wrote another pamphlet for the information of Europeans who might want to come to America. The climate, Penn said, was delightful. It was not too cold in winter, nor too hot in summer. He thought it much better than the climate of England. The land was fertile and would produce abundant crops of grain, fruit, and vegetables. Valuable timber grew in the forests, and the woods swarmed with game and wild fowl. Among the animals that he mentioned were elk, deer, beaver, rabbits, squirrels, bear, wild cats, panthers, wolves, and foxes. Wild turkeys, he said, grew as large as forty or fifty pounds. Great flocks of wild pigeons darkened the sky in their flight and ducks and wild geese were numerous. The waters swarmed with fish. Penn thought that nobody need ever go hungry in Pennsylvania. In August, 1683, there were already 4,000 people in Pennsylvania, with about eighty houses in Philadelphia.

Penn made friends of the Indians. Although the laws of England declared that the land belonged to the king and gave him the right to sell it or give it away, Penn thought that the red men, too, had a right to the land because they used it for their homes and hunting grounds. He determined, therefore, that he would buy the land from the Indians. He sent a letter to the Indians the very first thing, telling them that he would always be fair to them and wished to have their friendship.

"My friends," he wrote, "There is one great God. He made you and me and the world, and everything that is in the world. He has commanded us to love and to help and to do good to one another.

"The king of the country where I live has given me a great province in your part of the world: but I desire to enjoy it with your love and consent, and that we may always live together as neighbors and friends. I desire to win and gain your love and friendship by a kind, just, and peaceable life; and the people I send are of the same mind. They will treat you fairly. If you have a dispute with any of them, if they do anything that you do not like, the matter shall be settled by submitting it to an equal number of your people and mine.

"I shall shortly come to see you myself, at which time we can discuss everything more fully. In the meantime I am sending my agents to treat with you about land and a firm league of peace. Let me desire you to be kind to them and to the people. I wish you to receive the presents which I have sent you as a token of my good will to you, and of my resolution to live justly, peaceably, and friendly with you. I am your loving friend, William Penn."

When Penn came to America, he visited the Indians in their homes, and convinced them of his goodness and fairness. The next summer he met a number of chiefs near Philadelphia and made a treaty which both the Indians and the white men kept for seventy years. Later he made other treaties, by some of which the Indians sold him land.

Many years later, a governor of Pennsylvania gave a talk to a large gathering of Indians and reminded them of their treaties with William Penn. This is a part of his talk:

"My friends and brothers: You remember that the great William Penn, the father of this country, when he first brought the people with him over the broad sea, took all the Indians by the hand. He found them to be a sincere, honest people. He took them to his heart, and loved them as his own.

"He then made a strong league and chain of

The Pennsylvania colonists profited from Penn's Indian treaty. The purchase of the land kept peace, and peace encouraged the fur trade.

friendship with them, by which it was agreed that the Indians and the English, with all the Christians, should be as one people. Your friend and father, William Penn, always had a warm affection for all

the Indians, and commanded his governors whom he
sent to this country to treat the Indians as his children. He continued to love them until his death."

Because of the fairness of Penn and his colonists,
there were no wars with the Indians for many
years. This was one of the reasons why the population of Pennsylvania increased so rapidly. People
knew that they could go there and be safe from
the Indians.

It was easy to earn a living. As in all of the
colonies, the first occupation in Pennsylvania was
farming. The colonists had to raise the food they
and their livestock ate. But Pennsylvania quickly
became an important commercial colony, also. In
the first place, the fertile soil was capable of pro-
ducing far more grain and other foodstuff than the
colonists could use, and they naturally wanted to
sell the surplus that they did not need. In the
second place, the forests and streams of the colony
were the homes of great numbers of fur-bearing
animals and caused the development of a valuable
fur trade with England. Finally, at Philadelphia,
the broad, deep Delaware River gave Pennsylvania
one of the best ports on the Atlantic coast. We may
say that geography gave the Pennsylvanians an
abundance of things to sell and furnished them a
safe and easy means of sending the goods to market.

The location of Philadelphia between the Delaware and Schuylkill (skōōl′kǐl) rivers gave it great

advantages for commerce. It grew quickly into the largest city in the English portion of North America, though it was many years younger than New York, Boston, or Baltimore. A few figures will show us how rapidly it grew. When Penn wrote that there were eighty houses in Philadelphia, some of them were hardly better than Indian wigwams. The next year he wrote that there were 357 houses, and that some were built of brick. By 1700 there were 2,000 houses in the thriving little city.

Although there were many large farms in Pennsylvania, there were very few slaves, for the Quakers were opposed to slavery. A great many people came, however, as redemptioners, or indentured servants. These servants became free, you remember, after serving their masters a few years, and were given land for their own use.

The population of Pennsylvania in 1700 was around 16,000. By 1750 there were 200,000 people.

How Democracy Began in Pennsylvania

Penn had rights as landowner and governor. William Penn was given a charter granting him the territory bounded on the north by New York, on the south by Maryland, and on the east by the Delaware River and New Jersey. He had the same rights and powers in Pennsylvania that Lord Baltimore had in Maryland. He could sell the land or rent it and he could govern the country by laws which the colonists approved. The date of the king's grant was 1681.

Penn's charter from the king did not describe the southern boundary of Pennsylvania very clearly. Apparently, it was intended to give Penn the territory north of Maryland and south of New York. Almost immediately, however, a dispute arose between Penn and Lord Baltimore about the boundary between Pennsylvania and Maryland. The dispute dragged on for seventy years and was finally settled by a compromise. The boundary was then surveyed and marked in order to avoid future misunderstanding. The surveyors who marked the line were Charles Mason and Jeremiah Dixon, so the boundary between Pennsylvania and Maryland is sometimes called the Mason and Dixon line.

It was Penn's idea that he himself would be the governor of Pennsylvania, but, since he spent only four years in America, the colony was governed most of his lifetime by a governor whom he appointed. After Penn's death, however, one of his sons was governor of Pennsylvania for many years.

The people elected the legislature. It was Penn's wish from the beginning that his colonists should make their own laws. For that purpose he proposed that they should elect two bodies to represent them, a council of seventy-two members and a larger body which he called the assembly. The colonists decided, however, that one body of representatives would be enough for them so they let the council pass the laws. The result of this change was that the laws of Pennsylvania were made by a legislature of *one house*, that is, by a single group of representatives all working together in one room, or *house*. All other colonies then had *two-house* legislatures.

The legislature and the governors disagreed. The governor could propose laws that he wanted, but the legislature had to pass them before they could go into effect. On the other hand, the legislature could pass laws that it wanted, but they could not go into effect until the governor signed them. Thus the legislature and the governor had to act together in the making of the laws.

Misunderstandings and ill-feelings arose about the laws. In spite of Penn's desire to benefit the colonists and be fair, the legislature often disagreed with the governors who carried out Penn's instructions. It tried to tax the proprietor's vacant lands, and protested about the rents which many colonists refused to pay on the lands that Penn had let them have.

Some of the colonists felt that Penn was greedy, and he felt that the colonists were ungrateful. Penn declared that he had spent a great deal more in buying land from the Indians and in surveying and deeding it to the colonists than he received from the colonists during his lifetime, and his statement was probably correct. His last years were saddened by these quarrels for, in addition to his expenses in Pennsylvania, he lost a great deal of money through the dishonesty of the manager of his property in England. He was even compelled to spend nearly a year in prison because he could not pay his debts. After Penn's death, however, his lands in Pennsylvania made his children and grandchildren very wealthy.

The Mixture of Colonists in New Jersey

Dutch, Swedish, and English settlers came. New Jersey, which is really a peninsula bounded on the east by the Hudson River, on the west by the Delaware River, and on the south by the ocean, was regarded by the Dutch as part of New Netherland. The first settlements were made on the two river fronts by the Dutch, who had the center of their government at what is now the city of New York.

Some Swedish colonists settled in the Delaware valley, but they were conquered by Governor Stuyvesant, the last Dutch governor of New Netherland.

The New Jersey country came to the English by their conquest of New Netherland and was included by the king in the territory he gave to his brother James, Duke of York. James gave the territory of New Jersey to two friends, Lord John Berkeley (bûrk′lĭ) and Sir George Carteret (kär′tẽr-ĕt). These two noblemen, after making some settlements, sold their rights to some Quakers.

ENGLISH
SCOTCH
WELSH
2,880,000

NEGROES
760,000

SCOTCH-
IRISH
200,000

GERMANS
150,000

INDIANS
80,000

DUTCH
IRISH
JEWS
HUGUENOTS
SPANIARDS
SWEDES
?

Adapted from "We and Our History" by A. B. Hart.
Courtesy, The American Viewpoint Society, Inc.

This graph shows from what nations and races the population of the thirteen American colonies came. What were the four largest groups?

Penn helped to give New Jersey self-government. All of New Jersey finally came into the ownership of William Penn and some of his Quaker friends. While the territory was under the control of the Quakers, a good many colonists came to New Jersey, some from New England, but most of them from Europe. Penn helped to give them the right to make their own laws. After 1702, when New Jersey became a royal colony, the king appointed the governor, but the people kept the right to make their own laws. For more than a quarter of a century New Jersey had the same governor as New York; but it was finally given its own governor.

Delaware and Pennsylvania Under the Same Governor

Dutch and Swedes first settled Delaware. The beginning of Delaware was like that of New Jersey. The first settlements were made by Dutch and Swedish colonists. The country came to the English by the conquest of New Netherland in 1664, and the king gave the territory to his brother, James. James granted it to William Penn in 1682, and its history after that time goes on as a part of the history of Pennsylvania.

Delaware and Pennsylvania had the same governor. If you will look at the map, you will see that Pennsylvania does not touch the Atlantic Ocean. The Delaware River is wide and deep and ships could sail right up to the front street in Philadelphia, but Penn wanted a port nearer the ocean. He, therefore, made a bargain with his good friend, James, the Duke of York. James gave him Delaware, and Penn agreed, for his part of the bargain, to govern the territory and to sell lands there and give James half of the money that was collected from the sale of the lands.

This agreement was made in 1682, about a month before Penn sailed upon his first voyage to America. Upon his arrival, Penn put both of his colonies under the same government. The inhabitants of Delaware sent representatives to the Pennsylvania legislature, and the governor of Pennsylvania was their governor also.

For a good many years Delaware and Pennsylvania had the same laws. Then the time came when the people of Delaware wanted a separate legislature, and, instead of sending representatives to Philadelphia, insisted on electing a legislature to make their own laws at home. But Pennsylvania and Delaware continued to have the same governor until the end of colonial times.

WHAT DID WILLIAM PENN DO?

1. What did Penn do to get Pennsylvania?
2. What did Penn do to get settlers?
3. How did Penn make his colony attractive?
4. How did Penn govern his colony when he spent only four years in America?
5. How did Penn get a seacoast for his colony?
6. What did Penn do to provide for different classes of settlers?

FACT AND FANCY

1. Write a brief story of William Penn's life for your scrapbook. Tell whether you admire him or not, and why.
2. The first ten laws passed by the people of Pennsylvania are given in Southworth's *Builders of Our Country*, Volume I, pp. 192-193. Try to get the book and read them. Perhaps you can copy them and post them on the bulletin board to show how religious freedom was established in Pennsylvania.

3. Pretend that you are William Penn in England after your return from America, and tell your classmates about the conditions, resources, and government in your colony. The pictures in *The Pageant of America* (Yale University Press), Volume I, pp. 246-255, will help you to make your talk interesting. To get more information about Pennsylvania read Hart's *Colonial Children*, pages 144-149, Foote and Skinner's *Explorers and Founders of America*, pages 225-234, or Coe, Fanny E., *Founders of Our Country* (American Book Company), pages 108-116.

4. Make a picture map of the central colonies. Look at the maps on pages 288 and 169 before you begin. Show:

   a. the occupations
   b. the products traded
   c. colonists from different nations
   d. three large cities of today that were begun in colonial times

5. Dramatize Penn's treaty with the Indians.

PICTURES AND STORIES TO ENJOY FOR UNIT THREE

1. The following references will tell more about the middle colonies:

Foote, A. E., and Skinner, A. W., *Explorers and Founders of America*, pp. 168-194.

Gordy, Wilbur F., *Colonial Days* (Scribner's Sons), pp. 173-184.

Coffman, Ramon, *Our America*, Chapter XIII.

Coe, Fanny E., *Founders of Our Country* (The American Book Company), pp. 218-232.

Hart, Albert B., *Colonial Children*, pp. 140-144.

Gordy, Wilbur F., *Our Patriots*, pp. 39-43.

2. Look at the pictures in *The Pageant of America* (Yale University Press), Volume I, pp. 226-240, 246-255, or see "The Beginning of Wall Street," p. 171 in Woodburn and Moran's *Finders and Founders of the New World*. Look at New York streets today in *Compton's Pictured Encyclopedia*.

3. Read these stories just for fun:

Moore, A. C., *Nicholas*, a Manhattan Christmas Story (G. P. Putnam's Sons).

Otis, James, *Stephen of Philadelphia* (American Book Company).

Leetch, Dorothy L., *Annetje and Her Family* (Lothrop, Lee and Shepard Company).

A SHORT STORY OF UNIT THREE

PEOPLE OF MANY NATIONS CAME TO THE MIDDLE COLONIES

From the beginning of colonial times great advantages for both trade and farming have attracted a mixed population to New York, Pennsylvania, New Jersey, and Delaware.

New York began as a Dutch trading post. A Dutch trading company interested in trade with the East sent Henry Hudson to search for a northwest passage to India. He found, instead, the rich

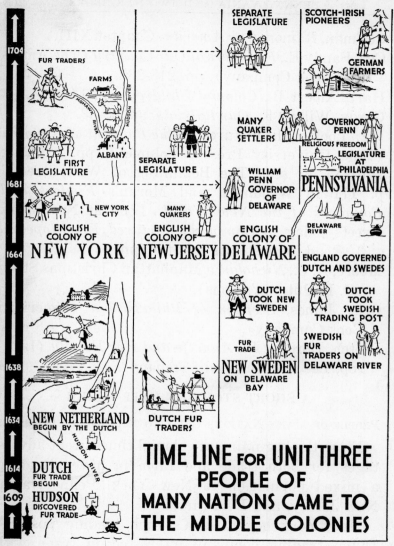

1704

FUR TRADERS

FARMS

MOHAWK RIVER

HUDSON RIVER

ALBANY

FIRST
LEGISLATURE

SEPARATE
LEGISLATURE

SEPARATE
LEGISLATURE

MANY
QUAKER
SETTLERS

SCOTCH-IRISH
PIONEERS

GERMAN
FARMERS

GOVERNOR
PENN

RELIGIOUS FREEDOM

WILLIAM
PENN
GOVERNOR
OF
DELAWARE

LEGISLATURE
AT
PHILADELPHIA

PENNSYLVANIA

1681

NEW YORK
CITY

MANY
QUAKERS

ENGLISH
COLONY OF
NEW YORK

ENGLISH
COLONY OF
NEW JERSEY

ENGLISH
COLONY OF
DELAWARE

DELAWARE
RIVER

1664

ENGLAND GOVERNED
DUTCH AND SWEDES

DUTCH
TOOK NEW
SWEDEN

DUTCH
TOOK
SWEDISH
TRADING POST

FUR
TRADE

SWEDISH
FUR
TRADERS ON
DELAWARE RIVER

1638

NEW SWEDEN
ON DELAWARE BAY

NEW NETHERLAND
BEGUN BY THE DUTCH

DUTCH FUR
TRADERS

HUDSON RIVER

1634

1614

DUTCH
FUR TRADE
BEGUN

1609

HUDSON
DISCOVERED
FUR TRADE

TIME LINE FOR UNIT THREE
PEOPLE OF
MANY NATIONS CAME TO
THE MIDDLE COLONIES

Follow the time line upward, starting at the foot of the page.

fur trade with the Indians up the Hudson River. In order to develop this trade, the Dutch West India Company started trading posts and brought over settlers. These settlers became the landowner's tenants, cultivating his fields, cutting his wood, working on the roads, and obeying him in many things. New Netherland had religious freedom, but the Dutch company did not permit the colonists to engage in the profitable fur trade or to take part in their own government. As a result, the colony did not grow rapidly.

Seeing its great advantages for trade and claiming that it really belonged to them, the English seized the Dutch colony in 1664 and changed its name to New York. This change of ownership was very important because there was then no break in the line of English colonies along the Atlantic coast, a fact which helped these colonies to unite into our nation. The Dutch settlers naturally expected that they would have a democratic government under the English, but it was twenty years before New York secured a representative assembly to make its laws. The colony grew in population; its trade became more important; and the English were careful to continue friendly relations with the Indians. Through the powerful Iroquois, New York controlled the fur trade and held back the French, who occupied the St. Lawrence Valley and tried for a hundred years to drive the English from New York.

Early Pennsylvania, New Jersey, and Delaware all had some Dutch and Swedish settlers, but they owed their rapid settlement to William Penn. Penn wished to provide homes in America for the Quakers and other unfortunate people who were denied religious freedom in Europe. In 1681, when he secured Pennsylvania from the king in payment of a debt, he already owned a share in New Jersey. The next year he bought Delaware. By publishing glowing descriptions of his colonies and by promising religious freedom and cheap land, Penn attracted many immigrants from England, Wales, Scotland, Ireland, and Germany.

There were four good reasons for the prosperity of these colonies: first, the rich land; second, the trading advantages of the country; third, Penn's policy of giving the people religious freedom and a right to make their own laws; and fourth, his success in making friends of the Indians. Pennsylvania and New Jersey each elected its own legislature and had a governor appointed by the proprietors. Delaware at first sent representatives to the Pennsylvania legislature. Later it set up its own legislature, but continued to have the same governor as Pennsylvania to the end of the colonial period.

THE COLONIES AS A WHOLE

1. Make a map of the thirteen colonies. Color each colony a different color and indicate with a

heavy line the three separate groups of colonies which you have studied.

2. Identify each of the following words or groups of words with one of the thirteen colonies:

a. patroon
b. the "starving time"
c. Lord Baltimore
d. House of Burgesses
e. Mayflower compact
f. Roger Williams
g. Harvard University
h. Quakers

3. What? Who? Where? and Why? (a game to play). Your teacher begins the game by asking some boy or girl the question "What?" The pupil should name some event of colonial days, for example, the founding of Jamestown. The pupil who answers the first question correctly then calls on someone else and asks, "Who?" The one called upon must give the name of some important person or persons connected with Jamestown. If the answer is correct that pupil may call on someone else and ask, "Where?" and he in turn will ask "Why?" If anyone fails to answer, he loses his chance to ask a question until a new "What?" is asked by the teacher.

Our life today, when nearly everything is made in factories, is very different from life in colonial days. What is each member of this colonial family doing, and how is the same thing done today?

UNIT FOUR

New Ways of Thinking and Living Began in America

Many inventions have made living today a very different thing from what it was when the first white settlers came to our shores. It was not until about 1750 that Benjamin Franklin discovered electricity, and that the steam engine was invented in England. Few colonists lived long enough to see a steam engine draw a train of cars, and no one dreamed of such a miracle as electric lights. Since colonial times, our manner of living, occupations, homes, dress, amusements, education, and means of travel have all undergone great changes.

No home or village or town is as complete in itself and as independent of its neighbors today as in colonial times. Then, the people of each home or small community for the most part raised their own food, made their own clothes, provided their own amusement, and often were responsible for their own defense. There was much work to do, and there were not very many people to do it, so that no one who could work needed to dread unemployment.

It is difficult for us now to imagine the sort of

world in which the colonists lived three, or even two, hundred years ago. Most of the work was done by hand. All members of the earlier colonial families had to work, although by 1700 many indentured servants and slaves supplied the wealthier families with labor. Homes were much less comfortable than they are now, for most of the articles that make our houses comfortable and convenient had not yet been invented. There were almost no public amusements such as we have today. Everyone went to church, but there were very few public schools. Roads were few and very bad. Travelers went mostly by boat or on horseback.

We have noticed that none of the colonies were at first governed by the English king or Parliament. They were begun by trading companies such as the London Company in Virginia and the Massachusetts Bay Company in Massachusetts, or by individuals such as Baltimore in Maryland and Penn in Pennsylvania. The early settlers were allowed to govern themselves in local affairs and to elect legislatures to make laws for the colony. Hardly was a colony successfully begun before the English government began trying to control it for the profit of England. But this did not prevent the growth of representative government, freedom of religion, and freedom of the press. It was such new ways of living and thinking as these in America that led to the creation of our nation.

If you study life in colonial times carefully, you will find it very different from your own life, yet you will see that it was the foundation from which our life today has developed.

The following chapters will help you to understand how new ways of thinking and living began in colonial times:

Can you tell why the ways of living and thinking listed in this cartoon are the foundations of democracy?

Outline of Chapter X

X. Life in the Northern Colonies

  A. How the Colonists Made a Living

    1. Farming was not very profitable.

    2. People turned to trading and fishing.

    3. Manufacturing often furnished a living.

  B. Labor

  C. Homes in Early New England

    1. The pioneers lived in log cabins.

    2. Better New England houses developed.

    3. Colonial homes had few comforts.

    4. Kitchens served as dining and living rooms.

  D. How People Amused Themselves

    1. Grown-ups combined work with play.

    2. Young folks enjoyed sports and games.

  E. Going to Church

  F. The First Schools in America

    1. New England had the earliest colleges and public schools.

    2. The first public schools were not free.

    3. It was difficult to get a good education.

  G. Travel in Colonial Days

    1. Early travel was largely by water.

    2. Land travel was slow and uncomfortable.

    3. Inns were few and poor.

CHAPTER X

Life in the Northern Colonies

How the Colonists Made a Living

Farming was not very profitable. For the first few years after they came to America all the New England settlers were farmers. Food was their first need, and every new day brought its own hard strug-

Details adapted by courtesy First National Bank of Boston

Here you see John Winthrop, the younger, inspecting an iron pot cast at Lynn, Massachusetts, where he helped to set up the first successful iron works in what is now the United States.

gle for enough to eat. In the short summer months corn, beans, and pumpkins must be grown on the thin, rocky soil, or the family would starve. At other seasons land must be cleared, wood chopped, fences built, and the cabin made larger and more comfortable. Everything needed to be done at once, and every family had to do everything for itself. There was little labor to be hired.

People turned to trading and fishing. As the number of settlers increased, more and more of them made a living at other kinds of work than farming. Some men turned to fur trading and store keeping. Many built ships and engaged in trading or fishing on the sea. In trade and commerce colonists found opportunity to gain wealth which would give them more importance in the community.

The waters of the ocean were still alive with fish, as in the days when John Cabot reported that he could dip them up in baskets, so that fishing became a paying business. Small boats carried fishermen beyond the harbors to the open sea, where they caught cod, mackerel, and other kinds of fish. The choicer portions of these were salted, dried, and packed for shipment to European countries, where many religious fast days on which people did not eat meat created a great demand for fish. The poorer portions were cured to be shipped to the West Indies, where slave-owners bought them for their slaves.

Whale oil and candles were in demand in England and in other European countries, as well as in colonial homes where candles and whale-oil lamps shed a soft light during the long winter evening. Therefore, whaling was a profitable occupation.

Manufacturing often furnished a living. Since people lived near each other in small towns, they found it convenient to share work with each other. The blacksmith was an important man in every settlement. Every village had its carpenter and its shoemaker. A tannery was set up in each large town to manufacture leather.

Before the grain could be used, it had to be ground into flour. It would have been expensive and inconvenient for each colonist to own his own mill. Instead, one man would put up a mill beside a stream and grind the grain into flour for all of his neighbors. The men who brought their grain to be ground into flour paid the miller in money or in flour or wool, or something else that they raised on their farms.

In the same way, many sawmills were built. These mills produced lumber for shipbuilding, shingles and clapboards for the colonial homes, and staves for barrels.

The forests in the new world furnished plenty of wood for ships. The sturdy oak tree made solid timbers and boards; the tall, straight fir was used for masts; the pine provided the pitch and tar for calking the seams and turpentine for preserving the wood. Hemp, from which ropes were made, grew in the fields. The New England shipyards were busy and noisy places. Shipbuilders in England objected to this growing colonial industry because some of their skilled workers left England for America and also because English shipbuilders wanted to sell ships to the colonies.

As some of the colonies contained iron ore, men began to set up forges along the rivers. One of Abraham Lincoln's ancestors set up one of the earliest forges in Massachusetts. These workshops turned out bar iron and pig iron to be shipped to England. Some of the iron mills manufactured nails, hoes, kettles, guns, chains, and anchors to be sold in the colonies. The iron manufacturers in England did not like this, so they persuaded Parliament to pass laws limiting the manufacture of iron in the colonies.

Many things were home-manufactured. Much of the manufacturing in colonial times was done by women. Every girl learned to dry fruits and to preserve them in spices, to "try out" lard, and to pack meat in salt brine where it kept for months. Mother and daughters had to "dip" a great supply of candles, to spin and weave cloth for clothing, and to knit warm stockings and mittens.

Many yards of cloth were made in every household. The women spun and wove linen and wool

In the New England colonial house, of which this clapboard house was a common type, the family provided its own light and water. How are light and water supplied for most modern homes?

into cloth for the clothing of the family. In those days, a new woolen dress meant many hours of labor. First the wool had to be sheared from the sheep and washed until it was clean. Then it had to be combed or carded until the fibers were all untangled and straight. These fibers were then spun into long threads which were woven into cloth. When the cloth was dyed, the colonial mother was ready to begin a dress for her daughter or a suit for her son or husband. From the first most people wore roughly woven, home-spun clothes. Some colonial women made such fine woolen cloth that even a rich man was proud to wear it to church on Sunday. For their best garments, however, most wealthy people imported cloth from England.

Labor

Most colonial families were large, and everybody had to do his share of labor in the home, for it took many hands to feed and clothe the family. The women and girls did the work about the house, tending the younger children, working the garden, cooking, churning, spinning, weaving, sewing, and knitting. The boys did such chores as chopping wood, keeping up the fires, and feeding the animals. As soon as they were large enough, they went to work with their fathers in the field or shop or fishing boat.

Slaves were not profitable on the small rocky farms in New England, but some well-to-do families owned and used slaves for servants. Most of the slaves were Negroes, brought from Africa or the Spanish West Indies. A few of them were Indians.

Many New England families had white servants whom they had helped to come to America by paying their fare across the Atlantic. These indentured servants were bound to serve their masters from five to seven years. After serving their time, they became free, and either continued to work for wages or set up in some occupation for themselves. Many were skilled in some trade.

Homes in Early New England

The pioneers lived in log cabins. The first houses of the Pilgrims at Plymouth were mere huts built of logs with floors of dirt and roofs of brush and straw. The cracks between the logs were filled with mud. The doors and windows were solid wooden shutters without glass, and when they were closed the cabins were dark, except for the little light that came through the cracks. It was impossible to heat such shacks. The roofs leaked, and sleet and snow blew through the cracks in the walls. No doubt, much of the sickness of the Pilgrims during the first terrible winter at Plymouth was due to the fact that they were often wet and always cold.

For a year or two, these cabins contained little furniture, and most of it was home-made. Chests and trunks in which the colonists brought their few belongings from Europe were used as seats. Stools were made by sawing off thin sections of a log and fixing peg legs in the slices thus formed. Tables and benches were made in the same way, by splitting a log several feet long, smoothing the flat side with an axe, and fitting legs in the under side. Bedsteads were simple frames of poles built into the corners of the room.

Better New England houses developed. After a time the settlers built larger and more comfortable houses. Though many houses continued to be built of logs, sawmills, run by the swift rivers and creeks, were soon turning out lumber enough for the needs of the colonists. Boards took the place of the straw roofs, and oiled paper or thin skins were stretched over the windows to let in the light. The furniture of the poorer homes, though much better than the rough furniture of the first cabins, was still homemade, and the floors were covered with rag carpets and with rugs made of corn shucks.

As the houses continued to improve and to grow in size, a very beautiful way of building them, known as the New England colonial style, developed. These better houses were owned by well-to-do colonists who could afford to bring glass windows, rugs, carpets, curtains, and furniture from England.

Colonial homes had few comforts. Even the finest houses had few of the comforts which houses now have. The windows and doors were without screens, and flies and mosquitoes swarmed in at will. Whale-oil lamps, tallow candles made at home, and pine

Compare what you see in this colonial kitchen with the furnishings of a modern kitchen. Why was the kitchen in New England a more comfortable eating place than a dining room would have been?

knots were the only means that people had of lighting their homes. There was no running water in a colonial house, no bathroom, no telephone, and no radio.

Colonial homes were very uncomfortable in winter. The only means of heat was the great fireplace, which burned long logs and filled the room with a cheery glow but left it chilly and uncomfortable at even a short distance from the fire. Roaring wood fires in the huge fireplaces could not warm the large rooms. Warming pans were used to warm the beds in rooms that had no fires. These warming pans were brass or copper pans with close-fitting tops and long wooden handles. They were filled with glowing coals and were moved back and forth between the sheets until the damp chill was removed.

Kitchens served as dining and living rooms. There was always a cheerful fire blazing in the huge fireplace of the kitchen, which was the most comfortable room in the house. All the cooking was done in the fireplace, for there were no cookstoves. A long iron crane, hung with stout pothooks, swung from the side of the fireplace. The housewife could swing pots and kettles over the fire and boil pork and vegetables while the bread was baking below in cast-iron pans, or ovens, covered with hot ashes and coals. The spinning wheel stood in the corner, and dried apples, onions, and peppers strung on twine hung in long loops from the ceiling. The long rifle, which was a necessary article in every house, rested on deer horns over the mantel or door. Beside it hung cow horns filled with powder and shot.

In general, the family ate in the kitchen, although the better colonial houses had dining rooms, and dining room furniture improved with the size and comfort of the houses. If you have ever lived in a hunting camp, or picnicked in a park, you will have some idea of the dining table and tableware in early colonial houses. The tables were narrow and made of rough boards. The seats were benches without backs. The "silver" consisted of knives and spoons, for forks had not come into use in England when the first colonists came to New England. It is said that John Winthrop brought the first fork to Massachusetts when Boston was three years old. There were some silver spoons, but most people used table ware made of pewter which is a metal made from tin and lead. Colonists made their own spoons by melting old pewter mugs and worn-out pans and pouring the metal into a mold. Few tables boasted china or even earthenware dishes. People ate from wooden trays called trenchers. Usually two people, sitting side by side, ate from the same trencher, though a good carpenter or wood-carver sometimes made trays for each member of his family.

The kitchen was the room in which the members of the family spent most of their time when in the house. There by the warm fire the children gathered after supper in the long winter evenings to pop corn and tell stories. There the father read the Bible and said the evening prayers.

The New England poets of later days were fond of describing the great fireplaces and the home life that went on about them. James Russell Lowell

Chopping and carrying in wood for the fireplace was one of the common chores which kept boys busy in colonial times. What changes in our ways of living have made these tasks unnecessary in most homes today?

puts his description in the words of an old back-woodsman:

> "A fireplace filled the room's one side
>   With half a cord of wood in—
> There warn't no stoves (till comfort died)
>   To bake ye to a puddin'."

John Greenleaf Whittier's *Snow-Bound* describes the family life around the cheerful fire during the cold New England winter:

"Shut in from all the world without,
We sat the clean-winged hearth about,
Content to let the north wind roar
In baffled rage at pane and door,
While the red logs before us beat
The frost-line back with tropic heat;
And ever, when a louder blast
Shook beam and rafter as it passed,
The merrier up its roaring draught
The great throat of the chimney laughed.
The house dog on his paws outspread
Laid to the fire his drowsy head,
The cat's dark silhouette on the wall
A couchant tiger's seemed to fall;
And, for the winter fireside meet,
Between the andirons' straddling feet
The mug of cider simmered slow,
And apples sputtered in a row.
And, close at hand the basket stood
With nuts from brown October's woods.
What matter how the night behaved!
What matter how the north wind raved!
Blow high, blow low, not all its snow
Could quench our hearth-fire's ruddy glow."

How People Amused Themselves

Grown-ups combined work with play. Life for
the Pilgrims and other New England people meant
much work and little play. They did not think it

right to take much time for pleasure. Their religion discouraged gaiety and good times. The grown-ups hunted bear and deer for meat, and wolves and foxes for sport. Sometimes all the people of a community gathered in a neighbor's barn and helped him husk his corn; sometimes the women met at quilting parties and gossiped while making quilts. People enjoyed these meetings which brought old and young together.   After the work was done, they talked and ate, played games, and sang hymns.

Young folks enjoyed sports and games. Children in those early days were expected "to be seen and not heard." Nearly every family had a large number of children, but nobody seems to have paid much attention to their amusement. The old books tell us little about how they played. No one then, of course, dreamed of some of the pleasures that you enjoy. There were no picture shows, no Boy Scout troops, no Camp Fire Girls, no public parks or swimming pools.   Still, colonial boys and girls probably got a good deal of fun out of life.

Such sports as fishing, hunting, and trapping were then a part of every boy's life; and boys and young men enjoyed wrestling, running races, and jumping as they do now. Skating was a popular winter sport which, judging from the accounts in old newspapers, was not without danger. Reports of skaters breaking through the ice and drowning are frequent. One of the most common games was to see who could cover the greatest distance in three hops, or in a hop, skip, and jump. Marbles became the fashion about the middle of the eighteenth century. A few toys were brought in from Europe and sold to the children of the rich, but the only dolls that most of the children had were made of rags at home.

Benjamin Franklin's story of his early life in Boston shortly after 1700 shows that boys were very much the same two hundred years ago, as they are today. He says:

"Living near the water, I was much in and about it, and I learned early to swim well, and to manage boats. When on a boat or canoe with other boys, I was commonly allowed to manage things, especially in any case of danger, and upon other occasions I was generally a leader among the boys. Sometimes I led them into scrapes. I will mention one such instance.

"There was a salt marsh on one side of the mill pond. On the edge of this, at high water, we used to stand to fish for minnows. By much trampling we had made it very soft and muddy. My plan was to build a wharf there for us to stand upon, and I showed my comrades a large heap of stones, which were intended for a new house near the marsh. These would very well suit our purpose.

"So, in the evening, when the workmen were gone, I gathered together a number of my playfellows. We worked very hard, just like so many ants.

Sometimes two or three of us were needed to carry out one stone. Finally, we brought them all away and built our little wharf.

"The next morning the workmen were surprised at missing the stones. They began to ask who moved them. They found us out and made complaint. Several of us were punished by our fathers. And, although I said for excuse that it was a useful kind of work, my father convinced me that nothing was useful which was not honest."

Going to Church

The Pilgrims and Puritans who settled Massachusetts had come to America for religious freedom and suffered many hardships and dangers to worship God in the way they thought right. They always went to church on Sunday in spite of cold or danger from Indians. Going to "meeting," as church services were called, was one of the greatest pleasures of the grown people in New England. They attended church twice on Sundays and once on week days in the evening, and listened to long sermons. The children, too, were taken to "meeting."

The early churches were bare and uncomfortable, without glass in the windows or fires to keep them warm in winter. The women and girls sat on one side of the church, and the men on the other. The boys sat in the gallery, or balcony, where a stern old man kept his eye on them and rapped them on

The church was the most important building in a New England colonial town. It served not only as a place of worship but often as the courthouse and the town hall where the town meetings were held. This shows the interior of one of the later colonial churches.

the head with a long stick when they nodded or misbehaved. In winter it must have been very tiresome to the children to sit quietly through the long sermons which they could not understand.

The grown people, as well as children, sometimes found it hard to keep awake. The women sleepers did not fare so badly, for the usher gently brushed their faces with a fox tail or a rabbit's foot to wake them up. But the men who went to sleep were usually wakened by a hard rap with the knob of a long stick, sometimes with amusing results. One man protested that a mistake had been made in tapping him on the head. He was not asleep, he said; he was merely nodding his head in approval of the preacher's sermon. Another time, a man was sleeping so soundly that he could not immediately remember where he was when he was rapped on the head. He promptly rose and knocked the usher down. Perhaps this incident amused others at the meeting, but the result was anything but amusing for the unfortunate sleeper. He was convicted next day of being "a common sleeper at public worship" and sentenced to be severely whipped.

The First Schools in America

New England had the earliest colleges and public schools. We have already seen that some of the New England leaders were among the best educated men of their day. This was true of John Winthrop, John Eliot, Thomas Hooker, the Mathers, Roger Williams, and numerous others. They showed their belief in the value of education by founding Harvard University in 1636, when the colony of Massachusetts Bay was only five years old. A minister named John Harvard left his library and a sum of money for a college, and the governor and legislature voted enough more money to start the school at once.

The Massachusetts legislature passed a law in 1647 requiring every community with fifty families in it to set up a school to teach reading and writing. Connecticut passed the same sort of a law three years later. The colonists in New England generally settled in villages, and each village kept up a school.

The first public schools were not free. These early public schools were not free schools. The parents had to pay something for the support of the schools, and the pupils had to do the work of the school that is now done by the janitor. Some parents furnished wood for the school. The boys had to bring in the wood after it was cut and keep up the fire. They had also to bring water from the spring or from a neighboring well.

The teacher rarely received his small pay in money. He was paid in all sorts of things—Indian wampum, beaver skins, corn, wheat, and vegetables, or even chickens, eggs, and ducks. In some schools it was the duty of one of the boys to sit at the window and call out to passers-by, begging them to buy the teacher's "truck."

It was difficult to get a good education. School was kept six days in the week, beginning at seven or eight in the morning and closing at four or five in the afternoon, with recess for lunch from eleven to one o'clock. The boys and girls really had to study on Sundays, too. Usually on Mondays the teacher

The passing of the famous Massachusetts school law encouraged every town in colonial New England to provide for a school. How does your schoolroom differ from the one in which these colonial boys and girls are studying?

called all the classes together and examined them on what they had learned from the sermon at church the day before.

The teachers were strict and often whipped the pupils for very slight offenses. One of the old rules of a school in Massachusetts said: "The rod of correction is a rule of God, necessary sometimes to be used upon children. The schoolmaster shall have full power to punish all or any of his scholars, no

Schools today commonly provide fine playgrounds, gymnasiums, and teachers of athletics. Can you think of reasons why the boys and girls in our great cities need training in sports and games more than colonial children did?

matter who they are. No parent or other person living in the place shall hinder the master in this."

In the primary schools little was taught but reading, writing, arithmetic, and the catechism, a book of questions and answers on religion. Schools were bare and uncomfortable. There were no blackboards and maps, no charts and globes, very little paper and ink, and, strangest of all, hardly any books for the boys and girls to read.

The books used in the elementary schools in those days were very different from our readers and storybooks with their beautiful pictures. Children learned to read and spell chiefly from the *New England Primer* and the catechism, and arithmetic was taught by problems given out by the teacher. Sometimes pages were cut from books, fastened on a flat piece of board which ended in a handle, and covered with thin, transparent sheets of cow horn, just as we now put glass over pictures in frames. By this means, the pages were saved from wear and tear, and at the same time one book furnished reading matter for several classes. A page between horn covers like this was called a horn book.

In spite of the difficulties a great many New England boys and girls managed to get a very good education. Benjamin Franklin wrote of his early education in Boston:

"I was sent to school at eight years of age. My father intended to make me a minister of the church. I must have learned to read very early, as I do not remember when I could not read. Later my father sent me to a school for writing and arithmetic. I learned good writing pretty soon, but I failed in the arithmetic. At ten years of age my father took me home to help him in his business.

"My father was a candle maker and soap boiler. He put me at work cutting wick for the candles, filling the candle molds with tallow, keeping the shop, and going on errands. I disliked the business. I wanted to go to sea; but my father declared against it.

"From a child I was always fond of reading, and all the little money that came into my hands was laid out in books. My father's little library was chiefly religious books, most of which I read.

"My liking for books at last caused my father to make me a printer. I now had a chance to read better books. Knowing the boys who worked for booksellers, I could sometimes borrow a small book, which I was careful to return soon and clean. Often I sat up in my room reading the greater part of the night when the book was borrowed in the evening and had to be returned early in the morning."

Travel in Colonial Days

Early travel was largely by water. When the colonists first came to America, they settled in small villages or on farms that were close together. They frequently traveled from one town to another by water, as this was easier than the journey overland. On every river there were boats to be used by the traveler and by the farmer who took his produce to market.

A long trip on the ocean in the small ships of the time was far from a pleasure. The food was poor, and drinking water was scarce. Discomforts were shared by all alike, whether gentle-folk or servants. Boston helped trade and travel by sea by building a lighthouse as early as 1716.

Land travel was slow and uncomfortable. In most cases the only way one could get from one village to another on land was by way of rough trails through the forests. Men and women usually traveled on foot or on horseback because there were few roads and all of them were poor. The trails through the forest were marked by blazing the trees, that is, marking them by cutting gashes in the bark. On many of these trails the trees grew so close to the forest path that the branches scratched the faces of horseback riders. There were few bridges. On coming to a stream, a traveler had to ford it. Sometimes he waded; sometimes he was carried on the back of an Indian guide; sometimes he sat on his horse as the horse swam across.

In 1704, Mrs. Sarah Kemble Knight made the trip by horseback from Boston to New York in seven days. This trip took her through the most settled parts of the colonies, but the difficulties and dangers of her journey would have discouraged any but a brave woman.

Part of the time she traveled with guides whom she hired; part, with the carrier of the mail. Once her guide deserted her after dark, just as she came to a swift stream that had to be forded, and left her to cross on her horse as best she could. At Providence Ferry, she was taken in a canoe, and the trip was so rough that she said she dared not move even her tongue "a hair's breadth." In some places, the road was so narrow that the branches brushed her and her horse as they slowly made their way through the forest.

Travel by carriage was sometimes possible but never very comfortable because the roads were very rough and the early carriages had only leather straps in place of springs. When the traveler came to a stream, the horses had to be unhitched and allowed to swim across. The carriage was set on two canoes and paddled over, or horses and carriage were carried across by a ferry.

Inns were few and poor. Travelers had difficulty in getting food and in finding a place to spend the night. Many were given shelter and food by kindly farmers who were glad to get any news that a stranger might bring. In the larger towns there were taverns or inns. Often these were dirty and provided poorly cooked food. The beds were sometimes far from clean, and no attempt was made to provide the traveler with a room that he could have as his own for the night.

When Mrs. Knight made her trip from Boston to New York, she found stopping at the dirty inns for food and lodging very unpleasant. One night, having been given a room next to the kitchen, she was unable to sleep because two men talked in loud tones in the outer room all night. They were still talking when Madam Knight rode off at four o'clock in the morning.

DESCRIBE AS THOUGH YOU WERE THERE

1. Try to get one or more of the following books from your school or public library, and learn more about life in Massachusetts. The readings will help you with the activities that follow.

Hurley, B. D., and Sartorious, I. C., *School Boys of Long Ago*, Part Two, Our Changing World (Thomas Nelson and Sons), pp. 66-74.

Gordy, Wilbur F., *Stories of Early American History*, pp. 140-153.

Halleck and Frantz, *Founders of Our Nation*, pp. 179-197.

Hart, Albert B., *Colonial Children*, pp. 152-155, 180-182, 201-215.

Faris, John T., *Real Stories From Our History*, Ginn and Company), pp. 38-44.

Bailey, Carolyn Sherwin, *Children of the Handcrafts*, pp. 11-33. Look at the illustrations of the shoemaker's shop on page 15 and of the furniture of a New England kitchen on pages 22, 23, and 27.

2. Describe each of the chief ways in which the New Englanders made a living.

3. Describe a New England home in colonial times.

4. Give a description of a New England church scene of colonial days.

5. If it were possible for you to step into a Puritan school, what would you see? What would you miss that your school has today?

6. Describe the difficulties of travel in New England in colonial times.

PRETEND YOU ARE A PURITAN

1. Imagine that you are a boy or a girl living in New England in colonial times and write a letter to a cousin of your own age in England telling how you spend a day here in America.

2. Plan a meal that a Puritan family would be apt to serve.

3. Make a hornbook, using cellophane and cardboard.

Outline of Chapter XI

XI. Life in the Middle Colonies
  A. Making a Living
    1. Farming was profitable.
    2. Trade and manufacturing flourished.
  B. Labor
    1. Big families provided workers.
    2. There were some slaves.
    3. Many settlers came as indentured servants.
  C. Houses and Furniture
    1. The poor had small, wooden houses.
    2. The rich had great houses.
  D. Food and Cooking
    1. Food was grown and preserved at home.
    2. Cooking was done in fireplaces.
  E. Dress
    1. Most people wore homemade clothes.
    2. Rich people imported their clothing.
  F. Amusements
    1. Often work was combined with play.
    2. Sports, parties, and games were common.
    3. The larger cities had music and plays.
  G. Schools and Education
    1. Public schools were few.
    2. Three great colleges were begun.
  H. Travel and Communication
    1. Stagecoaches and stage boats were used.
    2. Mail service was slow and uncertain.
    3. Travelers carried the news.

The white men found the Indians dipping oil to use as medicine, from the oil springs in western New York and Pennsylvania, but they did not guess that wells of valuable fuel lay underneath the ground.

CHAPTER XI

Life in the Middle Colonies

Making a Living

Farming was profitable. The valleys in the middle colonies were wider than those in New England, and the land was far more fertile. It was easy to raise large crops of wheat, rye, oats, and barley. Apples, peaches, and grapes grew plentifully. Cattle and sheep grew fat on the long grass in the pastures. The rivers were wider and deeper, too, than most of those in the northern colonies. This made it possible for a farmer to live farther away from the seacoast, because he could get his crops to market by boat. As a result of these two geographical advantages, most of the settlers in the middle colonies became farmers.

One person sometimes owned a great deal of land, but there were many small farms owned by the farmers who worked them. The farmer in New York, Pennsylvania, Delaware, and New Jersey raised wool and flax for clothing, as well as all the food needed in his home. The wool, grain, beef, pork, and peas that he did not use he sold to merchants who exported it to England. In fact, because they produced so much grain, the middle colonies were called the bread colonies.

Trade and manufacturing flourished. The thick forests and the irregular eastern coast with many great harbors making it easy for vessels to leave and enter the ports suggested to some the best means of making a living. English merchants and business men wanted the furs from the beaver, the mink, and the otter that were so plentiful in the dense woods. They needed the wood in the forests for building ships or for burning in their iron and glass furnaces. They wanted the tar, rosin, and pitch from the pine trees for their ships. They needed the fish from the ocean for food and oil. Young men who loved adventure left the fertile fields for trade and the sea.

Skilled workmen in the shipyards of New York and Pennsylvania built ships with which merchants carried on a thriving trade. The larger ships sailed across the Atlantic loaded with furs, grains, peas, livestock, salt pork, barrel staves, and shingles. They returned carrying the brocaded silks, fine woolen cloth, polished furniture, soft carpets, coffee and tea, and other luxuries purchased by wealthy colonists. Smaller ships carried grain, salt pork, and peas from the middle colonies to ports along the coast, and brought back cotton and tobacco from the South to the middle colonies and to New England.

Some sturdy ships sailed into the cold waters of the far north in search of whales. Some were used for fishing nearer home. Others engaged in the trade with Europe and the West Indies.

As there was plenty of timber in the forests, sawmills were built to make lumber. By about 1700 there were at least forty sawmills in New York. In Pennsylvania, the manufacture of lumber was so important that the legislature passed a law that all staves should be of "good sound well-seasoned oak timber for hogsheads, tierces (small kegs) and barrels." Much of the lumber was shipped to England.

Many grist mills run by wind and water ground grain for the colonists and manufactured flour for trade. There were some iron mills turning out bar iron and pig iron to be shipped to England. Clay gave some people their occupation, for it was made into pottery, into pipes for smoking tobacco, and into bricks for homes.

Labor

Big families provided workers. Most families were large. A father expected his sons to help on his farm or in his business and his daughters to help their mother. The farmer tried to raise all the food for his family and his stock. His wife had to store much of the food for the winter. But girls and boys married very young because the abundance of land offered each young man a sure way to earn a living for himself and his family. The sons and daughters of the rich did not wish to spend long hours of each day in the fields or in a kitchen. There were not laborers enough in his family to meet the needs of the owner of much land.

There were some slaves. Although there were some Negro slaves and a few Indian servants, the need for workers in the middle colonies was not filled largely by slaves as it was in the South. The following advertisement from a New Jersey paper shows that the Indians did not take kindly to the life of slavery:

Most of the people of the middle colonies were farmers, and one of their amusements was the husking bee when the neighbors gathered together to share the work of husking the corn in harvest time.

"On the eighteenth of September, there ran away from Thomas Hill of Salem an Indian man named Pompey. He is of medium height, is about thirty years old, and his face is scarred by smallpox. He wears a yellow coat with horn buttons, a linen shirt, and a pair of white yarn stockings. Pompey took with him a little black pacing horse, branded on the side with the letters 'H. M.' Whoever takes up this Indian and brings him to his master shall receive a suitable reward."

Many settlers came as indentured servants. The need for labor was supplied chiefly by indentured servants. Large numbers of young men and women, as we have already learned, promised to work in the middle colonies for the man who paid their passage across the Atlantic. The term of labor was usually five, six, or seven years. During this time the employer furnished the servant with food, clothing, and shelter. At the end of the term of service, the servant was free. His employer usually gave him some clothes, a small amount of money, and an axe. In a country where there was so much fertile land, it was easy for the newly freed man to get fifty acres for himself and to become an independent farmer. The fact that he worked for himself had a great deal to do with making him think for himself and desire to share in the government.

Houses and Furniture

The poor had wooden houses and homemade furniture. Since wood was very plentiful, most of the homes were built of that material. The poor had no rugs or carpets, but sanded their floors. A poor man slept on a bed that he made himself, sat on a homemade chair, and ate from a homemade table. His wife stored her linen in a homemade bureau.

Usually she set her table with pewter plates, knives, and spoons.

The rich had great houses and imported furniture. Some homes of the wealthier classes were built of stone or of brick. The Van Cortlandt Manor house in the colony of New York, erected in 1681, was of stone and was built to withstand Indian attacks. The walls were thick and had slits in them for guns. In Philadelphia one good citizen built a home of brick in which the cellar was connected, by means of a passage, with the river. This allowed goods to be shipped right to the door.

The wealthy furnished their homes with furniture imported from London. Their tables and chairs were of mahogany and other fine woods. They had chairs and sofas covered in leather or in strong, costly cloth. Instead of pewter, there were silver spoons and imported china dishes on their tables.

Food and Cooking

Food was home-grown and home-preserved. Few, if any, in the middle colonies went hungry, because there was plenty of food. Fish, beef, pork, or lamb; bread, vegetables, and fruits were to be found on most tables. Cane sugar had to be bought, and the poor used honey, or, in New York, maple sugar, instead. Tea and coffee were imported, but these were luxuries and the poor man could get along without them. Cider, rum, and beer were plentiful.

Learning to bake bread, pie, and cakes in the brick oven by the kitchen fireplace was part of the education of every colonial girl. Where is the bread that you eat made?

Girls were taught to dry fruits and to preserve them in spices; to smoke hams or sides of bacon; and to pack meat in salt brine.

Cooking was done in fireplaces. In the fireplace, huge iron kettles hung over the flames. In these kettles vegetables and meat were cooked. Meat to be roasted was hung on the spit and carefully turned while cooking. Bread and pies were baked in the brick ovens at the sides of fireplaces in the old Dutch homes.

This quilting party is being held in the living room of a well-to-do home of later colonial times. The walls are of polished wood panels, and the handsome hand-made chairs are probably the work of a furniture maker.

Dress

Most people wore homemade clothes. In the winter, the poor wore homespun wool dresses and shirts, knitted stockings, deerskin coats, and heavy boots. In summer, coarse linen was used instead of woolen cloth. The little boys and girls wore no shoes and stockings in the summer, except at church on Sunday. It was not uncommon to see a small boy trudging to church with stockings and shining shoes under his arm to keep them clean. When almost at the church, he would sit down beside the road and put them on.

Almost everyone had a "best" suit or a "best" dress which was worn on Sundays and on important occasions. Sometimes a man would will his "best suit" to his son. Clothes were worn until the cloth in them was worn out. When an older member of a family outgrew a dress or a pair of trousers, a younger member received it. The poorer colonists were not troubled because their clothes did not fit well or were out of style. They wanted their clothing to last a long time.

Rich people imported their clothing. It was very different with the rich. When they wore their best, their clothes showed their wealth. Both men and women wore silk, velvet, linen, or wool that had been spun and woven in Europe.

The men wore powdered wigs, gaily-colored coats, satin waistcoats, lace or embroidery at neck and wrists, long silk hose, and buckles on their shoes.

The wealthy man's wife or daughter was even more richly dressed. She, too, wore a powdered wig. Her best dress of silk or satin was made with a wide skirt and a tight-fitting waist. Party dresses were of brilliant colors and were trimmed with lace or gold embroidery. Rings, bracelets, and necklaces were often worn.

Amusements

Often work was combined with play. Most of the colonists, particularly those who were farmers, had little time for play. In the middle colonies, as in New England, the sharing of work was often turned into a picnic, or party.

In the country districts the building of a new home would be the occasion for a "house-raising" in which all the neighbors would unite to help build the frame of the house. Men loaned what tools they had. All worked until rafters and ridge-pole were in place and the frame of the house complete. The women, too, shared in the work, for it was their part to prepare the food.

In a similar manner, the finishing of a bed-covering served the women as a social occasion. They often met and quilted the cover with small, even stitches as they talked over the neighborhood news.

Husking-bees, when the harvest was in the barns, brought the neighbors together to husk the corn, and lucky was the man who found a red ear of corn, for this gave him the right to kiss the maiden of his choice.

Spelling-bees were one of the simple amusements of colonial times which are still sometimes held, though most communities having modern ways of amusement no longer hold them.

The singing school was a favorite amusement, because practicing with the church choir or for village celebrations, gave the young men opportunities for seeing the girls home.

Sports, parties, and games were common. In the winter the young people skated, or went sleigh riding if the roads were passable. In the summer, they picnicked, rode horseback, and paddled canoes on lakes or rivers. Sometimes there were horse races.

At evening balls and parties, young and old joined in the stately dances of colonial times, known as the minuet or the cotillion.

The men played games such as billiards and cards. By 1700 a coffee house, similar to those which were such popular men's clubs in England, was opened in New York City.

The larger cities had music and plays. Music and the theater provided entertainment in the larger cities. By the middle of the eighteenth century, the "Orpheus Club" entertained audiences with music in Philadelphia, and symphony concerts were played by an orchestra in New York City. In 1750, the "Beggar's Opera" was given in New York. The building was lighted by candles, arranged on a barrel hoop hung from the ceiling, and other candles were placed in front of the stage to serve as footlights.

By the middle of the eighteenth century, also, an English actor and actress with their company visited the colonies. For twenty years this company played in New York and in other large towns south of New

The largest town in the colonies was Philadelphia. There
the wealthy led a lively social life. They entertained in handsome three-story brick houses, and went in chairs and coaches
to plays and parties.

England. The plays they acted were written by
Shakespeare and other noted authors. The settlers
of the middle and southern colonies thus had an
opportunity to see some of the best plays ever
written.

Schools and Education

Public schools were few. The people of the middle colonies were much slower than the colonists of New England in starting public education. They had few schools supported by taxes. Most of their schools were supported by the churches. The Dutch in New York had church schools. The Quakers and Germans in Pennsylvania each established schools in connection with their churches. Some fathers had private teachers for their sons and later sent their boys to England or to Boston to finish their education.

In all the primary schools the children were taught reading, writing, and arithmetic. If the school was supported by the church, special instruction in the Bible and in the beliefs of the church was added. Horn books were used because books for children were so few, and those few were not to be compared with the wonderful books in our schools today. Such schooling as there was was for boys. Girls were expected to stay at home to be educated in the duties of the housewife.

Three great colleges were begun. Three of the middle colonies had colleges in colonial times. King's College, which was to grow into the great Columbia University of today, was opened in New York; Princeton College was started in New Jersey; and the College and Academy of Philadelphia was the beginning of the University of Pennsylvania. If a boy wished to study medicine or law, however, he usually went to Europe to complete his education.

Travel and Communication

Stagecoaches and stage boats came into use. Travel in the middle colonies was not much easier than in New England, but the first public stagecoach began running between New York and Philadelphia. The stagecoach, which ran at regular times and carried both mail and passengers, was a great improvement over the old way of carrying mail and traveling on horseback. The coaches used four horses, or sometimes six where the roads were poorest. The passenger sat in a box-like, covered wagon,

Compare the trip this sleepy young colonial traveler will make in the "Flying Machine" with the comfort and speed of a modern journey between Philadelphia and New York City.

with his small, brass-studded, pigskin trunk under his seat.

The stage line that operated between Philadelphia and New York about 1750 advertised that, "The Flying Machine, a good stage wagon set on springs," took only two days to the trip. This meant when the weather was good, going from five o'clock in the morning until nine or ten o'clock at night. Today fast trains passing under the Hudson River through a tunnel make the same trip in two hours.

President Quincy of Harvard College, writing of a journey to New York from Boston, said that the stagecoach usually stopped at an inn about ten o'clock at night. All passengers were warned that the coach would start at three in the morning, and at three or earlier, the sleepy passengers were roused. They dressed by candlelight, and with the aid of a lantern proceeded on their way. Sometimes the driver had to arrange the loose planks in a bridge before he could cross it. Sometimes the passengers would be asked to help lift the coach out of a muddy rut. If there were deep ruts on the right side of the road, the driver would call, "gentlemen to the left," whereupon all the passengers would lean over the side of the wagon to prevent it from overturning.

Regular passenger boats, or stage boats, came into use. For example, a stagecoach operated from Brunswick to Trenton, New Jersey, and a boat from Trenton to Philadelphia. However, people wishing

There was a post office for all the colonies after 1690, but post riders made slow and irregular trips until Franklin became postmaster. Then the time for sending mail from Boston to Philadelphia fell from three weeks to six days.

to journey from New York to Boston, Philadelphia, or Charleston more often engaged passage with a trading vessel, and made the whole trip by water.

Mail service was slow and uncertain. Mail delivery was everywhere slow and uncertain. Letters were generally carried by travelers. Sometimes one traveler would carry a letter part of the way toward its address and leave it at an inn to be picked up by another traveler going farther in the right direction weeks or months later. When a very important letter had to be written, two or three copies were made and sent by different hands to be sure that at least one copy would arrive.

The first regular mail delivery on the American continent was begun, you remember, by the governor of New York. The mail started from New York for Boston on New Year's Day, 1673, and it was planned to make one trip each way every month, but the plan was not carried out. The old Boston Post Road between Boston and New York is now a famous highway over which automobiles go from one great city to the other in a day. How horrified the owners of the cars would be if they were compelled to take one month for the round trip!

Travelers carried the news. There were no newspapers until the eighteenth century. Because mail was so slow and travelers were so few, people knew very little about what was going on outside their own neighborhoods. The arrival of a stranger at the village inn or at the blacksmith's shop always brought people crowding around to ask him the news of the places that he had passed through.

A story is told of Benjamin Franklin which shows how eager the people were for news, and how many questions a traveler was asked. Franklin traveled a good deal, and, according to the story, he grew so tired of answering questions that he made it a practice to say when he arrived at an inn: "My name is Benjamin Franklin. I was born at Boston, am a printer by profession, am traveling to Philadelphia, shall have to return next month, and have no news. Now what can you give me for dinner?" The story is probably only partly true, for Franklin liked to talk too well to shut off conversation with such a blunt speech.

CAN YOU GIVE THE REASON?

1. Explain why the geography of a region does not control occupations today as much as it did in colonial times.

2. One historian tells us that some of the indentured servants came to be among the most respected citizens of a community. Explain how this would be so.

3. Why do women have more time to take part in public affairs today than they did in colonial times?

LISTS TO MAKE

(Consult a geography for present-day occupations and products.)

1. List the raw materials produced in the middle colonies in colonial times.

2. List the raw materials produced in the same territory today. How many items on your lists are the same?

3. Make a list of the articles manufactured by the middle colonies. Check those that are still manu-

factured in the same region today. Add at least five other articles that are made in that region today.

4. Write the names of the occupations of the middle colonies and after each occupation named give at least two reasons why it was natural work for the colonists to do. List at least five of today's occupations for this region.

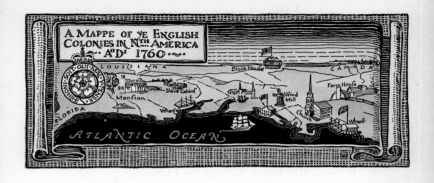

Outline of Chapter XII

XII. Life in the Southern Colonies
  A. Making a Living by Farming
  B. Labor in the South
    1. Indentured laborers became backwoods farmers.
    2. Negro slavery was beginning.
  C. Home Life in the South
    1. The early settlers lived in log cabins.
    2. Later the southern colonial mansion developed.
  D. Dress
  E. Amusements and Social Life
  F. Education in the South
    1. There were few schools.
    2. Early teachers were often indentured servants.
    3. What was a plantation school like?
  G. Travel in the South

CHAPTER XII

Life in the Southern Colonies

Making a Living by Farming

Nearly everybody in the South lived in the country. Of course there were doctors and lawyers and preachers and merchants, but many of these owned farms which they rented, and some worked on the farms themselves or directed the work of their slaves. Most of the work of carpenters, blacksmiths, and brick masons in the South was done on the farms by indentured servants or slaves. Williamsburg in Virginia, Baltimore in Maryland, Charleston in South Carolina, and Savannah in Georgia were the only important towns.

The principal crops raised for sale were tobacco and rice, which were shipped to England. But every man, whether he was a great planter owning thousands of acres of land and a hundred slaves or a poor backwoods farmer, raised food for his own people and for his work animals. Grain and potatoes and beans were a steady crop for winter food; vegetables were grown in spring and summer; and everybody tried to raise enough hogs to supply meat for his family and servants.

Labor in the South

Indentured laborers became backwoods farmers.
Although most of the stories that are written about
old times in the South describe the life on the
great plantations, it is important for us to remember that in colonial times nearly everyone in the
South lived on small farms. Many white people
came to the South as servants, just as they did to
New England and to the middle colonies, in order
to pay the cost of their fare across the Atlantic.
When they had worked out their fare, they were
given small farms in the backwoods.

Negro slavery was beginning. Most of the farmers
in the South in colonial times did their own work
and helped one another. There were really very
few colonists who were wealthy enough to own
slaves. The first Negro slaves in the English settlements were brought to Virginia, you remember,
by a Dutch ship in 1619, the same year in which
the Virginia settlers gained the right to elect their
legislature and govern themselves. In the beginning,
however, there were more indentured servants than
slaves.

There were, however, many more slaves in the
South than in New England or in the middle colonies. The growth of slavery in the South, which
had a very important influence upon the later history of our country, was largely the result of geography. Slavery grew chiefly because the climate

The mansions of the South were built along the rivers where water transportation could be used. Here guests are arriving at Mt. Vernon, George Washington's beautiful home on the Potomac River.

and the nature of the soil in the South made large plantations, growing one kind of crop, profitable. As some of the tobacco and rice plantations became very large, the planters began to use slave labor in the fields. After the beginning of the eighteenth century, that is, after about 1700, most of the work on the large southern plantations was done by Negro slaves.

Home Life in the South

The early settlers lived in log cabins. The first homes at Jamestown, like those in other early settlements, were one-room log cabins with roofs of grass or brush or rough boards. The cracks between the logs in the walls were filled with mud. The chimneys were built of sticks or branches plastered over with mud to keep them from catching fire.

As time passed, the settlers built larger houses by adding other rooms, halls, and porches to their first one-room cabins. These larger southern houses were all very much alike. If a farmer wanted a new two-room house, he built two log pens with a hall between them, and covered all with the same roof. Then he added a long porch, often called the "gallery," running the whole length of the house in front. If he wanted more room, he added "shed rooms" at the back, one room on each side of the hall. Sometimes a separate cabin, joined to the main house by a platform which was usually called "the passage," was built to serve as a kitchen.

The furniture in these log houses was much like that in early New England. The cooking was done at a fireplace. The floors were sometimes carpeted with deerskins or bearskins. Tables, beds, and chairs were handmade. The chairs had rawhide bottoms, with the hairy side of the skin turned out to make a sort of cushion. Tables and bedsteads were of plain lumber, and usually no effort was made to make them beautiful. No house was without a spinning wheel and a rifle. The spinning wheel stood in one corner of the main room. The rifle, powderhorn, and shot horn hung on pegs or deer horns over the door. Saddles, bridles, and farm harness hung from wooden pegs fixed in the walls of the hall and porch. No southern farmhouse was complete without a pack of dogs sleeping on the porch or in the hall.

Later the southern colonial mansion developed. As more and more people in the South became wealthy, the log houses gave place in towns and on the great plantations to fine buildings in what is now known as the "southern colonial" style. These were large two-story houses of wood or brick, having wide porches with beautiful columns in front. George Washington's home at Mount Vernon is a fine example of one of these great colonial mansions.

The owners of these fine homes bought their furniture in Europe and spent a great deal of money to make their houses attractive. But, like all houses in colonial times, southern colonial mansions lacked bathtubs, screens, and modern lights. They were large and airy, but our simpler, modern homes are far more comfortable.

The wealthy colonial planters living in these plantation homes enjoyed an easy, pleasant life. At daylight in the winter months, a Negro boy made great wood fires in the bedrooms, while other servants were milking the cows and feeding the horses. When the master had eaten breakfast, he mounted his horse. Perhaps he made the rounds of the plantation, setting the Negroes to work at the different tasks. He oversaw such work as plowing, mending fences, digging drainage ditches, splitting rails, chopping wood, and killing hogs and curing meat. Or perhaps he gathered his hounds and rode off to join the neighbors in a fox hunt.

In the meantime, the mistress was giving her day's orders to the house servants and making her daily visit to the Negro "quarters," as the cabins where the Negroes lived were called.

The children, whose teacher usually lived in the house, began their lessons right after breakfast. After dinner, which was served by the Negro servants at about two o'clock in the afternoon, they had music and dancing lessons.

Dress

The dress of both men and women would look very strange to us, if we could look in at one of these great plantation houses. The men wore long coats and knee breeches made of velvet or satin, ruffled shirts trimmed with the finest lace, long silk stockings, and low shoes with silver buckles. They wore their hair long and tied in a queue, or braid, at the back, and sprinkled it with powder to make it white. The women's dresses had very tight waists and very long, wide skirts. The skirts were worn over circular frames called hoops, so that they stood out like big bells.

Amusements and Social Life

Life in the South was somewhat gayer than in the other colonies. The people took their church duties less seriously than the New England Puritans or the Pennsylvania Quakers, and all classes gave more time to amusements and social life.

Nearly all of the early southern colonists lived near the water, on rivers or on the seacoast. Though the mild climate deprived them of the winter sport of skating, the boys had fine times swimming, fishing, paddling canoes, and sailing or rowing boats.

Hunting and horse-racing were two of the greatest sports in the South. The boys hunted rabbits, squirrels, 'possums, and coons. Usually an old Negro went along with the boys, especially when they went to hunt 'possums or coons, for they hunted those at night. The men gathered in parties with great packs of dogs, sometimes as many as fifty dogs, and hunted bear, deer, and foxes. Both men and women enjoyed going to the horse races, which were held at the largest town in each county.

Hunting the foxes, bears, and deer that roamed their fields and woods was a favorite sport of the southern planters in colonial times. Why do state laws now limit the sport of hunting wild animals?

Young and old were fond of parties and dancing. Here is a description of the end of the day in one of the great plantation houses: "Half after eight we were rung in to supper. The room was well lighted and splendid, four very large candles burned on the table where we supped, three others in different parts of the room; a gay, sociable party; and four well trained waiters! So soon as we rose from supper, the company gathered round the fire and played games. Here we had great fun, but the party broke up by ten and we all retired to our rooms." The most fashionable ball of the year was given by the governor and his wife at the capital. All the important people in the colony were invited to the governor's ball, and everybody wanted to be there without fail.

Education in the South

There were few schools. For a long time there were no public schools to which the common people in the South could send their children. One reason for the small number of schools was that the homes in the South were very far apart. The colonists did not settle in villages which could keep up a school as in New England and the middle colonies. Settlement was made up of large plantations along the river banks and small farms in the backwoods. The backwoods farmers lived too far apart or were too poor to keep up a common school to which their children might go.

The South had fewer schools than either New England or the middle colonies. The College of William and Mary, which is older than any college in the United States except Harvard University, was established at Williamsburg, Virginia, in 1692. Some of the well-to-do plantation owners sent their sons to England to be educated. Some kept private teachers on their plantations to teach their own sons and daughters and the children of the neighborhood. While the South had some of the best educated men in America, very few of the poor people could read or write.

Early teachers were often indentured servants. Many of the teachers in the early South were indentured servants, serving for five or six years to repay the cost of their voyage to America. Some of these were brought over by ship captains and sold to the highest bidder. An old book tells us that hardly a ship arrived in early Maryland which did not advertise that it had a schoolmaster for sale.

Although some of these indentured servants had fine characters, most of them were not the sort of men that were needed to make good schools. One old writer said that it seemed to him that the colonists took better care of their hogs than of the education of their children. Sometimes such school teachers ran away from their masters before they had served out their time. A description of one such escaped teacher was printed in an old newspaper: "Ran away. A servant, clothed in damask breeches and vest, black coat, with a broadcloth cloak of copper color and wearing black stockings."

What was a plantation school like? A young student from Princeton College in New Jersey spent a year in one of the great Virginia plantation houses about the end of the colonial period, and he described his work in a diary which he kept. He says:

"*Monday, November 1.* We began school. The school consists of eight pupils: two of Mr. Carter's sons, one nephew, and five daughters. The eldest son is studying Latin. The second is studying English grammar, reading English books, and studying arithmetic. The nephew is reading and writing and studying arithmetic. The eldest daughter is reading in a magazine, writing, and beginning arithmetic. The second is reading now out of the spelling book, and beginning to write. The next is reading in the spelling book. The fourth is spelling in the beginning of the spelling book. And the last is beginning to learn the alphabet.

"In the morning so soon as it is light, a Negro boy knocks at my door to make a fire. After the fire is kindled, I rise, which now in winter is usually at seven o'clock or a little after. By the time I am dressed the children enter the schoolroom, which is under the room I sleep in. I hear one lesson from each. Then the bell rings for eight o'clock. The children go out, and at half past eight the bell rings for breakfast. After breakfast, about half after nine, we go into school and sit until twelve. Then the bell rings and they go out for noon. After dinner is over, which, when we have no company, is about half after three, we go into school and

Colonial girls seldom went to school. Most people then thought that a housewife's training was all the education any woman needed.

sit till the bell rings at five, when the children are free till the next morning.

"*Saturday, December 18.* Mr. Goodlet was barred out of his school last Monday by his scholars, for Christmas holidays; but my scholars are of a more quiet nature, and have consented to have four or five days now, and to have their full holiday in May next."

Travel in the South

Travel was difficult and uncomfortable in all the colonies and more so in the South than in New England or the middle colonies. On long journeys, people traveled as much as they could by water.

The planter boarded his boat at his own wharf on the plantation and had his slaves row him down to the mouth of the river. There he took a sailing vessel for Baltimore, Philadelphia, or London.

There were, as we have noticed, few roads in any of the colonies, and fewest of all in the South. All of the roads were bad. Short trips were made on horseback. Heavy carriages were mainly for show. The well-to-do planters owned coaches or carriages which were driven by proud Negro coachmen and drawn by four or six horses. But these were used only when the mistress went calling in town, and when they were polished up for the governor's ball.

As a result of poor roads, there was little travel. There were some inns, however, and not all of them were uncomfortable. One tavern in Baltimore, "The Indian Queen," boasted that every room had a bell with which to call for service, just as in our own time hotels often advertise "every room with bath and radio."

We can learn something about traveling conditions in the South from George Washington, who was born on a plantation in Virginia on February 22, 1732. His father died when he was eleven years old, and he was brought up by his mother and his older brother, Lawrence, who was like a father to him. Washington worked hard at school and learned arithmetic so quickly and so well that he was able to survey and measure land when he was only sixteen years old. He liked to write about things that he saw and did; and we can read in his own words about the first surveying trip that he made into the western part of Virginia.

His diary tells us the number of acres that he surveyed each day; how he swam his horses across the overflowing rivers; how he shot deer and wild turkeys. It tells us about the people that he saw, the sort of houses that he stayed in, and the Indians that he met. He says of his first surveying trip:

"On Friday, March 11, 1748, I began my journey in company with George Fairfax and we traveled forty miles.

"On Tuesday, the 15th, we worked hard till night and then returned to Pennington's, got our supper, and were shown to our room. I undressed and got into bed. To my surprise I found it to be nothing but a little straw, without sheets or anything else but one thin blanket. I was glad to get up as quickly as I could and put on my clothes. Had we not been very tired, I am sure we should not have slept much that night. I promised myself that I would never sleep in such a place again. I would rather sleep by a camp fire in the open air. But the next night, at another place, we had a good feather bed with clean sheets, which was a very agreeable change.

"On Saturday, March 26, we stopped for the night at the cabin of a settler. When we came to supper, there was neither a cloth on the table nor a knife to eat with. But as good luck would have it we had knives of our own.

"Tuesday, March 29, shot two wild turkeys.

"Saturday, April 2: Last night was a blowing and rainy night. The straw that we were sleeping on caught fire, but luckily one of the men waked up and put out the fire before it burned us.

"The next night was much more blustering than the one before. The wind blew our tent entirely away, and we had to spend part of the night without shelter."

Western Virginia was crossed only by Indian trails when the sixteen-year-old Washington traveled through it surveying wild forest lands for the great landowner, Lord Fairfax. Here the boy is shown watching an Indian war dance.

One day the young surveyor met thirty Indians coming from the warpath. They had one scalp. Washington gave them something to eat and drink, and afterwards they showed him a war dance. They built a great fire and seated themselves around it in a circle. The chief made a speech and then, "The best dancer jumped up, like a man just awakened from sleep. He ran and jumped about the ring in a very funny way, followed by the rest." Their music was made by a rattle and a drum. The drum was a pot half full of water, with a deer skin stretched over it. The rattle was a gourd with shot in it, "and a piece of horse's tail tied to it to make it look fine."

FIND THE DIFFERENCE

1. How did the homes of later Virginia differ from those of early Jamestown?

2. What amusements were carried on in the southern and middle colonies that were not carried on in New England?

3. How did travel in the South differ from travel in New England?

4. How did the interest in farming differ in the South and in New England?

5. If you had lived in colonial times would you have preferred to be educated in Massachusetts or in Virginia? Why?

Picturing Colonial Life in the South

1. Keep up your scrapbook by finding or making pictures for each group of colonies so that you may help in making a History Picture Exhibit at the end of the term.

2. Draw a picture of a rich southern planter's mansion.

or

Build on your sand table a southern plantation with mansion, slave quarters, barns, tobacco fields, wharf, etc.

See *The Pageant of America* (Yale University Press), Volume III, Chapter III, and other books that you may find in the library, for pictures of life in the southern colonies that will help you with this activity. Stories that will give you excellent pictures of plantation life are Lucy Fitch Perkin's *Colonial Twins in Virginia*, D. L. Leetch's *Tommy Tucker on a Plantation*, and Elizabeth Coatsworth's *The Golden Horseshoe*.

3. Collect pictures of comforts and conveniences which we have today that were unknown in colonial Virginia.

4. Try making some pen-and-ink or crayon sketches of colonial travel, furniture, clothing, punishments, and amusements in the South. The following references will give you ideas:

Willis, Carrie Hunter, and Saunders, Lucy S., *Those Who Dared*, Part III, pp. 95-118.

Gordy, Wilbur F., *Stories of Early American History*, pp. 149-156.

Perkins, Lucy Fitch, *Colonial Twins in Virginia*.

Many of the references given at the end of the unit will help you, too.

Outline of Chapter XIII

XIII. Government in Colonial Times
- A. Democracy in the American Colonies
  1. All colonies developed self-government.
  2. Who had the right to vote?
  3. Freedom of the press was secured.
- B. England's Government of the Colonies
  1. Colonial business was regulated.
  2. Colonial self-government was limited.
  3. Did England mean to oppress colonists?
- C. Laws Controlling Colonial Business
  1. The trade laws were called "navigation laws."
  2. What was the first navigation law?
  3. What was the second navigation law?
  4. What was the third navigation law?
  5. Colonial manufacturing was checked.
  6. Some laws favored the colonists.
  7. The colonists disobeyed the trade laws.
- D. How Self-Government was limited
  1. Trading New England lost its self-government.
  2. Massachusetts led the defense of self-government.
  3. Massachusetts won back its legislature.
  4. England planned to appoint all colonial governors.

CHAPTER XIII

Government in Colonial Times

Democracy in the American Colonies

All of the colonies developed self-government. All of the colonies were not governed exactly alike in local matters, but in larger matters the colonies were governed in very much the same way. In all of them the people of the colony had developed the right to help in the central government of the colony.

At the head of the government was the governor. In some colonies the voters elected him; in some he was appointed by a proprietor; and in the royal colonies he was appointed by the king. Then there was the legislature, usually composed of two groups of men. One group was elected by the voters. The other group was sometimes elected and sometimes appointed by the governor. The legislature passed the laws for a colony, including the laws for the collection of taxes and the spending of money. In all of the colonies, the people claimed the right, through the legislature, to pass tax laws and denied the right of the king and Parliament to tax them without the consent of the legislatures. Thus we see that in large matters that were important to the whole colony both the governor and legislature had great power.

For matters of local government each colony was divided into counties, and the counties were further divided into still smaller districts. These smaller districts in New England were generally called towns, or townships; in the southern colonies they were sometimes called parishes, or sometimes precincts; while in the middle colonies they might be called either precincts or townships.

In the South the officers of the county carried on the most important matters of local government. In the New England colonies the towns, or townships, governed themselves. In the middle colonies, sometimes local matters were looked after by the county and sometimes by the township.

In the New England townships all of the voters met together in *town meeting* to elect officers and pass local laws or ordinances. Much the same sort of thing was done in the southern parish meetings, though most of the matters were decided by the county officers who were appointed by the governors. In the southern counties, particularly in Virginia, the justices of the peace or county judges not only held court but had a good deal of authority in directing local affairs.

It was the duty of town or parish officers to look after the highways, to keep them in repair, and to build bridges and open new roads when necessary.

They had to see that the laws were obeyed and
that peace was preserved. They had to see that
care was taken of the poor. And it was their duty
to keep the churches and schools in good repair.

Taxes for the necessary expenses of the townships and parishes were collected by the constables,
or by special tax collectors, after being voted by
the town or parish officers. In the North the taxes
were usually based on property, and each man
paid in proportion to the value of his property.
In the southern colonies, the tax was based on the
number of persons, so much for each. In Virginia,
for example, a man was required to pay not only
for himself and the members of his family, but
also for each servant or slave that he employed.

Who had the right to vote? In none of the colonies did all of the people have the right to vote.
Women, servants, and slaves could not vote, nor
could even all free men. Only men who owned land
or other property were allowed to vote, and in some
of the colonies people had, also, to belong to a certain
church.

Freedom of the press was secured. One of the
most important happenings in colonial times was
the trial of Peter Zenger (zĕng′ẽr), in New York
in 1735. Zenger was a young printer and newspaper
editor. His paper was *The New York Weekly
Journal*. Zenger printed articles which criticized
the governor, and the governor wanted the court

Peter Zenger's trial established the right of freedom of the press in our country. Do people today depend largely upon newspapers for information about what public officers are doing? Do newspapers criticize the government?

to punish him. Zenger's trial was of great importance to all the colonists, because, if the court decided that his newspaper could not criticize the governor and other government officers, freedom to speak and write what one honestly believed would come to an end.

Zenger's friends employed Andrew Hamilton, a very able Philadelphia lawyer, to defend him. Hamilton convinced the jury that Zenger and all other newspaper editors must be allowed to print the truth about public officers; and the jury set Zenger free. Freedom of the press was one of the most valued principles of free government in the American colonies, and later in the American nation.

England's Government of the Colonies

Colonial business was regulated. The English colonies in America were founded by groups of merchants, such as the London Company in Virginia and the Massachusetts Bay Company in Massachusetts, or by individual owners, such as Baltimore in Maryland and Penn in Pennsylvania. Hardly was a colony begun, however, before the national government in England began trying to control for the benefit of the business men of the home country the ways in which the colonists made their living.

Colonial self-government was limited. In spite of the fact that the colonies were governed without expense to the national government, Englishmen believed that colonial government should be managed for the benefit of English business. In order to carry out this idea, the Parliament of England passed laws to control the trade and manufacturing of the colonists, and the king appointed officers to enforce the laws.

Did England mean to oppress the colonists? It is important for us to remember that the English government did not mean to oppress or mistreat its colonists. The English colonists enjoyed far greater rights and privileges than did the colonists of Spain, Portugal, France, or Holland. The truth is that practically all European people of that day thought that the purpose of a colony was to benefit the business of the home country. They regarded it as the first duty of the colonist to sell the home country things that it could not produce for itself and to buy the things that the home country had for sale.

Laws Controlling Colonial Business

The trade laws were called "navigation laws." The first step that the English government took to control the trade of the colonies was to pass the navigation laws. There were a great number of these laws, but we will study only the three that mattered most to the people of the American colonies. Although the date of each law is given for clearness, it will be necessary to remember only that all three were passed about the middle of the seventeenth century, that is, about the time that England took New York from the Dutch. Notice that these laws were passed before some of the colonies had been begun.

What was the first navigation law? The main purpose of the first navigation law, which was passed by Parliament in 1651, was to increase the use of English ships and to furnish work for English sailors. It declared that goods which were shipped to England and to its colonies from Asia, Africa, and America must be carried in English ships. It declared, also, that goods from the continent of Europe must be carried either in English ships or in ships owned in the country that produced the goods.

You can see that this law gave English and colonial shipowners a great advantage and furnished work for many English and colonial sailors. Suppose that you were a business man living in England or Ireland in colonial times and wanted a cargo of French goods. You could ship it in a French vessel or in an English vessel, but you could not ship it in a Dutch ship. Suppose you wanted to buy some rice and tobacco from America. You could ship it only in an English ship, and three-fourths of the sailors on that ship must be English subjects. An English ship meant a ship owned by an English subject, whether he lived in England, in the American colonies, or in any of England's other possessions.

What was the second navigation law? The second navigation law, passed in 1660, forbade the colonists to sell certain goods anywhere except in England or in some other territory governed by England. The goods named in this law were tobacco, sugar, indigo, and cotton. Later laws added a great number of other colonial products to the list. Among

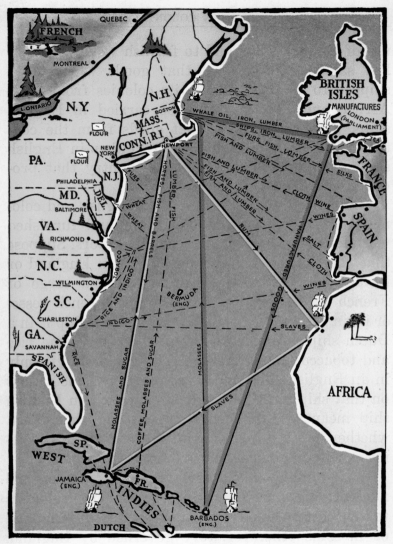

List the products carried by the Rhode Island ships in the profitable, three-cornered trade with Africa and the West Indies. Would the navigation laws interfere with the trade with the sugar planters of Cuba? Why?

them were rice and all sorts of materials that were needed in shipbuilding, such as tar, pitch, turpentine, ship masts, and hemp for ropes and rigging.

The effect of this law was to give merchants in England the profits from the trade in these particular products. These goods, you see, were supposed to be carried only in English ships manned by English sailors, and the colonists could sell them only in England or in some other territory governed by England.

What was the third navigation law? The third navigation law, passed in 1663, declared that colonists who wished to buy the products of other European countries must buy them from merchants in England. If you lived in colonial Virginia, for example, and wanted some lace handkerchiefs and silver buckles made in France, you could buy them only from England.

The effect of the third law, like the second, was to give English merchants most of the profits of the colonial trade to and from Europe.

Colonial manufacturing was checked. Other laws passed by Parliament forbade the colonists to manufacture certain sorts of goods, such as woolen cloth, hats made of beaver skins, and iron tools. Colonists could make these things for their own use and could sell them to their neighbors, but they could not ship them out of the colony in which they made them. For example, a cloth-maker or

When the American forests were full of fur-bearing animals, making fur hats was profitable. The furs were dipped in a steaming liquid, rolled and beaten into felt, and then shaped on hat blocks.

a hat-maker in Massachusetts could not ship cloth or hats to New York or Virginia, nor could he ship them to England or France.

The object of these laws was to keep the colonists from building mills and shops and manufacturing goods that would compete with goods made in England. The manufacturers and merchants in England wanted to have the profits from the sale of woolen cloth, beaver hats, and iron goods.

Some laws favored the colonists. As we have seen, the first navigation law gave colonial shipbuilders and colonial sailors the same advantages that it gave shipbuilders and sailors in England.

The English government also passed laws giving the colonists certain advantages in the English market. For example, it paid the colonists a bounty for certain shipbuilding products, such as masts and hemp, and it made raising tobacco in England or Ireland unlawful so that Englishmen would have to buy colonial tobacco.

The colonists disobeyed the trade laws. Even before some of the colonies were established, the efforts of the king and Parliament in England to control the ways in which the colonists made their living caused discontent in America. The trade laws were annoying, but at first the colonists offered little open objection. Nevertheless, the laws were not really fair, and the colonists, for the most part, did not obey them. The New England merchants, particularly, went on trading with the French and the Dutch as before.

If the English leaders had been able to read the signs of the times, they would have seen in colonial discontent the promise of a dangerous conflict and might have changed the policies of the national government.

How Colonial Self-Government Was Limited

Trading New England lost its self-government.
The government in England knew that the colonial
merchants, particularly in New England, were not
obeying the navigation laws but were trading with
French and Dutch ships. It was in order to enforce
the trade laws, as well as to protect the colonies
from the French and the Indians, that the king
took control of the government of the New England
colonies. You remember how Governor Andros was
sent out to govern all of New England as well as
New York and New Jersey (See page 172). The
English government thus brought about half of
the colonies under a single governor who ruled
from Boston.

You will remember that the colonists in Massachusetts had governed themselves for fifty years
under the charter of the Massachusetts Bay Company. It gave members of the company the right
to elect their own officers and to make their own
laws. Before the king could get control of their
government, he had to take away this charter. The
year before the king sent Andros out to be governor
of all the territory from Maine in the north to the
Delaware River in the south, a high court in England declared the charter of Massachusetts no longer
in force.

The Massachusetts colonists thought it hard
enough to have a governor appointed by the king,

but that was not the worst of their troubles. When their charter was taken away, they lost the right to elect a legislature and pass their own laws. Governor Andros created a council of representatives from all the colonies under his authority, and this council acted with him in making the laws. You can imagine how little the Massachusetts Puritans enjoyed having councilmen from Rhode Island, New Jersey, and New York help to make the laws for their colony.

The governor and the council fixed the taxes that the people had to pay. Governor Andros appointed officers to enforce the navigation laws. He discovered that very few people had a good legal title to the lands that some of them had been living on for fifty years. He insisted that they must get a good deed from him and pay a fee for it. He "borrowed" one of the churches in Massachusetts so that a preacher of the Church of England could hold services in it when the Puritan congregation was not using it.

Massachusetts led the defense of self-government. The people of Massachusetts were used to having their own legislature fix their taxes, and they denied that Governor Andros and his council had a right to tell them how much they must pay. They did not deny the right of Parliament to pass the navigation laws, but they disliked the governor for enforcing these laws which hurt their trade with the French and the Dutch. They had bought their land from the Indians, had improved it, and had lived on it for years. They declared that they ought not to have to pay the king for land they already owned. The Puritans had left England to avoid practicing the religion of the Church of England, and they did not want any church but their own to be established in Massachusetts.

It is easy to understand the anger of the Puritans in Massachusetts who had ruled themselves so long. Puritan writers declared that Governor Andros was a tyrant, but the worst that can fairly be said of him is that he was blunt and impatient in manner. He was a good officer who did his duty in carrying out his instructions and enforcing the laws. Parliament had passed the laws, and the advisers of the king had given the governor his instructions. The colonists were really quarreling with the English government.

Four years after Massachusetts had lost its charter, the news reached Boston that Parliament had driven King James II from his throne and had invited William and Mary to be the new rulers of England. The leaders in Massachusetts arrested Governor Andros and set up a government of their own. They hoped the old Massachusetts charter would be restored by the new English government, but they were disappointed. After some months, they allowed Andros to go back to England, from which he was sent back to America in a little while to be governor of Virginia for four or five years.

Massachusetts won back its legislature. After three years, Massachusetts received a new charter from the king. It gave back to the colonists the right to elect a legislature, but gave the king the right to appoint the governor. The laws passed by the colonial legislature had to be sent to England for the approval of the king, and he could veto them if he did not wish them to go into effect. It was by this charter that Plymouth was included in Massachusetts. It is easy to see that people in Massachusetts were less free to govern themselves under the new charter than they had been under the trading company's charter.

England planned to appoint all colonial governors. What the English government did in Massachusetts was part of a general plan to limit the power of the colonists to govern themselves. The plan had been started when the king began appointing the governor in Virginia in 1624. It was carried out slowly, but steadily. Before the end of colonial times, eight of the thirteen colonies were royal colonies, that is, had governors appointed by the king.

By giving the king the right to appoint the governor and requiring the governor to send colonial laws to England for the king's approval, the national government could exercise a great deal of power in the colonies.

FIND THE CAUSES AND THE RESULTS

1. of the trial of Peter Zenger
2. of the passing of the Navigation Acts
3. of the removal of Governor Andros
4. of the decrease in colonial self-government

FIND CONNECTIONS BETWEEN MODERN AND COLONIAL PROBLEMS

1. In a newspaper or magazine find an example showing the freedom of the press today in criticizing our government.

2. Try to find in a newspaper examples of present-day trade laws. Discuss these laws in class to see why each is needful.

3. Find out whether you live under a township government, under a county government, or under both.

4. Find out what people can vote today who could not have voted in colonial days. What people cannot vote today? (Use a civics book or a voters' guide or handbook as a reference.)

THEN AND NOW

1. If you are interested in reading about life in the English colonies as a whole, the following books will give you a good picture of colonial life. This library list will help you with the activities and questions that follow.

Gordy, W. F., *Stories of Early American History*, Chapter XVII.

Long, J. A., *Early Settlements in America*, Chapter XI.

Bailey, Carolyn Sherwin, *Boys and Girls of Colonial Days* (A. Flanagan Company), for those who like stories that are easy to read.

Prescott, Della R., *A Day in a Colonial Home* (Marshall Jones Company).

Stone and Fickett's *Everyday Life in the Colonies* (D. C. Heath and Company).

Smith, S. C., *Made in America* (Alfred A. Knopf).

Phelan, Margaret S. G., *Candle Light Tales*, Our Changing World (Thomas Nelson & Sons).

Warren, Maude R., *Little Pioneers*, American Life Series (Rand McNally and Company).

Hogan, Louis J., *Extra! Extra!* Our Changing World (Thomas Nelson and Sons). Perhaps you can read Chapter III and tell the class what it says about newspapers in colonial times.

2. Name ten conveniences your home has that a colonial home did not have, and tell the chief reasons why you can have more conveniences.

3. Why have you a better chance than a colonial child to be educated in the affairs of the world?

4. Why is travel easier now than in colonial days?

5. What improvements make it possible to receive news more quickly today than in colonial times?

6. What would be the effect on the government

TIME LINE FOR UNIT FOUR
NEW WAYS OF THINKING AND LIVING
BEGAN —
IN AMERICA

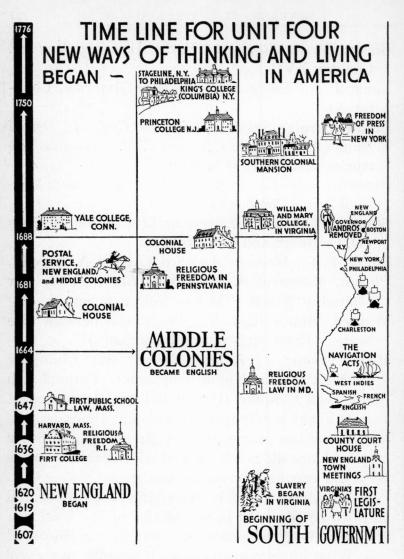

1776
1750
1688
1681
1664
1647
1636
1620
1619
1607

STAGELINE, N.Y. TO PHILADELPHIA
KING'S COLLEGE (COLUMBIA) N.Y.
PRINCETON COLLEGE N.J.

SOUTHERN COLONIAL MANSION

FREEDOM OF PRESS IN NEW YORK

YALE COLLEGE, CONN.

COLONIAL HOUSE

WILLIAM AND MARY COLLEGE, IN VIRGINIA

NEW ENGLAND GOVERNOR ANDROS REMOVED BOSTON
N.Y. NEWPORT
NEW YORK
PHILADELPHIA

POSTAL SERVICE, NEW ENGLAND and MIDDLE COLONIES

COLONIAL HOUSE

RELIGIOUS FREEDOM IN PENNSYLVANIA

CHARLESTON

THE NAVIGATION ACTS

MIDDLE COLONIES
BECAME ENGLISH

RELIGIOUS FREEDOM LAW IN MD.

WEST INDIES
SPANISH FRENCH
ENGLISH

FIRST PUBLIC SCHOOL LAW, MASS.

HARVARD, MASS.
RELIGIOUS FREEDOM R.I.
FIRST COLLEGE

COUNTY COURT HOUSE
NEW ENGLAND TOWN MEETINGS

NEW ENGLAND
BEGAN

SLAVERY BEGAN IN VIRGINIA

BEGINNING OF
SOUTH

VIRGINIA'S FIRST LEGISLATURE

GOVERNM'T

When and where do you find the beginnings of religious freedom? of public schools? of freedom of the press?

298

of the United States if freedom to criticize it had not been established in colonial times? Can you name any countries that do not have freedom of the press today?

7. Make a list of five different beliefs or customs or ideas that are ours today that were begun in colonial times?

A SHORT STORY OF UNIT FOUR

New Ways of Thinking and Living in America

Three hundred years ago, most of the work was done by hand. The use of steam, gas, and electricity for running machinery and for lighting and heating homes had not yet been discovered. Life in our times is very different from colonial life because of the invention of many machines to take the place of hand labor.

The colonists at first made a bare living by fishing, fur trading, and farming. Later, as more settlers came to America, people in New England and the middle colonies turned to trade. Many made a living by carrying freight to England and to other colonies, especially to the West Indies. In the South, people made their living almost entirely by working on farms and plantations.

There was much work to do in the colonies, and not very many people to do it, so no one who could work needed to dread unemployment. All members of the earlier colonial families had to work; but, with the coming of more and more people, indentured servants and slaves supplied the wealthier families with labor.

The home life of the people was very much the same whether they lived in New England, in the middle colonies, or in the South. Nearly everybody lived in the country on scattered farms or in tiny country villages. Boston, New York, Philadelphia, and Charleston were the only towns of any size. The single city of Chicago today contains more people than all the colonies at the close of colonial times. Throughout the colonial period, many of the colonists lived in log houses furnished with homemade furniture and wore homespun clothing. Some grew rich enough to build beautiful colonial mansions of lumber and of brick, and had fine furniture and handsome clothes brought from England.

Life in the middle and southern colonies was somewhat gayer than in Puritan New England. People took their church duties less seriously; and all classes gave more time to sports and amusements. Education, other than what work gave, was confined to the fortunate few except in New England, where our first public schools were begun. Travel was slow, inconvenient, and often dangerous; and mail service was uncertain.

Government in the thirteen English colonies was more democratic than in any other country of colonial times. The colonists in America managed their

Young Benjamin Franklin printed his *Pennsylvania Gazette*
sheet by sheet on a hand-run press. Today huge presses
driven by electric power can roll off fifty thousand entire
newspapers, of many sheets each, in an hour.

affairs in town meetings, elected representative
legislatures to make laws, and helped to establish
freedom of religion and of the press. Nevertheless,
colonial self-government was limited. Only part
of the people were allowed to vote even in the most
democratic colonies; and the English government
attempted to limit self-government in two ways.
First, England tried to control the trade and manu-

facturing of the colonies for the benefit of the home country. Second, it tried to control the governments of the colonies through governors appointed by the king of England.

There is a saying that "coming events cast their shadows before them," meaning that by carefully studying causes and effects we can often foresee that certain things are likely to happen before they actually do happen. If people in England had been wise enough "to read the signs of the time," they might have changed their policies. It was plain that new ways of living and thinking were beginning in the American colonies, which might lead to a new nation.

UNIT FIVE

People in the Colonies Spread Westward

If we use our imaginations, we can see the settlement of our country as a thrilling moving picture. In the first scene we have Jamestown and Plymouth. The settlers arrive from England in their queer-looking ships. They unload their chests and trunks. The ships sail away. People build log cabins, clear land, and plant their crops. And always they are in danger of their lives from the tomahawks and scalping knives of Indians angered by the loss of their lands.

The next scene shows colonial hunters pushing into the forests, hunting deer and beaver and bears and panthers. They want the skins for clothing and rugs and bedding. They want furs to ship to England.

Following the hunters come men and women and children, leaving the old settlements by the sea to make new homes in the western woods. We see them on the trail, usually walking with their long rifles on their shoulders, perhaps with all their belongings in a pack on one shaggy horse, sometimes in wagons. They select a wooded hilltop near the bank of a running stream. Out come the axes.

The earliest western settlers were hunters and fur traders.

Trees are felled. A little field is cleared. Soon smoke is rising from cabin chimneys, and corn is growing in the clearings.

So the scenes shift up the rivers, through the forests, and across the Appalachian Mountains. There French trading posts bar the way of the pioneer until France loses her colonies late in colonial times. Then the first important settlements west of the mountains are planted in Kentucky and Tennessee. Always the movement is toward the west, and always Indians are near with tomahawk, knife, and torch.

Later scenes move on across the broad Mississippi, across the high, dry plains of the far West, across the Rocky Mountains, and finally to the shore of the rolling Pacific. When the picture ends, we see the United States as it is today.

Unit Five shows how the people in the colonies spread westward in:

Chapter XIV. Taking the West from France

Chapter XV. Moving West in Colonial Times

Outline of Chapter XIV

306

CHAPTER XIV

Taking the West from France

How the Contest for the West Began

English settlers spread westward. Throughout
the colonial period, population moved steadily westward. From the first settlements on the seacoast
the people moved quickly up the rivers. You will
remember that there were eleven "plantations" or
settlements in Virginia in 1619 when the first legislature was elected. Ten of these settlements were
up the James River, west of the first settlement at
Jamestown. Boston and its neighboring villages
were settled in 1630. Six years later Thomas Hooker
and his church people moved westward to the Connecticut River and began the settlement that grew
into Connecticut.

In general, the lines of travel followed the course
of the rivers flowing into the Atlantic. The streams
were the first highways, and the most valuable
lands were on the river fronts. The first settlers,
of course, chose land close to a river's mouth. Newcomers went up a little farther and a little farther.
Then they filled in the lands between the rivers.

The same sort of movement went on in all of the
colonies. Why did people move? The answer is

that they hoped to improve their condition by every move. They moved to get better land; to get a better location on a creek or river; to find a more healthful situation. They moved sometimes in order to enjoy greater political freedom. By starting a new settlement they could make their own rules about voting and holding office.

By the middle of the eighteenth century, settlers were pushing up the eastern side of the Appalachian Mountains and looking toward the lands beyond.

Courtesy Bureau of Visual Instruction, University of Texas

Many Spanish missions aided Spanish trade in the southwestern part of what is now the United States. This Texas mission, the famous Alamo, was built in the early 1700's.

Father Marquette was a French missionary, Joliet a fur trader.

French and Spanish traders held the West. England was, you remember, not alone among the European nations in sending colonies to the new world. While the English colonists were fastening their hold upon the Atlantic coast, the Spanish were pushing their settlements northward from Mexico, and the French were moving up the St. Lawrence River, around the Great Lakes, and down the Mississippi River to the Gulf of Mexico.

Only a year after the English had started Jamestown, Samuel de Champlain (shăm′plān) had founded Quebec, from which French fur-traders and missionaries spread rapidly westward and southward. A year later the Spaniards established a frontier church and trading post at Santa Fe (săn'tà fā') in our present state of New Mexico. Thus the three years: 1607, 1608, and 1609, set the stage for a contest among three great European nations for the territory that became the United States.

A few French held a vast empire. The French fisherman, Jacques Cartier (zhäk' kär'tyā), had given France a claim to the St. Lawrence Valley seventy-three years before Quebec was founded. French fur-traders and missionaries, moving west and south from Quebec, gave France a claim to all the territory drained by the great Mississippi River. Father Marquette (mär-kĕt') and Louis Joliet (jō'lĭ-ĕt) explored the upper Mississippi River, and Robert Cavelier de la Salle (kà'vē-lyā' dē là sàl') led a party to the mouth of that great stream.

The French founded scattered settlements to protect their broad claims. Montreal (mŏn'trē-ôl') was at the head of navigation on the St. Lawrence. Biloxi (bĭ-lŏk'sĭ) and Mobile (mō-bēl') held the northern coast of the Gulf of Mexico. New Orleans (ôr'lē-ănz) guarded the lower part of the Mississippi Valley, Kaskaskia (kăs-kăs'kĭ-ä) and Vincennes (vĭn-sĕnz') held the present states of Illinois and Indiana. These widespread settlements served as trading posts and as centers of religious influence which kept the Indians faithful to France.

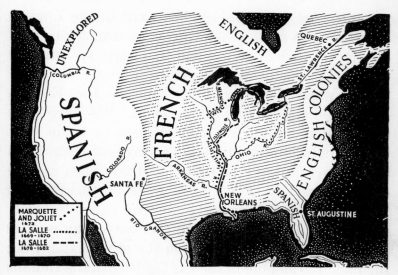

By the time Georgia was begun, there were three countries in control of the country which has become the United States. What were they, and which had the least land?

France did not give its colonies self-government. The French colonists had none of the freedom that English colonists enjoyed. The governor came from France and ruled according to the king's instructions. The people not only had no share in the making of the laws; they were even forbidden to meet together for the purpose of drawing up petitions to ask for things that they wanted.

In religion, too, the French colonists had less freedom than the English. The French government would permit none but Catholics to go to its colonies. The result was that the many French Protestants who fled from France went to the English colonies or to some other European country instead of giving their energy and industry to building up the French empire in America.

Nor were the French as free as the English colonists in matters of commerce. We have seen that England required the colonists to trade with the mother country and tried to prevent them from selling certain sorts of manufactured goods outside of the colony in which they were made. But the people in each colony were allowed to trade freely with the Indians and among themselves, as well as with England. The French, on the other hand, were forbidden to engage in the fur trade with the Indians unless they had a permit from the governor; and about the only farm product they were allowed to ship to France was wheat. As a result of such strict control by their government, the French colonists were few and poor.

Of course, it is possible that not many Frenchmen would have gone to the French colonies had the government given them more freedom. The French loved their country more than most European people. They liked to stay at home. Few cared to go to Canada, where the climate was cold and living hard.

Whatever may have been the true cause, there were only 80,000 white people in the French colonies in 1750 when the English colonies had grown to 1,250,000.

Every spring the "coureur du bois," or runners of the woods, sent out by the French fur-trading company led fleets of Indian canoes loaded with furs down the rivers to the French forts to trade.

Three wars brought little change. The movement of the English settlements to the west and the advance of the French fur-trading posts to the south naturally brought conflict. At the end of the seventeenth century, that is, about the end of the sixteen hundreds, the French and English colonists began to make war upon one another.

A great history telling the story of the first three wars between the French and English in America has been called *A Half Century of Conflict*. The three wars took their names from English rulers. The first was King William's War, lasting from 1690 to 1697. The second was Queen Anne's War, lasting from 1701 to 1713. The third was King George's War, lasting from 1745 to 1748 in the time of King George II. These dates are not particularly important, except that they keep the story straight and show that these three wars were spread over more than half a century.

Though the English settlers greatly outnumbered the French, the French were more successful in handling the Indians than were the English. The French leaders led or sent many Indians against the English frontier settlements. Savagely they attacked the borders of New York and New England, which were nearest to the French settlements on the St. Lawrence River. The stories of terror and suffering endured by the colonists would fill many books. We will take time here to tell two: the story of Hannah Dustin and the story of the massacre of Deerfield, Massachusetts.

Hannah Dustin lived on a farm near Haverhill, Massachusetts, with her husband and eight children. When the Indians attacked the house during the

last year of King William's War, she begged her
husband to take the children and try to escape. She
herself was sick in bed, so sick that she had a nurse.
Thomas Dustin and the children managed to get
away, but the Indians captured the two women,
Hannah and the nurse. In spite of Mrs. Dustin's
weakness, the Indians compelled her to get up and
walk. Finally, she and her nurse found themselves
in an Indian lodge on an island up the river, where
there was a white boy who had been a captive for
about a year. With this boy the two women planned
to escape. One morning just before daybreak, they
killed ten Indians and scalped them. Then they got
into a boat and paddled down the river to safety.

The Deerfield massacre occurred during Queen
Anne's War. A company of Indian warriors commanded by a Frenchman stole upon the village
during one of the coldest nights of the winter and
attacked it before dawn. They killed 47 people and
burned the village to the ground. Then they led
away 120 men, women, and children as captives.

The English in their turn made attacks on Canada.
During Queen Anne's War, a force of English colonists and soldiers captured Port Royal, the capital
of Acadia (ä-kād'ĭ-ä), as the French called Nova
Scotia. A treaty of peace allowing England to keep
Acadia made the only lasting change of territory
during the first three wars. We shall see how tragic
this change was for the French colonists.

How France Lost the West

A race for the Ohio Valley started. The fourth and last war started in the race for the Ohio River Valley that began shortly after 1750. The purpose of the English to take possession of the Ohio Valley and use it as a gateway to the West was clear. The French began to build a line of forts from Lake Erie to where Pittsburgh now stands at the forks of the Ohio River. If the French fur-traders could crowd into this region and win the friendship of the Iroquois Indians from the English, they might shut the English out of the West and might even conquer the northern colonies. The governor of Canada built one fort on the southeast shore of Lake Erie, and two others, Fort Le Boeuf (lĕ bûf') and Fort Venango (vē-năn'gō), in the northwest corner of the present state of Pennsylvania.

It was not known at the time whether the Ohio territory belonged to Pennsylvania or to Virginia. The Quakers in the Pennsylvania legislature were, however, opposed to war, and certainly would take no steps to check the advance of the French. It was the governor of Virginia who sent a message to the commander of the two French forts on the Ohio, warning him that the territory belonged to England and requesting him to withdraw from it.

George Washington appeared as a leader. The messenger to the French was a young Virginia surveyor, George Washington, who was to play such

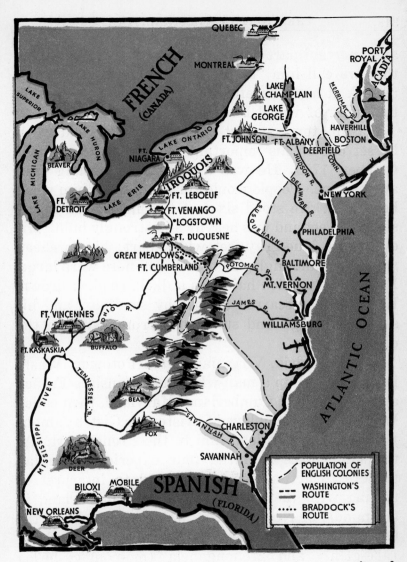

The French and Indian War was a struggle for possession of what is now our Middle West. This map shows how far English population had spread by 1750.

an important part in the history of the United States that we call him "the father of his country." Let us look at him, therefore, on his first appearance on the stage of world history.

Washington was just twenty-one years old when he set out on his important journey at the end of October, 1753. He was a fine-looking young man at this time. People would turn to look at him when he passed. He stood six feet two inches tall in his stocking feet and was heavily and strongly built. His eyes were blue-gray, set wide apart; his forehead was broad and high; his mouth and nose were large. His straight, thick hair was a dark, reddish brown. His face was scarred a little by smallpox, and his skin was rough and sunburned from living in the open air.

At Alexandria, Virginia, on the Potomac, Washington picked up a man who could translate French and English. At Cumberland, Maryland, then called Wills Creek, he employed Christopher Gist, a famous frontier guide, to lead him to the French fort. At the same place he hired four experienced Indian traders to act as "servitors" and to interpret in talking with the Indians. Leaving Cumberland in the middle of November, he was at the forks of the Ohio River a week later. Here, where the Allegheny (ăl′ē-gā′nĭ) and Monongahela (mō-nŏng′gä-hē′lä) Rivers meet to form the Ohio, Washington recorded in his diary that he thought the land "extremely

well situated for a fort." Very shortly a fort was
to be built there, which would grow into the modern
city of Pittsburgh, Pennsylvania.

At Logstown, some thirty miles north, Washington held some conferences with the Indians, and they
promised to be faithful to the English. Four chiefs
went with him from Logstown to Fort Venango.

Early in December he was at Fort Le Boeuf and
delivered his message. The French commander said
that "the country belonged to the French; that no
Englishman had a right to trade upon those waters;
and that he had orders to make every person
prisoner who attempted it on the Ohio or the waters
of it." The reply that Washington carried back to
the governor of Virginia was that the French king
owned the territory, and that the French commander
would not withdraw. The answer that the English
colonies made to this was war.

Franklin tried to unite the colonies. During the
summer of 1754, when the war began, the English
colonies held an important meeting at Albany on
the Hudson River. Representatives from seven colonies met there to make plans for defense of the
frontiers.

Benjamin Franklin, who was sent by Pennsylvania, offered a "Plan of Union." He proposed that
all of the colonies should send representatives to a
congress every year, and that the congress should
be given power to make and carry out plans for

defense of all the colonies. Since the carrying out
of such plans would cost money, Franklin suggested
that the congress should have the power to tax the
colonies.

The Albany Congress accepted Franklin's plan,
but the legislatures of the different colonies rejected
it. It was an important step toward union, however,
because it, at least, made the colonies think about
uniting.

The French and Indian War began. At the forks
of the Ohio River, you remember, was the place
that Washington had chosen for a fort on his
journey to warn the French. The governor of Virginia had sent a small force there to establish a
trading station.

The French, too, saw that the nation that held the
forks of the Ohio would be able to control a large
part of the Ohio Valley and the territory west of
the mountains. In the spring of 1754, the French
built a fort there and called it Fort Duquesne
(doŏ-kān'), after the governor of Canada.

When the governor of Virginia learned that the
French had seized the position, he ordered Washington to go with three hundred men and help the English settlement there. Washington was met at Great
Meadows, about fifty miles south of Fort Duquesne,
by a larger force of French and Indians. He had
built a fort there and named it Fort Necessity. He
defended his position ably at first, hoping vainly

for more help from the colonies. Then he surrendered the place on condition that he and his men should be allowed to return to Virginia without giving up their arms.

This was the beginning of the last stage of the struggle between the French and the English, which was known as the French and Indian War. It lasted from 1754 until 1763.

The French held the Ohio. Almost exactly a year later, Washington went again to the Ohio Valley to face another defeat. This time he was a colonel in the army of General Edward Braddock (brăd'ŭk), who commanded 1500 trained soldiers from England and nearly 500 Virginia colonists.

Braddock had had long experience on the battlefields of Europe, but he knew nothing about how to fight Indians in the forests of the New World. Unfortunately, he failed to take the wise advice of Washington and other colonial officers who joined him in Virginia. He marched through the wilderness of western Pennsylvania with his soldiers in close ranks, in spite of the fact that there might be an Indian sharpshooter behind every rock and tree.

When Braddock was within eight or nine miles of Fort Duquesne, the French and Indians attacked. Braddock was taken by surprise, and his men fell by scores without being able to see the hidden enemies who shot them. The English soldiers became panic-stricken. Finally, General Braddock was killed, and Washington led the retreat of what was left of the army. But for his skillful rear-guard defense, nearly all the English would have been killed or captured.

Washington wrote his mother: "The Virginia troops showed a great deal of bravery, and were nearly all killed; for I believe that, out of three companies that were there, scarcely thirty men are left alive." He wrote bitterly of the panic of the British soldiers, whom he blamed for the defeat. In spite of the brave efforts of their officers, he said, "they broke and ran as sheep before hounds, leaving the artillery, ammunition, provisions, baggage, and in short every thing a prey to the enemy; and, when we endeavored to rally them, . . . it was with as little success as if we had attempted to stop the wild bears of the mountains, or the rivulets with our feet."

We must remember, however, that Washington was a very young man, writing under the bitter disappointment of defeat. The British soldiers were not cowards. The trouble was that they were not prepared for the sort of fighting that they met in the woods of western Pennsylvania. They ought to have been trained to find shelter behind rocks and trees and baggage wagons at the first shot from the enemy.

For three years longer the French held Fort Duquesne. Then, their Indian allies deserted them, and they abandoned it without firing a shot. The English then took possession and renamed it Pittsburgh, in honor of the great English statesman who was helping to govern England.

The war became world-wide. From the Ohio Valley the French and Indian War spread to the New York and New England frontiers, to Canada, to Europe, and to far-away India. Wherever the interests of French and English subjects clashed, there was war.

The fighting in Europe had a most important influence upon the war in the colonies, especially upon the terms of the treaty of peace which ended the war. We must remember this fact, but it is not necessary for us to follow the history of the war in Europe. We are interested mainly in finding out what happened in America.

The French attacked the northern frontier. While the struggle was going on in the West, there was fighting on the frontiers of New York and of the New England colonies.

There were two important gateways between New York and Canada, one on the Niagara River about where the city of Buffalo now stands, and the other by way of Lake George and Lake Champlain. During the three years of the struggle for the forks of the Ohio, there was fighting for both these gateways. In most of the fighting in New York the French were successful. The only English victory was won near

Crown Point on Lake George in the second year of the war. This success was probably won by a Connecticut commander, but Sir William Johnson claimed and was given credit for it.

Whether or not Johnson was responsible for the victory on Lake George, we know that his services were very important in keeping the powerful Iroquois Indians friendly with the English. Living among them along the Mohawk River not far from Albany, Johnson used all his skill and power to keep the Indians loyal and helpful. As superintendent of Indian affairs for New York, he enlisted and equipped the Six Nations of the Iroquois for war against the French. It was with the aid of these powerful savages that the battle of Lake George was won and that the colonial frontier was protected from the French.

Sir William Johnson's work in keeping the Iroquois Indians faithful to England was the most important feature of the struggle on the northern frontier. If these Indians had joined the French, the history of our country might have been very different. Certainly the English colonies would have suffered a great deal more than they did in the conflict with France over the West.

French settlers were removed from Canada. One of the most distressing incidents of the French and Indian War occurred in Acadia, which appears on modern maps as Nova Scotia. The French farmers

Reproduced from The Pageant of America. ©Yale University Press

The poor French farmers of Acadia were cruelly torn from their homes in the fight for control of North America.

living in this territory refused to take the oath of allegiance to England. They loved France, and there was always danger that they would assist the French garrison located near them. To rid themselves of this danger, the English commanders determined to move the Acadians and scatter them throughout the other English colonies.

The removal took place in the second year of the war. Nearly six thousand people—men, women and children—were loaded on ships and carried away to be scattered through the English colonies from Massachusetts to Georgia. They were allowed to take some of their household goods, but they had to leave their homes, cattle, and other property behind. It was a cruel fate, and was probably not necessary to assure the English conquest of Canada.

Henry W. Longfellow, in his poem, *Evangeline*, has told the story of how the people of one French village were scattered on strange shores:

> Far asunder, on separate coasts, the Aca-
> dians landed;
> Scattered were they, like flakes of snow,
> when the wind from the northeast
> Strikes a slant through the fogs that darken
> the Banks of Newfoundland.
> Friendless, homeless, hopeless, they wan-
> dered from city to city,
> From the cold lakes of the North to the sul-
> try Southern savannas,—
> From the bleak shores of the sea to the lands
> where the Father of Waters
> Seizes the hills in his hands and drags them
> down to the ocean, . . .
> Friends they sought and homes; and many,
> despairing, heart-broken,
> Asked of the earth but a grave, and no
> longer a friend nor a fireside.

Some of these French settlers wandered far westward to the French settlements in Louisiana—"The lands where the Father of Waters seizes the hills in his hands, and drags them down to the ocean." Others managed to make their way back to Canada, where the English no longer feared them after the war ended. It is a pity that all of them could not have been restored to their homes and families.

The English took Quebec. The war that began with the failure of the English army in the woods of western Pennsylvania ended in the complete defeat of the French and the victory of the English in Canada, in 1759.

The last important battle was fought in the city of Quebec, which is built on a high cliff on the north bank of the St. Lawrence River. The sides of the cliff are very steep, but the land at the top, where the city stands, is open and level. Here the French made their last stand against the English. They knew that if Quebec fell, they could not hold Canada or any part of America. The English knew that if they could take Quebec, they could take Canada and drive the French from America.

The English commander who led the attack on Canada was General James Wolfe. He was a brilliant military leader with a great deal of experience though he was only thirty-one years old. When the king sent Wolfe to America, some men who did not like him complained that he was mad. "Mad, is he?" King George replied. "Well, I hope he will bite some of my other generals so that they too will become mad." The French commander who defended Quebec was the Marquis de Montcalm (mär′kwĭs dē mŏnt-käm′).

When General Wolfe arrived in front of Quebec, he found it defended by Montcalm with his Indian friends and about eight thousand French soldiers. Wolfe shelled the town with his cannon, but could do little harm because it was so high and so well protected by the steep, rocky cliffs. For weeks the English ships lay in the river, both above and below Quebec, but there seemed no way to reach the French on the heights.

For a time Wolfe was quite ill, and while he was in bed he told his officers to hold a council and see if they could find a way to get to Montcalm or make him come out. The officers held the council and went over all the plans they could think of, but none of them promised much success. While he was still on his cot, weakened with fever, Wolfe said to his doctor: "I know you can not cure me, but patch me up so that I may be able to do my duty for a few days."

When he was better, Wolfe made a plan to get at the French which was so daring that he did not tell it to any of his officers until he was ready to start. It was September, and whatever was done had to be done quickly before winter put an end to the fighting. Wolfe had found a way to send his men up the cliff to the very gates of Quebec. At one point there was a rough trail that led upward over rocks and through bushes to the top of the cliff. It was so steep that even a goat would have found it hard to climb in the dark, but Wolfe determined to send his men up that path at night. The French kept a small guard at the top, but they never dreamed of an attack there because they did not believe that an army could climb the cliff.

While the gunboats kept up a steady firing from the river to hold the attention of the French, Wolfe started a little party of twenty-four men up the trail. Others and still others followed. They beat off the guards and passed the word down the line that the way was open. The English climbed more rapidly then, since they no longer had to steal up the trail without noise. When morning dawned, forty-eight hundred of Wolfe's best soldiers were in line ready to meet the French, and General Wolfe himself was there to command. He had scaled the steep cliff with his men.

Montcalm could hardly convince himself that the enemy was at hand on the level ground around the city. There were only two courses now from which to choose: he could withdraw from Quebec and save his army to fight again, or he could risk a battle. He chose to fight.

The battle was won by the English almost from the first. In a little while the French forces were in retreat. Both Wolfe and Montcalm were fatally wounded. Neither lived to see the city surrendered.

The capture of Quebec decided the result of the war in America, but peace had to wait upon the end of the struggle in Europe. The treaty that ended the war was not signed until four years later.

When France Withdrew From America

England and Spain divided North America. The French and Indian War changed the map of North America. Though the struggle began for control of the Ohio Valley, it found the English at the end in possession of most of the French territory. The treaty was signed at Paris in 1763. It gave to England, Canada and all the French territory east of the Mississippi River except the island upon which New Orleans was built near the mouth of the river.

Toward the end of the war Spain had joined France against England. When peace was made, England got Florida from Spain.

In the general settlement that followed the war, the French gave Spain all the territory that France claimed west of the Mississippi River, and also the Island of Orleans east of the river.

France had ceased to be an American power. All North America was now divided between England and Spain.

The treaty of 1763 opened the West. The object of the French in the French and Indian War had been to hold the English to the narrow strip of

The Treaty of Paris, ending the French and Indian War in 1763, gave the English the country as far west as the Mississippi River. Who owned the land west of the Mississippi?

land between the Appalachian Mountains and the ocean. The object of the English colonists, which they had secured by the treaty, was to take possession of the Ohio Valley and use it as a gateway to the West. In 1763, England took possession of Canada and of the western lands between the Appalachian Mountains and the Mississippi River. The English colonies could now spread across the mountains into the western country as far as the Mississippi. The colonists were ready to go, even though the English government reserved the land as Indian territory.

Some Things to Think About

1. What were the chief differences between the English and French colonies? Consider:
    a. the reasons for colonizing
    b. the government
    c. settlers
    d. religion
    e. advantages in case of war
2. Why were the Iroquois Indians important in the French and Indian War?
3. Why was Benjamin Franklin's plan of union important?
4. What results of the French and Indian War can you give other than the changes in territory?

Mapping the Disputed West

Make a picture map of North America. Look at the maps on pages 311 and 317 before you begin. Locate on your map:
    a. three important rivers
    b. the explorations of the French in the Mississippi Valley
    c. two important Spanish cities
    d. three important French forts
    e. the western edge of English settlement at the beginning of the French and Indian War
    f. the Iroquois Indians

The rivers were the colonial highways to the West. Floating
west with a boat load of cows, horses, and household goods
was far safer and easier than taking the Indian trails.

Outline of Chapter XV

XV. Moving West in Colonial Times
    A. Going West Into Kentucky
        1. Daniel Boone was a "long hunter."
        2. Boone started settlement in Kentucky.
    B. Going West Into Tennessee
        1. Bold pioneers settled eastern Tennessee.
        2. People followed the rivers westward.
    C. The West at the End of Colonial Times

CHAPTER XV

Moving West in Colonial Times

Going West Into Kentucky

Daniel Boone was a "long hunter." There was a thin, blue-eyed, yellow-haired young wagon driver named Daniel Boone in General Braddock's army when it marched against the French. When the English soldiers were fleeing after the battle, he unhitched his team and escaped on one of the horses to his father's home in the mountains of western North Carolina.

Daniel Boone had lived most of his twenty years in the woods on the western edge of the colonial settlements, and from early childhood had been familiar with the dangers and delights of life in the forest. He spent most of his time in the woods, even after he married and settled with his wife and children on a little farm where he raised some corn and tobacco. The truth was that he could make more money by hunting and trapping than he could by farming. In one year he killed more than a hundred bears and an untold number of deer, and there was always a ready sale for deer skins at about a dollar apiece.

Hunters who went far into the trackless forests

and stayed a long time were called "long hunters."
Boone became the greatest of all the long hunters
of the colonial West. Dressed in buckskin coat and
leggings, wearing moccasins on his feet and a coon-
skin cap on his head, carrying his rifle on his shoulder, his knife and tomahawk in his belt, Boone would
tramp through the forests for weeks at a time. He
was a dead shot with his long, clumsy rifle. He could
follow the trail of a deer or a bear as silently as an
Indian.

Now and then, Boone met hunters who had gone
beyond the mountains into the country that is now
Kentucky. They told him that it was the most beautiful land they had ever seen. It was swarming with
fine game. The hunters had never seen so many
deer, bears, buffaloes, and wild turkeys. They described a hunter's paradise, a happy hunting ground.
The trouble was that Kentucky was part of the
Indian country and was the hunting ground of many
tribes of Indians. They did not live there, but one
might run into a hunting party or a war party at
almost any time.

In spite of the danger, Boone determined to go
and see Kentucky with his own eyes. He finally got
together a party of five men, and started across the
mountains. When he reached Kentucky, he knew
that the stories he had heard were true. The trees
were tall and beautiful, like trees in a park. The
open prairies were carpeted with grass and flowers.

Today our forests and wild game are so few that our government sets aside forest and game preserves, guarded by game wardens and forest rangers against lawless hunters, forest fires, and other dangers.

Herds of buffalo and deer roamed everywhere. In some places there were patches of salty earth which the animals came to lick, and near these salt licks the ground was packed as hard as a cement floor by the trampling herds. The hunters built a cabin and settled down to the business of killing deer and collecting valuable furs.

The summer passed. Winter was upon them,

In Daniel Boone's day, the whole country was covered with forests, and wild game roamed everywhere. Hunting wild animals for their furs and skins and clearing the land of trees were two of the main occupations of the pioneers.

and still they had seen no Indians. Perhaps they grew careless, for two days before Christmas, Boone and one of the hunters named Stuart were captured by a hunting party. Boone pretended to be perfectly happy. He laughed and joked with the Indians, joined in their games, and made them believe that he wanted to go home with them. After about a week of traveling in the direction of Canada, the Indians stopped guarding their prisoners. That was what Boone was waiting for. At night when the Indians were all asleep, Boone awakened Stuart, and they quietly stole away. They made their way back to their cabin, but found it deserted. Everything was gone: friends, skins, and horses. The other four hunters were never heard of again. No doubt, they were captured by another band of Indians while Boone and Stuart were away from the camp.

Most men facing such dangers would have been glad to leave Kentucky forever, but not Boone. He and Stuart moved the camp to another place, hid it more securely, and started again to gather skins and furs. They wanted to take back enough bales of skins to pay the expenses of the trip.

Just as powder and shot were running low, and Boone began to think that they might have to go home before they were ready, he came upon two men. From a distance they looked like white men, but he was not sure. Hiding behind a tree, he waited until they drew near. Then he called, "Hello, strangers, who are you?"

"White men and friends," was the answer. It brought Boone out of his hiding place, and to his surprise and joy, he saw that one of the men was his older brother, Squire Boone. The two newcomers had brought enough powder and shot so that the four men went on hunting together.

Every day Boone liked Kentucky better, but every

day it seemed to grow more dangerous. One morning Daniel Boone's hunting partner went off alone and did not return. For days the two brothers looked for him, but he was gone. Five years later, Daniel Boone found a man's bones and a powder horn with the name Stuart on it in a tree. Then he knew that the man must have been wounded and had hidden in the tree where he died. The loss of this man was too much for the other hunter. Leaving the Boone brothers, he started back to North Carolina, and that was the last that was ever heard of him. He did not get home. Whether he was captured, killed, or lost in the woods, no one knows. At the end of the summer, powder and shot were again getting low, so Squire Boone loaded the horses with furs and skins and took the trail for the east.

Alone, Daniel Boone tramped the country far and wide. Several times his camp was broken into and his supplies stolen while he was away. Once he saw a large band of Indians but managed to hide before they saw him. Another time he saw an Indian fishing. He told his friends later that the Indian fell into the river and disappeared. This was Boone's way of saying that he shot the Indian. At another time Boone met a band of Indians face to face. No doubt, the Indians thought they had him, but he jumped off a high cliff into the top of a tree below, slid to the ground, and escaped by swimming a river.

Squire Boone came back, and the two brothers hunted for another year. Finally they went home together, but Daniel Boone had made up his mind that Kentucky was the place for him. He would tell his neighbors about it, and perhaps some of them would go there to live.

Boone started settlement in Kentucky. Several years went by before Boone was able to lead his

The center of every new western community was a fort. In their advance into the Indian country, the western settlers had to protect themselves against the attempts of the natives to drive them back.

own family and other families to Kentucky. But, just the year before the American colonies declared their independence, he and some of his friends started the settlement of Boonesborough on the Kentucky River.

During the war for independence the Kentucky settlers suffered terribly from the Indians. Once the savages captured Boone's daughter, Jemima, and two other girls. On a Sunday afternoon the three girls had paddled in a canoe some distance down the river from their homes. They did not know, of course, that Indians were near. There had been peace for seven months, and the settlers had grown careless. Suddenly the canoe stuck on a sandbar, and before the girls could get it off, five painted warriors dashed out of the woods and seized them.

The girls were not missed until nearly sundown. Then the search began. One of the searchers found the canoe, picked up the trail, and the chase was on. The Indians traveled all night, but the rescue party led by Boone had to spend the night in camp. They could not follow the trail in the dark. Next morning the chase began again. Every now and then the searchers found little pieces of cloth that the girls had torn from their dresses to help mark the trail.

Just at dark the second night, Boone's party came in sight of the Indians making camp. The white men hid until the Indians were safely asleep. Then

Boone picked three of his most skillful trackers, and slowly they began to creep toward the camp. They knew that the Indians, if given a chance, would tomahawk the girls, who were "huddled at the foot of a tree only a few feet from the fire." Inch by inch Boone and his men crept forward. At a signal four shots rang out. Two of the Indians never rose. Three escaped "without their moccasins, and not one of them with so much as a knife or a tomahawk."

When the rescue party returned to the settlement they found that another band of Indians had burned the cabin and destroyed the young apple trees in the orchard.

The fame of Kentucky spread; and after the war with England, men, women, and barefoot children, with horses, dogs, and cows, thronged the roads to the beautiful country. People called it "Kaintuc."

But the crowds made Boone unhappy. He moved farther west to get "elbow room." This time he moved across the Mississippi to the banks of the Missouri River. He died there at the age of eighty-six, still looking toward the West with longing eyes. He wanted to go to Oregon.

Going West Into Tennessee

Bold pioneers settled eastern Tennessee. In the meantime, another bold pioneer, James Robertson, had led a group of settlers into what is now eastern Tennessee while his friend Boone was opening the way into Kentucky. The Tennessee pioneers built their cabins on the banks of the Watauga (wŏ-tô'gä) River, thinking that they were on the Virginia frontier.

Robertson, like Boone, was the son of a poor farmer. There were no schools where he lived as a boy, and he was a grown man with children of his own before he learned to read. His wife, it is said, taught him to read and write. Lack of education did not keep him from being a wise leader. He was thoughtful and honest and brave, and his neighbors trusted him. Whenever there was trouble of any sort, they looked to him to tell them what to do, and he did not fail them.

Robertson was aided by one of his best friends, John Sevier (sĕ-vēēr), who came to Tennessee from Virginia about a year after Watauga was settled. Sevier was a bold, dashing, handsome man, and, unlike Robertson, was well educated. He could make a good speech and write strong, forceful letters. The two leaders worked shoulder to shoulder when dangers and troubles threatened the people.

The Tennessee pioneers at first thought that they were in Virginia. After a year or two, however, they found that they were not in Virginia at all but in the Indian country where the English government had forbidden white people to settle. The king's officers ordered them to move back into Virginia or North Carolina.

Unwilling to give up their homes, they sent Robertson to talk to the Indian chiefs. The red leaders said that the white people might stay on their land if they would give the Indians about six thousand dollars worth of blankets, paint, rifles, ammunition, axes, and other tools. They wanted to be friends with the settlers. The settlers were willing to pay for their lands. To celebrate the bargain, they invited the Indians to a feast, and everyone had a good time playing games, running races, and joining in shooting contests to see who was the best shot. Everything went well until a white man, a stranger in the Watauga settlement, killed an Indian. Then all the Indians went home and prepared for war.

At the risk of his life, Robertson went to see the chiefs again and begged them not to go to war. He told them that his people were very sorry about the death of the Indian, and promised that they would do everything that they could to capture the murderer and punish him. Robertson succeeded in persuading the Indians to wash off their black war paint and put on the red, white, and yellow paint that meant peace. But the trouble was not yet ended; it was only delayed.

Two or three years later, a chief named Dragging Canoe stirred up all the young Indian warriors to fight. Robertson and Sevier with about forty men held the fort at Watauga, to which the women and

The western settlers boldly moved out from their forts into the woods, cut small clearings beside the clear forest streams, and built their lonely cabin homes.

children had fled for safety. The Indians camped around the fort for nearly three weeks, hoping to starve the people out.

It was during this siege that Sevier saved the life of the young woman he married a few years later. One morning some women went out to milk

the cows, thinking that the Indians had gone home.
Suddenly a dreadful war-whoop was heard, and the
Indians were upon them. Dropping their milk
buckets, the women ran for the fort, reached the
walls, and the gates were closed. For a moment
they thought that all were safe. Then a scream was
heard, and looking through a loophole, they saw
that a beautiful girl named Kate Sherrill had been
left behind. She was running as fast as she could,
and a painted warrior was reaching out to grasp
her hair. Sevier shot the Indian dead, and then,
jumping up on the top of the wall, reached down and
lifted the young woman over the wall to safety.

At last, the Indians gave up, went home, and made
peace again. They recognized that the white settlers were coming into Tennessee too fast for them.
By that time there were many little settlements
like the one at Watauga, and the Indians could
not hope to destroy them all. They had to make
peace or die fighting.

People followed the rivers westward. About ten
years after the Watauga settlement began, Judge
Richard Henderson wished to send a colony to
some land that he had bought in the central part
of Tennessee on the Cumberland River. He engaged
James Robertson to go ahead and choose a good
spot for settlement. Robertson selected a place
that later became the city of Nashville.

Robertson went overland to the new place of

settlement, but the colonists went all the way in
boats. They floated down the Watauga and Holston
rivers to the Tennessee River, and down the Tennessee to the Ohio River. Then they went up the
Ohio to the Cumberland River, and up the Cumberland to Nashville. It was a journey of nearly
a thousand miles. They started just before Christmas and were on the way until April.

They suffered many dangers and hardships. Sometimes ice blocked the river so that the boats could
not move. Smallpox broke out on one boat, which
had twenty-eight people on board. To prevent the
dreadful disease from spreading, this boat was
kept some distance behind the others. Indians along
the bank, seeing one boat separated from the rest,
attacked it and killed all the passengers. At another place, one of the boats that happened to be
in the rear got stuck on a rock. Before the people
could get it off, the Indians attacked them. Three
of the men jumped out of the boat and ran away,
but the captain, his wife, and a Negro woman managed to get the boat off the rock and escape. Once
a boat floated in too close to the shore, and the
Indians fired at it and killed one of the passengers.

When the little fleet of boats reached the Ohio,
the river was very high on account of rain, and it
was almost impossible to push the big, flat-bottomed
boats up the stream. To make matters worse, food
was running low, and the crews were already worn

Redrawn from an old painting of Knoxville, Tennessee

The fort served as a trading post as well as a refuge in time of attack by the Indians. This is White's Fort on the site of the present Knoxville, Tennessee.

out by the long voyage down the Tennessee River. The people on some of the boats decided that they would not try to go up the Ohio. They would go down the river to the Mississippi and float down the "Father of Waters" to Natchez (năch′ĕz), which is now in the state of Mississippi. Others said that they would go down to the Mississippi and then up the great river to the Illinois.

But the leader of the largest party said that he had started for the Nashville settlement and he was going there. On March 21, 1780, he wrote in his diary: "Set out and on this day worked very hard and got but little way. Passed the two following days in the same way, suffering much from hunger and hard work." A month later the settlers arrived at Big Salt Lick, and there they found Captain Robertson waiting at the place he had selected for his settlement.

The West at the End of Colonial Times

By the end of colonial times people were looking toward Ohio, and it was the first territory to be settled after Kentucky and Tennessee. At the same

Hauling freight in wagons across the mountains of the West was a terrible task. Narrow Indian trails furnished the only roads. The settlers depended chiefly on pack horses and boats.

time a few venturesome families were going to Alabama and Mississippi.

We can tell how rapidly people moved into the western country by looking at the early census figures. A *census* means a counting. Every ten years our government counts all the people in the United States, so that by looking at the census reports we can learn the population of any state or city. The first census was taken in 1790. At that time the population west of the Appalachian Mountains was just about 100,000.

As soon as the colonies became the United States, people began to pour westward. By 1800, the number of people west of the mountains had increased to nearly 400,000. Twenty years later there were more than 2,000,000 people beyond the Appalachians, and the westward movement had crossed the Mississippi River. By the middle of the century, it had reached the Pacific Ocean.

Is It True?

(Give proof for each answer.)

1. Is it true that people moved west for the same reasons that they crossed the ocean to America?

2. Is it true that the French and Indian War resulted in increasing the westward movement?

3. Is it true that people bettered their condition by moving west?

4. Is it true that the population of the West in 1800 was nearly four times as great as it was at the time of the first census in 1790?

STUDY THE LIFE OF THE PIONEERS

1. Read about life in the West. You will find good descriptions of pioneer life in the following books:

Hartman, Gertrude, *These United States* (The Macmillan Company), pp. 176-188.

Bass, Florence, *Stories of Pioneer Life for Young Readers* (D. C. Heath and Company).

Nida, W. L., *Following the Frontier*, has interesting pictures and stories of pioneer life. See Chapters X and XIV-XIX, particularly.

The Pageant of America (Yale University Press), Volume II, Chapters I, II, and III.

2. Draw or make a model of Boonesborough.

3. Study the route taken by the colonists who were going to the Nashville settlement. Trace it on a wall map. Show how the rivers helped westward travel and how the mountains hindered it.

4. Draw a series of pictures of early pioneer hardships.

or

Collect illustrations of early pioneer life for your scrapbook.

5. Arrange a bulletin board exhibit of the best illustrations on pioneer life.

6. Write a description of a day in a pioneer home.

or

Write an original story about pioneer life in colonial times.

ANOTHER VIEW OF THE WEST

1. Two interesting stories of the French and Indian War are named below. Try to read one of them.

Marshall, H. E., *An Island Story* (Frederick A. Stokes Company), pp. 434-441, tells how Canada was won.

Orton, H. F., *The Gold-Laced Coat* (Frederick A. Stokes Company), is a story about a French boy in the French and Indian War.

2. These tales of the West will interest you:

Faris, John T., *Nolichuchy Jack* (J. B. Lippincott Company).

Skinner, C. L., *Debby Barnes, Trader* (The Macmillan Company), a story of a little girl who fled from the Indians and found refuge with the Boones.

Meigs, C. L., *The Willow Whistle* (The Macmillan Company), a pioneer story about the West and the Indians.

Lange, D., *On the Fur Trail* (Newson and Company).

3. Write a paragraph explaining what effect life on the frontier had on people in colonial times.

4. Explain why Kentucky and Tennessee attracted so many settlers.

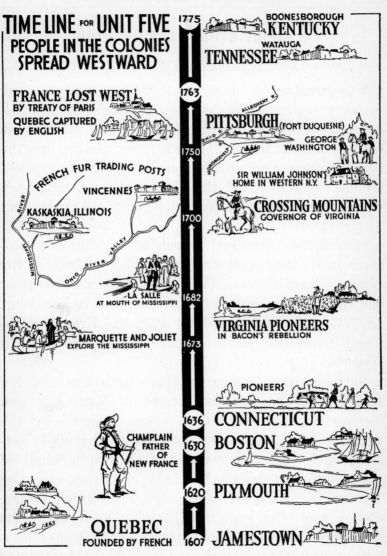

TIME LINE FOR UNIT FIVE
PEOPLE IN THE COLONIES SPREAD WESTWARD

1775

BOONESBOROUGH
KENTUCKY

WATAUGA
TENNESSEE

1763

FRANCE LOST WEST
BY TREATY OF PARIS

QUEBEC CAPTURED BY ENGLISH

PITTSBURGH (FORT DUQUESNE)

ALLEGHENY R.

OHIO R.

MONONGAHELA

GEORGE WASHINGTON

1750

FRENCH FUR TRADING POSTS

VINCENNES

KASKASKIA, ILLINOIS

MISSISSIPPI RIVER

OHIO RIVER VALLEY

SIR WILLIAM JOHNSON'S HOME IN WESTERN N.Y.

CROSSING MOUNTAINS
GOVERNOR OF VIRGINIA

1700

1682

LA SALLE
AT MOUTH OF MISSISSIPPI

VIRGINIA PIONEERS
IN BACON'S REBELLION

1673

MARQUETTE AND JOLIET
EXPLORE THE MISSISSIPPI

PIONEERS

1636

CONNECTICUT

1630

BOSTON

CHAMPLAIN
FATHER OF NEW FRANCE

1620

PLYMOUTH

QUEBEC
FOUNDED BY FRENCH

1607

JAMESTOWN

Notice how the English moved west to found homes, while the French were wandering explorers and fur traders.

A SHORT STORY OF UNIT FIVE

PEOPLE IN THE COLONIES SPREAD WESTWARD

The westward movement which peopled our country began about as soon as the first English colonists started clearing farms and plantations on the Atlantic coast. Slowly they pushed up the river valleys and spread out between the rivers. About the middle of the eighteenth century, they began to climb the eastern slope of the Appalachian Mountains.

It was the westward march of the English colonists and the southward spread of French fur traders from Canada that caused the contest over the Ohio Valley, called the French and Indian War. In 1763, as a result of this war, the French withdrew from the path of the English pioneers in America.

Settlers then began to move into the country which later became our states of Kentucky and Tennessee. All this country was claimed by the Indians, who fought fiercely to keep the white settlers back. Kentucky was the hunting ground of many different tribes, but they could not stop the westward march of such men as Daniel Boone. Boone took the lead in Kentucky and began the settlement at Boonesborough in 1775. James Robertson and John Sevier, the two great leaders in early Tennessee, had already settled with some of their neighbors on the Watauga River in eastern Tennessee. Robertson moved on after ten years to the Cumberland River, and there began the settlement that grew into the city of Nashville.

These bold pioneers opened the way to the West. At the close of colonial times, the roads to Ohio, Kentucky, and Tennessee were crowded with families going to the new lands beyond the mountains. By 1790 there were more than a hundred thousand settlers west of the Appalachian Mountains.

When the Second Continental Congress declared the American colonies a free nation in 1776, the people of Boston heard the Declaration of Independence read from the balcony of the Old State House. How is such news announced today?

UNIT SIX

The American Colonies Became the United States

Like all European nations, the English people thought that the main purpose of a colony was to benefit the mother country. They expected the colonists to trade only with English merchants, and to be willing to pay taxes to the English government when necessary. Steps were taken in early colonial times to control the government of the colonies by giving the king the right to appoint the governors. At the same time, Parliament passed the trade laws, called the Navigation Acts, in order to compel the colonists to trade with English merchants.

Nevertheless, England allowed its colonists more freedom to govern themselves than the colonists of any other nation enjoyed. The colonists grew to believe that their government should be carried on for their own benefit. They disobeyed the annoying trade laws and quarreled with their governors. But they did not revolt seriously until Parliament tried to tax them to help pay the cost of the French and Indian War.

The English government tried to tax the colonists in two ways. First, Parliament passed a stamp tax, requiring them to buy stamps to be put on certain things such as legal documents, playing cards, and calendars. Second, it passed a law requiring them to pay a tax on goods that they imported from England and other English territories.

The tax laws brought all of the colonies into union to defend their rights to self-government. First they held the Stamp Act Congress, and then they elected the First Continental Congress to beg the king and Parliament to withdraw the tax laws. This led to the American Revolution; and in 1776 the Second Continental Congress declared the American colonies an independent nation. The success of the Revolution created the United States of America.

The story of how the American colonies became the United States is told in:

Chapter XVI. When the Colonies United to Preserve Self-Government

Chapter XVII. When the American Revolution Brought Independence

Outline of Chapter XVI

XVI. When the Colonies United to Preserve Self-Government

    A. When Trade Laws Were Enforced

    B. When the English Government Passed Tax Laws

        1. The colonies defended their right to tax themselves.

        2. The English government passed the Stamp Act.

        3. Three famous Americans opposed the Stamp Act.

        4. The Stamp Act Congress met.

        5. The colonists disobeyed the Stamp Act.

        6. Parliament repealed the stamp tax.

        7. A tax was put on colonial trade.

    C. How the Colonies United

        1. The leaders aroused the people.

        2. Samuel Adams started Committees of Correspondence.

        3. The First Continental Congress met.

CHAPTER XVI

When the Colonies United to Preserve Self-Government

When Trade Laws Were Enforced

In colonial times, as we know, all the nations of Europe believed that the main purpose of a colony was to benefit the home country. They all tried to govern their colonies in such a way as to make them carry out that purpose. England allowed its colonists more freedom to govern themselves than the colonists of any other nation enjoyed. Nevertheless, people in England believed that all colonies ought to be managed for the profit of English merchants.

England's first efforts to obtain benefit from the colonies took the form of controlling their shipping, trade, and manufacturing, so as to compel the colonists to do their trading in England. For this purpose Parliament passed the navigation laws. These laws required the colonists to sell in England the goods that they shipped across the ocean, and to buy in England all the goods that they imported from abroad. Other laws forbade the shipping of certain manufactured goods outside the colonies,

The collecting of high customs duties and the seizing of smuggled foreign goods to enforce the navigation laws put an end to much profitable trade. Colonial ships lay idle, sailors were out of work, and merchants protested.

making it necessary for many of the colonists to buy such goods from England.

In this way, much of the profit of American trade went into the pockets of English merchants and made England rich. The colonists could not ship their goods directly to France or Holland and buy French or Dutch goods in return, but must handle the whole business through a merchant in England. All the tobacco and rice and timber and furs shipped across the ocean must go to England. If the colonists wanted to buy European goods, they must buy them from England. It was against the law to sell tools and other things made of iron outside of the colony where they were made. The colonists must only mine the iron ore and ship it to England. If the people of Massachusetts made more woolen cloth and more beaver hats than they could use and sold them to their neighbors in Pennsylvania or Virginia, they were disobeying the law. Iron and wool and furs must be shipped to England to be made into tools and cloth and hats. Then the colonists must buy tools and cloth and hats from England.

As a result of these trade laws, requiring the colonists to buy and sell in England, the colonists lost money. Sometimes they did not get as good a price for their goods in England as they might have secured in France or in Holland. Sometimes they had to pay more for what they bought in England than they would have had to pay in other places. They lost both ways.

The trade laws were very annoying, but, as long as the English government did not enforce them strictly, the colonists did not complain. It is necessary to remember, however, that the colonists resented these laws. At the same time that the navigation laws were passed, as you know, steps were taken to change the government of the colonies by giving the king the right to appoint the governors. This made it possible to enforce the Navigation Acts, when England decided to do so after the French and Indian War.

When the English Government Passed Tax Laws

The colonies defended their right to tax themselves. The first effort of the English government to tax the colonists came after the French and Indian War. The war cost a great deal of money, and Englishmen thought that the colonies ought to help pay the war debt.

The colonists said that they had already paid more than their share. They had sent soldiers into the war and had paid the soldiers and supported them while the war was going on. If necessary, they were willing to pay more, but they denied the right of Parliament to tax them. They did not object to paying part of the cost of the war against France; but they did object to being taxed by Parliament because there were no American members in it to help make the laws.

They declared that no tax could be placed upon them except by their own legislatures. Their idea of the proper way to handle the matter was for the king to ask them for a gift. Then each colony would pass a law requiring its citizens to pay whatever might be necessary to make up the gift that the English government wanted.

The English government passed the Stamp Act. It did not seem to King George III a kingly thing to beg gifts from the American colonists. He was a good man, but he was a little stupid, and he was very stubborn. He had been brought up with a very high opinion of his own importance and power. From the time that he was a little boy, his mother had repeated one sentence over and over again: "Be king, George; be king!" George grew up determined to follow her advice. He thought that the king of England should not have to take what his backwoods colonists chose to give him. Parliament should simply pass a law and have the Americans pay what the government needed. So a tax law was passed.

Parliament passed the law in the form of a stamp tax. The law required the colonists to buy stamps from officers of the government and to put them on legal papers and on various articles that they bought and sold, just as we have to put stamps on letters. Some of the things to be stamped were: deeds, wills, playing cards, newspapers, almanacs, and advertisements printed in newspapers. For example, when a man sold a piece of land, he had to give the buyer a paper called a deed; and this deed was not good unless it had a stamp on it.

Copied from a painting by Robert Reid

All three of the famous Americans opposing the stamp tax were lawyers. This picture shows Otis arguing the noted case against the use of the general search warrants, called Writs of Assistance, by customs officers at Boston.

Or, if a man wrote his will telling what he wanted done with his property after he died, the will was not good unless it was stamped.

Three famous Americans opposed the Stamp Act. Three men in America played a leading part in working against the Stamp Act. They were James Otis and Samuel Adams of Massachusetts and Patrick Henry of Virginia.

Otis was forty years old when the stamp tax quarrel began. He was a man of good education, a graduate of Harvard College, a lawyer, and a fine speaker. He was a member of the Massachusetts legislature when Parliament passed the stamp tax, and he made many speeches and wrote against the right of Parliament to tax the colonists. He did much to stir up the people and encouraged them to refuse to pay the tax. He was greatly admired by the colonists for his bold stand against the king and Parliament; and it was he who took the lead in calling a Stamp Act Congress.

Samuel Adams was a little older than Otis, and like him was a graduate of Harvard College and a Boston lawyer. Although he failed at law and at several other occupations, Sam Adams was a great politician. He was popular, knowing probably every man in Boston and calling most of them by their first names. He was a leader of the people, and had great power in the Boston town meetings. For nine years he was tax collector of Boston and a member of the Massachusetts legislature. He helped to organize the people against the Stamp Act.

Patrick Henry of Virginia was eleven years younger than Otis. He had grown up on a farm near Richmond. Until he was ten years old he went to the country school near his home and learned reading, writing, and some arithmetic. After that age, his father kept him out of school and taught him Latin and history. As a young man, he failed as a farmer and as a storekeeper, but was a brilliant success as a lawyer. He first attracted attention by a speech in one of his law cases in which he hinted that George III was a tyrant because he vetoed a law passed by the Virginia legislature. This speech immediately made him popular, and two years later his neighbors elected him to the legislature, where he served for eleven years. Later, he was five times elected governor of Virginia.

Patrick Henry had just taken his seat in the Virginia legislature when news arrived that Parliament had passed the Stamp Act. He believed that the English government had no right to tax the colonists, and he persuaded the legislature to adopt a strong statement against the stamp tax. The statement was published in the newspapers, and led the Americans to take up their motto, "No Taxation Without Representation."

The Stamp Act Congress met. What could the colonists do? For a time they did not know. Then they decided to call a Stamp Act Congress at New York, where the leading men of all the colonies could meet and help to decide on a plan. Twenty-seven of the leading men of America met in October, 1765, and for nearly two weeks discussed what they should do. In the end, they decided to ask Parliament to repeal the law, that is, to pass another law doing away with the Stamp Act.

The colonists disobeyed the Stamp Act. England was already shipping the stamps to America and appointing officers to sell them. Even if Parliament was willing to do what the Stamp Act Congress

In New York people agreed not to buy from England until the Stamp tax was repealed. Here members of the Stamp Act Congress are shown discussing an article in the *New York Gazette*, which declared, "It is better to wear a homespun coat than to lose our liberty."

asked, it would take weeks and months to carry the colonists' message by a slow sailing ship to England, to get the law repealed, and then to send that news back to America. In the meantime, the tax would have gone into effect, and the people would have been made to buy the stamps.

The people took the law into their own hands. They sent committees to the stamp officers in every town and asked them to resign their positions and not to sell the stamps. If the officer refused, a mob visited him the next night, rode him on a fence rail; broke into his house, smashed his furniture; and sometimes found and destroyed the stamps. When the time came for the stamps to be used, not a stamp was to be had in all America.

Parliament repealed the stamp tax. When the request of the Americans for the repeal of the Stamp Act reached Parliament, it caused a great debate. William Pitt, one of the wisest statesmen that England has ever had, took the side of the colonists. He said that Parliament had the right to pass laws for the Americans, but it did not have the right to put its hand into their pockets and take their money. Therefore, he said, Parliament ought to repeal the stamp tax.

Another member of Parliament, Colonel Isaac Barré (bà′rā), who had fought side by side with the colonists as an officer in the French and Indian War, and knew them, spoke for them. He called them "Sons of Liberty." They owed England nothing, he said, but England owed them much for settling America and bringing it under the English flag. He declared that they had already paid more than their share of the cost of the war by furnishing men and provisions for the army.

While the debate was going on, a committee made up of members of Parliament had a talk with Benjamin Franklin. Franklin was in London looking after the interests of the colony of Pennsylvania. He told the committee plainly that the colonists would never pay the stamp tax, and that Parliament might just as well stop trying to get money from them in that way.

In the end, Parliament did repeal the stamp tax. There seemed to be nothing else to do. The colonists had refused to buy the stamps, and Franklin said that they never would buy them.

But Parliament passed a law saying that it still had the right to tax the colonists whenever it pleased. The Americans paid no attention to this law. They thought it merely showed that Parliament was in a bad temper and wanted to have the last word. They were willing to let it talk as much as it pleased so long as it did not try to tax them without their consent.

A tax was put on colonial trade. Hardly had the stamp tax been repealed when Parliament tried to tax the colonists in another way. It passed a law requiring them to pay a tax on the goods that they bought from England. Thus, the navigation laws forced them to buy their goods in England, and this new law taxed them every time they did it. These new taxes on colonial trade were introduced in Parliament by an unwise young man named Townshend. For that reason they were called the Townshend Acts.

The colonists were very angry, and again they

insisted that Parliament had no right to tax them. They declared that they would buy nothing at all in England until Parliament withdrew the law. When the English merchants saw that they were about to lose all the American trade on account of the tax law, they were greatly alarmed and begged Parliament to repeal the law, which it did—all except a little tax on tea. Again the colonists had won.

The English government made a very great mistake when it tried to keep the tax on tea. It kept the tax just to show its power; and the colonists refused to pay the tax simply to show that their motto meant what it said, "No Taxation Without Representation!" In December, 1773, a number of ships carrying tea arrived in America. At Charleston, Philadelphia, and New York the people refused to use the tea, returned it, or stored it in damp cellars to rot. At Boston the people asked the governor to send the tea back to England, but he refused. Then a large party of men disguised as Indians in war paint and feathers, with tomahawks waving, boarded the tea ships in Boston harbor and dumped three hundred and forty-two chests of tea overboard into the bay. This famous Boston Tea Party led by Samuel Adams settled the question of paying the tea tax, but it made the king of England thoroughly angry.

King George III insisted that Boston must be

punished and the tea paid for. Parliament passed one law taking from the people of Massachusetts much of their freedom to govern themselves; and another law closing the port of Boston to all trade. The king made General Thomas Gage governor of Massachusetts and sent troops with him to Boston to enforce the laws.

How the Colonies United

The leaders aroused the people. The quarrel with England over the tax laws had been going on for fifteen years. During that time, James Otis, Samuel Adams, and Patrick Henry were the leaders in stirring the people to work together to resist the stamp tax and the tax on tea. They have been called the "pen fighters" of the Revolution. This statement means that their writings and their speeches were of the highest importance in uniting the American colonies in defense of democracy.

Samuel Adams started Committees of Correspondence. Adams saw that the greatest difficulty about getting the people to resist the harsh laws of the king and Parliament was to keep them informed of what was going on. As we know, the roads were bad, newspapers were scarce, mail was irregular, and there was little travel. It took a day's hard travel on horseback or coach to go a distance which a fast train today covers in half an hour. How could the people of Boston know

Samuel Adams and his Boston Committee of Correspondence speed a messenger on his way. They have just come from a meeting in the town hall on the second floor of Fanueil Hall. On the first floor was a public market.

what was going on in other towns? To meet this difficulty, Adams formed a Committee of Correspondence in Boston to write to the neighboring towns. The committee sent its letters by special messengers.

Soon other towns in Massachusetts followed the example of Boston and appointed committees of their own. Then Committees of Correspondence were formed in all the other colonies, from Massachusetts to Georgia. The Committees of Correspondence were Samuel Adams' most useful service in the American Revolution. It was by means of these committees that the people were united and prepared for war against England.

The First Continental Congress met. When news of the king's intention to punish Boston reached America, it seemed to the colonists that another meeting like the Stamp Act Congress was necessary to decide what they should do. Again Samuel Adams took the lead, and his Committees of Correspondence spread the call for the First Continental Congress. In answer to the call the Congress met at Philadelphia on September 5, 1774.

The First Continental Congress included some of the greatest men in America. The Congress sent a letter to the king begging for the repeal of the harsh laws against Boston.

When Patrick Henry returned from Congress to Virginia, he felt certain that war with England would soon break out. He wanted to raise soldiers to be ready for it, but many of the leaders in the colony objected. They hoped that Virginia could still keep out of war. In reply to them, Henry blazed out in one of his fiery speeches:

"If we wish to be free," he said, "we must fight. There is no retreat but in submission and slavery!

Our chains are already forged! Their clanking may be heard on the plains of Boston! The war is certain to come—and let it come. Why stand we here idle? Is life so dear or peace so sweet as to be purchased at the price of chains and slavery? Forbid it, Almighty God! I know not what course others may take, but as for me, give me liberty or give me death!"

The truth is that the people in the colonies did not want war with England and hoped that the government would decide to treat them fairly. But they were disappointed, and Patrick Henry had his way. The king and Parliament refused the petition of the First Continental Congress; and the members of the Congress had hardly reached their homes after their meeting at Philadelphia before war began in Massachusetts. It was then too late to try to stop it.

REPORT TO THE CLASS

1. Report on the colonial objections to the trade and navigation laws.

2. Tell of the purpose and work of the committees of correspondence.

3. Report on the Stamp Act and the Stamp Act Congress.

4. Tell of the purpose and work of the First Continental Congress.

5. Report on two famous Englishmen who took the side of the colonists in the quarrel between England and the colonies.

UNDERSTAND BOTH SIDES

1. Divide your paper into two columns. Head one column *England* and the other *American Colonies*. Under these headings state briefly what each side thought about the following:

    a. for whose benefit the colonies existed

    b. representation

    c. taxation

Reading the following books will help you: Chalmers, Eleanor M., *Talks about Our Country* (Benjamin H. Sanborn and Company), pages 35-36; Guerber's *Story of the Thirteen Colonies*, pages 214-233; Salisbury, Ethel, *The Story of Our United States* (Little, Brown, and Company), pages 219-226; or Gordy, Wilbur F., *Leaders in Making American History*, pp. 137-159.

2. Make two cartoons to illustrate the quarrel between England and her colonies: one to show the colonial viewpoint and one to show the English viewpoint.

3. Imagine that you are a colonist who has just returned from taking part in the Boston Tea Party. Describe to your family what happened.

4. Imagine that you are a Boston citizen who

attended the town meeting which ended in the Boston Tea Party. You did not approve of destroying the tea. What might you be saying as you watched the tea being thrown into the harbor?

5. Study the map on page 288. Write answers to the following questions:

    a. Why would England wish to control colonial trade?

    b. Which colonies would object most to England's enforcement of the trade laws?

    c. Why would England and the colonies disagree over colonial manufacturing?

Patrick Henry

Outline of Chapter XVII

XVII. When the Revolution Brought Independence

  A. The War in the North
    1. War broke out in Massachusetts.
    2. Washington saved Boston.

  B. The Declaration of Independence
    1. Who framed the Declaration?
    2. What did the Declaration mean?

  C. The War in the Middle States
    1. Washington was driven from New York.
    2. Washington won battles.
    3. The Americans spent a terrible winter.
    4. The tide turned in favor of America.

  D. Winning the Northwest
    1. The English held the Northwest.
    2. Clark captured Kaskaskia.
    3. Clark took Vincennes.
    4. Why was Clark's work important?

  E. The War on the Sea
    1. The American navy was founded.
    2. John Paul Jones captured English ships.

  F. War in the South Ended in Peace
    1. The English held the South.
    2. Greene took Georgia and the Carolinas.
    3. Lafayette took the field in Virginia.
    4. Washington ended war at Yorktown.

  G. The Beginning of the United States
    1. What were the terms of peace?
    2. Why was the treaty of peace important?

CHAPTER XVII

When the American Revolution Brought Independence

The War in the North

War broke out in Massachusetts. The quarrel of the colonists with the English government was bringing them nearer and nearer to blows with the governor of Massachusetts and his five thousand British soldiers in Boston. Governor Gage learned that the colonists were collecting guns, powder, and balls and storing them at Concord, some twenty miles from Boston. He saw that war might easily begin, and determined to take these arms away from the colonists before any fighting started. At midnight on April 18, 1775, he ordered eight hundred soldiers to march to Concord and seize the guns and the powder and balls.

Governor Gage expected to surprise the Americans and to remove their arms peacefully, but patriots in Boston had learned his plans. Paul Revere was sent riding swiftly through the night to knock on farmhouse doors and warn patriots along the way that the soldiers were coming. The sleepy-eyed farmers hurriedly dressed, seized their rifles, and set off in the chilly darkness to join their neighbors and try to keep the redcoats, as they called the English soldiers, from reaching Concord.

Henry Wadsworth Longfellow made Paul Revere's ride the subject of a poem:

"A hurry of hoofs in a village street,
  A shape in the moonlight, a bulk in the dark,
  And beneath, from the pebbles, in passing,
    a spark
  By a steed flying fearless and fleet.

          *   *   *

So through the night rode Paul Revere;
  And so through the night went his cry of
    alarm,

          *   *   *

  A cry of defiance and not of fear,
  A voice in the darkness, a knock at the door,
  And a word that shall echo forevermore!"

At daybreak on the morning of April 19 the English soldiers found their path barred by sixty armed colonists at the village of Lexington. To this day it is not known whether the English or the Americans fired first. When the firing was over and the smoke had cleared away, eight Americans were dead and ten were wounded.

The English went on to Concord and seized what military supplies the colonists had not had time to hide. It was twenty miles back to Boston, and news

Paul Revere rode from house to house warning people of the coming of the British soldiers. Compare this method of communication with our present method of sending out warnings in times of danger.

of the fight at Lexington had spread like wildfire. From every rock, fence, and tree angry colonists mowed down the worn-out English soldiers, whose bright red coats made easy targets on the long return march. When the roll was called in Boston, two hundred and seventy-three of General Gage's men were missing. The loss among the colonists had been only ninety-three.

Almost exactly two months later the English lost more than a thousand men in the Battle of Bunker Hill, just out of Boston. Governor Gage had written King George that the Americans would not fight, but he learned that they would. After the first shots at Lexington, men from all over New England took up their guns and marched toward Boston. In a little while there was an army of fifteen thousand men in camp at Cambridge across the river from Boston.

Washington took command and saved Boston. In the meantime, the Second Continental Congress met at Philadelphia and took charge of the war. The Americans saw that what the colonies needed now was a commander. John Adams, a member of Congress from Massachusetts, suggested George Washington for the office of commander-in-chief. He said that there was but one man in all America for the place and that Washington was the man.

Washington was now forty-two years old and one of the richest men in America. Twenty years had passed since he had been a young Virginia colonel and had his coat shot full of holes while trying to save Braddock's terrified soldiers from the French and Indians. From his brother, Washington had inherited the fine estate of Mt. Vernon and, when he married Mrs. Martha Custis, he had gained other plantations and many slaves. His great wealth had not kept him from being truly interested in the affairs of his country. Even before the war began, his fame had spread through all thirteen colonies. He was known as a man of action rather than words.

Washington accepted his election as commander-in-chief of the American army because he thought it was his duty to do so. He told Congress that he would take no salary for his service, but that he would keep an exact account of his expenses. Congress could repay him what he spent. He took command of the army at Cambridge, Massachusetts, on July 3, 1775, under a great elm tree near Harvard College.

In March of the next year, Washington forced the English army to give up Boston and leave New England. This ended the serious fighting in the North.

The Declaration of Independence

Who framed the Declaration of Independence? The colonists now faced the question: "What are we fighting for? Are we fighting for our rights as Englishmen, or are we trying to break away from England forever?" The colonists had been proud of England and proud of their English blood. For more than a year after the fighting at Lexington and Concord and Bunker Hill, they continued to hope that the king and Parliament would offer them peace on terms that they could accept. But month followed month, and the war went on. Finally, on July 4, 1776, they gave up hope of making peace with England, and the Second Continental Congress adopted the Declaration of Independence, the most famous document in American history.

Congress had already appointed a committee of five men to write the Declaration of Independence. The five were John Adams of Massachusetts, Benjamin Franklin of Pennsylvania, Roger Sherman of Connecticut, Robert R. Livingston of New York, and Thomas Jefferson of Virginia.

John Adams was a Massachusetts lawyer. He grew up on his father's farm near Boston. He graduated at Harvard College when he was twenty years old, and then studied law. He was successful as a lawyer but like his cousin, Samuel Adams, spent most of his time in government service. He took an important part in the Second Continental Congress. We have already seen him nominating Washington to be commander-in-chief of the American army.

Franklin, you remember, had been in England trying to persuade the English government to treat the Americans fairly. He was now a wise old man of seventy. After spending the past ten years in London looking after the interests of the colonies, he was certain that peace was no longer possible. He strongly favored a declaration of independence.

Sherman was a Connecticut judge, who during

The signing of the Declaration of Independence marked the beginning of a new nation.

his early life had earned his living as a shoemaker. He had educated himself by studying at home, and he was well educated although he sometimes used incorrect grammar and pretended to be an ignorant man. When he was sitting as a judge in court, however, he was very dignified and correct in his speech.

Livingston, the youngest member of the committee on the Declaration of Independence, was only thirty years old. He belonged to one of the richest families in New York, and was a graduate of what is now Columbia University in New York City. He was called home on business before the members of Congress signed the Declaration of Independence, so that you do not find his name among the signers.

Thomas Jefferson had been for six years a member of the Virginia legislature with Patrick Henry. He took Washington's place as a member of Congress from Virginia when Washington was elected to command the army. He was a graduate of William and Mary College in Virginia. Like Livingston, he was young, only thirty-three years old. He was a poor speaker and never made a speech when he could help it, but he was a great writer. Because of his skill and ability as a writer, the other members of the committee asked Jefferson to write the Declaration of Independence. Though both the committee and the Continental Congress made some changes before adopting it, the Declaration of Independence is almost wholly the work of Jefferson.

What did the Declaration of Independence Mean? The Declaration of Independence first listed the abuses that the king and Parliament were guilty of in their treatment of the colonists. A king who would permit such abuses, Jefferson wrote, was a tyrant, "unfit to be the ruler of a free people."

In voting for the Declaration of Independence, Congress declared that the colonists should no longer be ruled by England. From then on they were to be citizens of the United States of America.

All the members of Congress who were present signed the Declaration of Independence. John Hancock of Massachusetts, president of the Congress, signed first in a bold, large hand which, he grimly remarked, King George could read "without his spectacles."

The Americans now knew for what they were fighting. They were fighting for independence. But could they win it? The answer to that question depended largely on Washington and the friendship of France.

The War in the Middle States

Washington was driven from New York. After the British army gave up Boston, Washington moved most of his forces to New York. He placed a part of his army on the western end of Long Island, where Brooklyn now is, and built strong forts on both banks of the Hudson River. His object was to prevent the English from capturing the Hudson River and thereby dividing New England from the middle states. It was while Washington was taking his position here, during the summer of 1776, that

Congress adopted the Declaration of Independence.

But Washington was unable to hold New York. The British fleet and army were too strong. After the battle of Brooklyn Heights in August, he drew his forces back to Manhattan Island. Two or three battles on Manhattan Island compelled him to cross the Hudson River into New Jersey. Then the British drove him across the state of New Jersey into Pennsylvania.

Washington won battles at Trenton and Princeton. The English followed Washington's retreat across New Jersey in high hope, thinking that the end of the war was in sight. Many Americans, too, thought the war was nearly over and were in despair, when Washington very cleverly outwitted the enemy and proved himself one of the great generals of history. Crossing the Delaware River in storm and sleet on Christmas night, 1776, he captured a thousand men at the town of Trenton, New Jersey, with the loss of only four of his own soldiers, two of whom froze to death.

A week later Washington surprised and defeated another force at Princeton. The English soldiers were beginning to call Washington the "Old Fox," because they knew by now that he was a clever general.

After Washington's victories at Trenton and Princeton, the English commander withdrew his army to New York. Washington followed as far

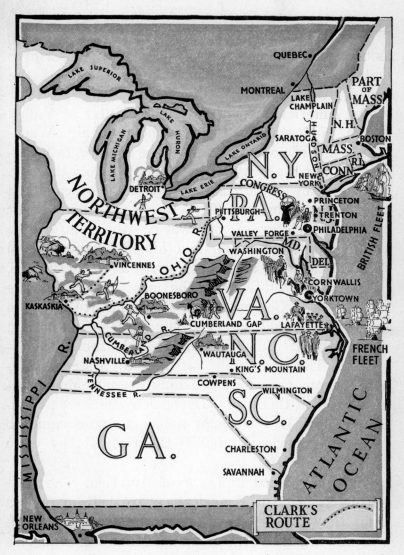

This map tells the story of the war for independence. Notice how close Valley Forge, Princeton, and Trenton are to Philadelphia, where Congress carried on the American government.

as the Hudson, and the two armies spent the winter watching each other from opposite sides of the broad river.

The Americans spent a terrible winter at Valley Forge. Next summer the game began again. Washington moved southward from the Hudson to Philadelphia, but his army was too small to hold the city. General Howe, the English commander, came on and forced him out. The English soldiers spent the third winter of the war in the comfortable city, while Washington and his men starved and froze in camp, twenty miles away, at Valley Forge.

This third winter was the most desperate time of the war. Congress had no money to pay the soldiers; it could not even supply them with food and clothing. But Washington held the army together. The men built log huts to protect themselves from the cold; Washington somehow managed to feed them; and Baron Frederick von Steuben (stū′bĕn), a German nobleman who came to help the Americans, drilled them until they were excellent soldiers.

The tide turned in favor of America. The next spring (1778) the Americans were better soldiers than they had ever been before. Their strength was due in part to the confidence that von Steuben's drilling had given the men, and in part to three events which raised their spirits high. The three events were these:

1. In October, 1777, an English army under General John Burgoyne (bûr-goin´) was captured by an American force at Saratoga (săr´ä-tō´gä), on the upper Hudson River.

2. In February, 1778, the friendly French nation joined with the United States in the war against England. Though the end of the war was still far off, the Americans now felt certain that they would win. French money and men and ships were a great help.

3. Still another thing that encouraged the Americans was the retreat of the English army from Philadelphia. It returned to New York, and the main army remained in New York for the next three years with Washington watching it from across the Hudson.

Winning the Northwest

The English held the Northwest. While Washington was keeping the main English army busy in New York, something very important was happening beyond the mountains in the West. It happened in the part of the territory that England had taken away from France in the French and Indian War. In this part of the country, which used to be called the Northwest Territory, are the present states of Ohio, Indiana, Michigan, Illinois, and Wisconsin.

You remember that France tried to hold the

Mississippi and St. Lawrence valleys by building forts and settlements in the Northwest. There was a fort at Kaskaskia (kăs-kăs'kĭä) in what is now southern Illinois, one at Vincennes (vĭn-sĕnz') on the Wabash River in Indiana, one at Detroit near the southeastern corner of Michigan, and others scattered here and there around the shores of the Great Lakes.

When England pushed the French out of this territory, it put its own soldiers in these forts, and they were, of course, still occupying them when the colonists began the Revolution.

Clark captured Kaskaskia, now in Illinois. Colonel George Rogers Clark wanted to drive the English out of the Northwest and take all that beautiful region for the Americans. Clark was, like Washington, a Virginian, a surveyor of the western lands, and a bold Indian fighter. He suggested to Patrick Henry, who was then Governor of Virginia, a plan for the conquest of the Northwest. Governor Henry told him to go ahead.

Clark promptly gathered two hundred men, loaded them on boats, and floated down the Ohio River to a spot as near Kaskaskia as the river went. There he hid his boats for future use and marched across the rolling hills of southern Illinois to attack the fort.

Marching quietly into the village of Kaskaskia on the night of July 4, 1778, the Virginians took

Marching a hundred men across the icy plains of Illinois and Indiana, George Rogers Clark took control of the Northwest for the Congress of the United States. Look at the map, page 389, and find his route.

the English soldiers by surprise and captured the fort without fighting.

Clark took Vincennes, now in Indiana. Clark's capture of Vincennes the following winter was another story. He started from Kaskaskia in February, after months of snow and rain. Streams were overflowing, and even the prairies were covered with water half way up to the men's knees. How could he get his men to Vincennes, two hundred and fifty miles away?

Colonel Clark tells the story of the long, hard march in his diary. He says:

"My object was now to keep the men in good spirits. I allowed them to shoot game on all occasions, and feast on it like Indian war dancers. Every night a different company provided the feast and invited all the other companies to be its guests. My officers and I shouted and ran and splashed through the mud and water as much as any of the men. So they got the idea that everything was a joke."

When they drew near the Little Wabash River, the whole country was under water. Colonel Clark built a boat and sent some of the men across the river to hunt a dry spot in which to camp for the night. They found a little hilltop about half an acre in size, and then began the labor of ferrying the men across.

"A scaffold was built on the opposite bank," Colonel Clark continued, "where the water was about three feet deep, and our baggage was ferried across and put on the scaffold. Then we swam the horses across and loaded them with the baggage at the scaffold. By that time the troops were across, and we began our march through the water.

"By evening we found ourselves encamped on a pretty hilltop, in high spirits, and each party laughing at the other because of something that had happened while the ferrying was going on. A little drummer made a lot of fun for the men by floating on his drum."

Once the food gave out and the men were nearly starving. A canoe filled with Indian squaws and their children came by and Colonel Clark found in it nearly a quarter of a buffalo, some corn, some tallow, and some kettles. "This," he says, "was a grand prize. We immediately made broth and served it to the men. Most of them got some, but many gave their portions to their weaker comrades. This little refreshment, and fine weather by the afternoon gave new life to the party."

Finally the little band arrived at Vincennes. Marching into the village, they surrounded the fort. The taking of Vincennes was not as easy, however, as the capture of Kaskaskia had been. The English soldiers at Vincennes were not taken by surprise; they were armed and ready to fight, and they did fight all one night. The next morning the commander surrendered.

Why was Clark's work important? Clark planned to march against Detroit and drive the English from that important position, but he' was never able to get a force strong enough to undertake the campaign.

His capture of Kaskaskia and Vincennes protected the new settlements that were being established in Kentucky. When peace was made, his conquest of the Northwest played an important part in fixing the boundary of the United States on the Mississippi River. England might have refused to surrender the territory west of the Appalachian Mountains if Americans had not been already in possession of it.

The War on the Sea

The American navy was founded. The Americans had no warships when the war began, but they owned many merchant vessels that were used for carrying freight, and their sailors were as skilful as any that sailed the seas. Congress, therefore, arranged to arm some of these merchant ships, and appointed officers to command them and to destroy English ships.

John Paul Jones captured English merchant ships. John Paul Jones was born in Scotland but had come to Virginia just before the war began to take possession of an estate left him in this country by his brother who had died. He was a young man, twenty-seven years old when the war began, and had been sailing the seas since he was a boy of sixteen.

Captain Jones became the most famous commander in the American navy. Hiding in the coves and harbors off the coast of France, he would dash into the English Channel and sink or capture English merchant vessels before the English warships could come to their assistance. English ship captains never knew where to expect him, and his name became a terror to English sailors.

Courtesy of the Chicago Historical Society

News of success in the fight for independence was spread by word of mouth. This was the way news was announced in the towns and cities of the colonies in 1781.

Jones's most noted battle was with the British man-of-war, *Serapis*. During the fight the captain of the *Serapis* asked him if he wanted to surrender. "No! I have not yet begun to fight," Jones shouted back. In the end, it was the warship that surrendered; but by that time Captain Jones's vessel, the *Bon Homme Richard*, was sinking. Young Captain Jones transferred his crew to the captured vessel, and wrote in his diary:

"No one was left aboard the *Richard* but our dead. The very last sign mortal eyes ever saw of the *Bon*

Homme Richard was the defiant waving of her un-conquered flag as she went down."

Congress made Captain Jones commander of a new ship, the *America*, gave him a gold medal, and voted him the thanks of the nation. The king of France gave him a gold sword and made him a knight.

War in the South Ended in Peace

The English held the South. While Washington was holding the main English army in New York, the English were successful in taking most of the South. They captured Savannah and Charleston, and held large parts of Georgia and South Carolina.

In the South the Americans fought in small bands, moving rapidly from one place to another under clever leaders. On their tough, shaggy ponies, they would swoop down upon an English force, strike a sudden blow, rush away to another place, and strike again. In this way, they captured powder and shot, food, and other supplies from their enemies, and lived mostly at the expense of the English. General Francis Marion, nicknamed "The Swamp Fox" because he moved so swiftly and secretly, gave the English the greatest trouble. They never knew when or where to expect him.

The fiercest fighting in the South was at King's Mountain and the Cowpens, on the border between North and South Carolina far to the west. Both of these battles were victories for the American soldiers.

Greene took Georgia and the Carolinas. After the war had been going on for more than five years, Washington sent General Nathanael Greene to take command in the South. General Greene came from the little state of Rhode Island. He had fought many battles and had proved himself to be one of Washington's best generals. It took him less than a year to drive the English army from Georgia and the Carolinas. At the end of 1781, England held only the city of Charleston.

To reward General Greene for his services, Congress gave him a gold medal and two English cannon taken in battle. Washington praised him by saying that General Greeene had done no more than he expected of him. The state of Georgia gave Greene a plantation called Mulberry Grove, and when the war was over he went there to live.

Lafayette took the field in Virginia. General Lafayette (lä-fā-yĕt′) was a young French nobleman, only nineteen years old, when the Americans declared their independence. But nothing could keep him from coming to the United States to help them. Congress made the young Frenchman a general and sent him to assist Washington at headquarters. Washington found that Lafayette was a skillful officer, and made good use of his services. Lafayette was commanding a force in Virginia in 1781 while Washington was still watching the main English army in New York, and while General Greene was driving the English out of the Carolinas and Georgia.

The English general in Virginia, Lord Cornwallis (kôrn-wŏl'ĭs), at first had more soldiers than the Americans had. He was sure he could capture Lafayette and all his men. So certain did he feel that he wrote a letter, saying, "The boy cannot escape me." But the boy did escape.

Lafayette managed to get more men, and the English army found itself in danger. Cornwallis had to retreat to escape capture. Slowly he drew back toward the seacoast and took his stand on the peninsula where the town of Yorktown stands. Lafayette saw that he had the English general in a trap and sent word to General Washington to come and help take the English army.

Washington ended the war at Yorktown. Fortunately the French fleet was in American waters, hoping to strike a blow that would end the war. Washington arranged with the French admiral to guard Yorktown from the sea and prevent the English warships from saving Cornwallis' trapped army. Then, leaving his camp in New Jersey so secretly that the English general in New York did not know that he was gone, Washington quickly joined Lafayette's army. He forced Cornwallis to surrender on October 19, 1781.

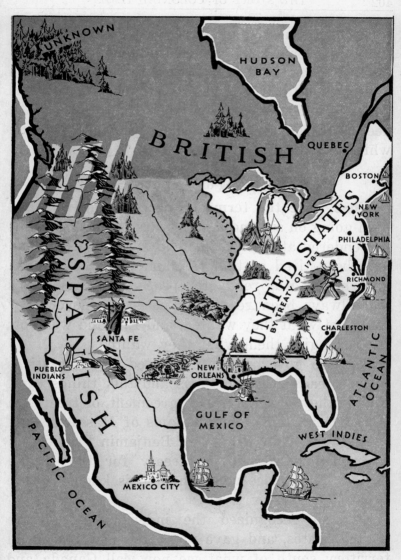

This map shows the United States as it began in 1783.

Of course the help of the French was very important. Five thousand French soldiers under Count Rochambeau (rō-shän′bō) were with Washington and Lafayette at the victory of Yorktown. It is doubtful whether without them and the French fleet General Washington could have won this battle which ended the war.

The Beginning of the United States

What were the terms of peace? The war had been going on six and a half years when Cornwallis surrendered at Yorktown. The English people had long been tired of the war, and now the English government was ready for peace. The Americans had always been ready for peace whenever they could get what they wanted, and England was now ready to give them what they wanted.

The two governments appointed representatives to meet each other in Paris and talk things over. Finally they signed a peace agreement, or treaty, on September 3, 1783. John Adams of Massachusetts, John Jay of New York, and Benjamin Franklin of Pennsylvania signed the treaty for the United States. This peace with England is known as the Treaty of Paris.

England recognized the independence of the United States, and gave up to the new nation all territory south of what we now call Canada and west as far as the Mississippi River. In the South,

Spain held what is now Florida and a narrow strip of land along the northern shore of the Gulf of Mexico, so that our southern boundary did not reach the Gulf.

Why was the treaty of peace important? It meant the creation of a new and democratic nation. It marked the beginning of the real independence of our government. It admitted that the United States had taken its place in the world.

WHAT IS LEADERSHIP?

1. Tell why you think leadership played an important part in America during the period of the Revolutionary War. Learn more about the leaders of this period by reading books you find in your school library, the public library, or at home. Look for some of the books which are listed below under the names of five great leaders.

a. Daniel Boone:

Foote, A. E., and Skinner, A. W., *Makers and Defenders of America* (The American Book Company), pp. 134-140.

Gordy, W. F., *American Leaders and Heroes* (Charles Scribner's Sons), pp. 222-233.

White, Stewart E., *Daniel Boone, Wilderness Scout* (Doubleday, Doran & Company).

Willis, Carrie Hunter, and Saunders, Lucy S., *Those Who Dared*, pages 123-143.

b. Patrick Henry:

Foote, A. E., and Skinner, A. W., *Makers and Defenders of America*, pp. 15-21.

Gordy, W. F., *American Leaders and Heroes*, pp. 140-155.

Nida, William L. and Stella H., *Pilots and Pathfinders*, pp. 174-178.

c. George Washington:

Brooks, E. S., *True Story of George Washington* (Lothrop, Lee & Shepard Company).

Hill, F. T., *On the Trail of Washington* (Appleton-Century Company).

Vollintine, Grace, *The Making of America* (Ginn and Company), Chapter II.

Gordy, Wilbur F., *American Leaders and Heroes*, pp. 116-134.

d. Samuel Adams:

Foote, A. E., and Skinner, A. W., *Makers and Defenders of America*, pp. 22-31.

Gordy, W. F., *American Leaders and Heroes*, pp. 156-164.

Willis, Carrie H., and Saunders, Lucy S., *Those Who Dared*, pages 109-118.

e. Benjamin Franklin:

Coe, Fanny E., *Founders of Our Country*, pp. 318-328.

Coffman, Ramon, *Our America*, pp. 190-198.

Brooks, E. S., *True Story of Benjamin Franklin* (Lothrop, Lee & Shepard Company).

Nida, William L. and Stella H., *Pilots and Pathfinders*, pages 166-172.

2. Arrange a program on *Leadership* to be given by your class. Here are suggestions:

    a. reports on American Leaders of the Revolutionary Period. Bring out leadership qualities by giving incidents to prove your points.

    b. talks on "Why Leadership Is Needed Today."

    c. class discussion on "How Can Sixth-grade Boys and Girls Develop Leadership Qualities?"

A MAP STORY OF THE WAR FOR INDEPENDENCE

1. Study the map on page 389. What does it tell you about the connection between Clark's capture of the Northwest Territory and the treaty provision about the western boundary of the United States?

2. Looking at the same map, explain how some of the English colonies took advantage of the statement written in their charters giving them claim to the land as far west as it extended.

3. What was taking place in the territory south of the Ohio River while the war for independence was being fought?

4. What foreign aid did the American colonists

receive that helped in the capture of Cornwallis and his army at Yorktown?

A LAST GLANCE AT UNIT SIX

1. Read stories about the Revolution:

Eggleston, George C., *Long Knives: The Story of How They Won the West* (Lothrop, Lee & Shepard Company).

Carter, Russel G., *A Patriot Lad of Old Boston* (Penn Publishing Company).

Perkins, Lucy F., *The American Twins of the Revolution* (Houghton Mifflin Company).

Curtis, Alice Turner, *A Little Maid of Philadelphia* (Penn Publishing Company).

Longfellow, Henry W., "Paul Revere's Ride."

2. Be sure to keep your scrapbook up to date with pictures relating to the quarrel between England and her colonies.

3. Write a good sentence telling why the Declaration of Independence is important to Americans.

A SHORT STORY OF UNIT SIX

THE AMERICAN COLONIES BECAME THE UNITED STATES

From early colonial times the English government, like all other governments of that day, had tried to control the trade and manufacturing of its colonies for the benefit of English merchants. Until

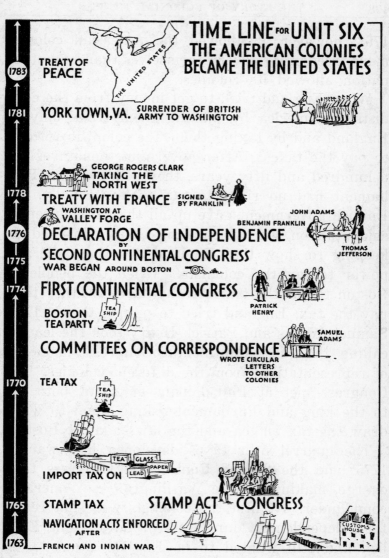

TIME LINE FOR UNIT SIX
THE AMERICAN COLONIES BECAME THE UNITED STATES

1783 — TREATY OF PEACE

1781 — YORK TOWN, VA. SURRENDER OF BRITISH ARMY TO WASHINGTON

GEORGE ROGERS CLARK TAKING THE NORTH WEST

1778 — TREATY WITH FRANCE SIGNED BY FRANKLIN

WASHINGTON AT VALLEY FORGE

JOHN ADAMS
BENJAMIN FRANKLIN
THOMAS JEFFERSON

1776 — DECLARATION OF INDEPENDENCE BY SECOND CONTINENTAL CONGRESS

1775 — WAR BEGAN AROUND BOSTON

1774 — FIRST CONTINENTAL CONGRESS

PATRICK HENRY

BOSTON TEA PARTY — TEA SHIP

COMMITTEES ON CORRESPONDENCE

SAMUEL ADAMS
WROTE CIRCULAR LETTERS TO OTHER COLONIES

1770 — TEA TAX — TEA SHIP

IMPORT TAX ON TEA GLASS LEAD PAPER

STAMP ACT CONGRESS

1765 — STAMP TAX

NAVIGATION ACTS ENFORCED AFTER

CUSTOMS HOUSE

1763 — FRENCH AND INDIAN WAR

Here you can trace through twenty years the important steps by which the American colonies became the United States.

407

1763, however, it allowed the American colonies more freedom to govern themselves than any other nation allowed its colonies.

When England tried to get money from the colonists in America by making them trade only in England and by taxing them, the colonists refused to pay the taxes. After governing themselves for a hundred and fifty years, they believed that Parliament had no right to tax them. Finally, the English government gave up all the taxes except a small tax on tea, which King George insisted on keeping to show that England had the right and power to tax the colonists. When the people of Boston threw the tea into the harbor rather than pay the tax, England tried to punish them. Then Samuel Adams and Patrick Henry took the lead in calling the First Continental Congress, made up of representatives from the different colonies. The Congress met at Philadelphia and sent petitions to the king and Parliament asking them to withdraw the tax on tea and the laws against Boston.

The quarrel over taxes developed into war in 1775, and the Second Continental Congress took charge, making George Washington the American commander. At first the colonists were not ready for independence. Many were proud of being English and still wanted to be English subjects. In 1776, however, the Second Continental Congress decided that England would not make peace on the terms America desired, and declared the independence of the colonies.

The war for independence can be divided into four parts: the war in the North, the war in the middle states, the war in the West, and the war in the South. At first Washington was successful, driving the English soldiers from Boston in the North. Then the English drove him from New York and Philadelphia in the middle colonies, compelling him and his men to spend a bitter winter at Valley Forge, Pennsylvania. During the third year of the war, fortune favored the colonies again. Franklin persuaded the French nation to join the Americans against England. George Rogers Clark won the West from the English. Captain Paul Jones captured many English ships on the sea. Finally Washington, with French help, captured the English army at Yorktown, in the South. Then England made peace, and the American colonies became the United States.

TODAY IN THE LIGHT OF COLONIAL TIMES

1. Use facts you have learned in your study of colonial times to explain each of the following quotations:

  a. "In America we are all immigrants or the descendants of immigrants."

  b. "Bring paper and linseed oil for your win-

dows and cotton yarn for your lamps."
(From a letter written by a colonist to an
Englishman who was coming to America.)

c. "Some things tended to separate the colonies from England, and some things drew
the colonies toward union among themselves."

d. "Geography is a maker of history."

e. "Our present history has its roots in the
past."

2. Ask the Bulletin Board Committee to prepare
a picture exhibit comparing *Colonial Times* and
Modern Times, using pictures gathered by the class.
If you have loose pictures which you have not put
into your notebook, you can contribute them for the
exhibit.

3. Have a notebook exhibit. Your collection of
pictures, cartoons, and drawings will be interesting
to the other members of the class. Appoint a committee to select the three most interesting and attractive notebooks for honorable mention.

4. Ask your teacher to allow you to have a meeting of the great personalities in colonial history.
Write on slips of paper the names of the important
people. Let each pupil in the class draw a slip and
prepare a short speech telling of the chief services
of the person whose name is on the slip.

5. Let one-half of the class represent our colonial
Past and the other half our modern *Present*. A

member of the *Past* group will make a statement of fact for colonial times. Then a member of the *Present* group will give a corresponding statement for modern life. Everyone in the class should take part. Example:

Past speaker: "In my time, I was educated by a tutor on my father's plantation in Virginia."

Present speaker: "In my time, I am being educated in a school paid for by public taxes" (or otherwise if you do not attend a public school).

Full-Page Maps and Time Lines

Pronouncing Key

In the index beginning on the next page, any proper name
or any unusual word is pronounced by the use of the following signs:

ă as in at	ĭ as in it
ā as in face	ī as in mine
ä as in father	ŏ as in not
ȧ as in ask	ō as in open
â as in ball	ô as in long
ĕ as in end	o͞o as in too
ē as in be	ŭ as in up
ẽ as in her	ū as in use

û as in turn

412

INDEX